Heartscapes:

True Stories of Remembered Love

Edited and Introduced by
Kate Harper and Leon Marasco

Spruce Mountain Press   Plainfield, Vermont

Published by: Spruce Mountain Press,
61 Katuah Road, Plainfield, Vermont 05667
www.ourpastloves.com

Publisher's Cataloging-in-Publication Data

Heartscapes: True Stories of Remembered Love / edited by Kate Harper and Leon Marasco–1st Spruce Mountain Press ed.

p.cm.
includes list of contributors/contact information
ISBN 978-0-9851409-0-8
1. Love-Anecdotes. 2. Interpersonal relationships
3. Oral History   I. Title
306.7
92

cover design by Tim Newcomb

To all storytellers,
with special remembrance
of our dear friend M. A.,
whose many tales—transcending time and
space—delighted and inspired us.

CONTENTS

Heartscapes: the inside story

xi

HEARTSCAPES: The Inside Story

In the 1958 movie, *The Inn of the Sixth Happiness*, reference is made to a traditional Chinese wish for these five Happinesses: Virtue, Tranquility, Wealth, Position, and Peaceful Death. The movie suggests that the Sixth Happiness might well be Listening to Stories.

*H*EARTSCAPES CAME INTO BEING as part of our personal journey, a quest that took us deep into the enticing (and many would say risky) world of past loves.

It was early in our life together, almost twenty years ago, when we began to explore what people do with their memories of past loves after they move into another significant relationship. We had discovered, through our own experience as a couple, that sharing fully what our previous loves meant to us contributed substantially to our emotional intimacy. But how, we wondered, do others handle this quite sensitive part of their pasts? We decided to ask. What we found became the basis for our book, *If Only I Could Tell You...Where Past Loves and Current Intimacy Meet*, published in 2006.

Then, in 2007, as part of our hope to foster greater awareness of the importance of past loves in today's relationships, we decided to sponsor a Past Loves Day Story Contest. Asking for true stories about former sweethearts, we suggested that each entrant write their story as if talking with a best friend. In response, the authors wrote with surprising emotional honesty, covering a wide range of experiences, in different times and places. And many thanked us for offering the contest, saying how important it was for them to have a chance to tell that personal love story.

Given the first contest's success, we made it an annual event. Over the years, the stories continued to touch us; while reading them aloud together, we often found ourselves momentarily sitting in silence, with moist eyes, immersed in the intensity of what we had just experienced. Occasionally, we laughed together when an author recalled a delicious, humorous moment.

As the stories from the contest accumulated, it was apparent that we were in possession of a treasure. This led us, in the spring of 2010, to decide that an anthology would be the best way to offer some of these compelling stories to a wider audience.

Here, then, are the 154 stories we felt best represent the emotional depth and variety found in the contest entries as a whole. Except for the very first group, where the authors all speak directly *to*, rather than *about*, the past love who inspired the "love letter," the stories are grouped under twenty-one loosely defined themes. But many stories might just as easily have been placed differently, to emphasize another aspect of that romance.

In a few instances, we were unable to make contact with the authors of stories we wanted to publish here. Fortunately, most of these may be read on our website, www.ourpastloves.com.

Every story in *Heartscapes* confirms the belief that human emotions are universal. Some express the nuances of different languages and diverse cultures, but the feelings themselves are reassuringly familiar.

To tell a story of such an intimate nature requires a certain kind of courage. You must recall, with tenderness, just what you still cherish about a special earlier love. And you must be willing to allow, in the telling, your heart to once again be touched.

We are grateful to all who chose to take the risk of sharing these stories, who invited us into the sacred space of their deeply personal memories of love and loss. They encourage each of us to remember an earlier love who is woven into the fabric of our being, to be open to what lingers in our own heart.

May "listening" to these stories become a Sixth Happiness in the lives of all who find their way to them.

—Kate Harper and Leon Marasco
Plainfield, Vermont, 2012

THINKING OF YOU...

Unlike the stories you will find in the rest of Heartscapes, each of these is like an unsent letter written directly to, not about, an earlier love. This approach creates a vulnerability, an intimacy, a sense that we, as readers, have come across something almost too private for us to witness, an unabashed willingness to speak from the heart.

The Necessary Selflessness of Love
by Joan L. Cannon

DEAR RON:

I wish I had written this a long time ago so you could have read it. Instead, you showed up in my poems. You never thought you were teaching me lessons for my whole life, for after we were no longer a couple—lessons I never forgot. I'm a widow now. Without you to show by your example, I might not have chosen such a good man for a husband.

Can you remember now what I was like at thirteen, a precocious but innocent thirteen, when you asked me for that first date? It's hard for me, and perhaps impossible for you.

I still wonder why you thought I was worth your time, since you were older, and not just in years. It was such a treat to have a properly dressed young man, down to his shined shoes, appear at the door to call for me. Handsome, six feet tall, with the manners to call my father "Sir." I was head over heels, as they used to say, in the first hour we spent together.

When the drinking age was lowered to include anyone in uniform, when the stress of war was with us every day, and when everyone our age was boiling with hormones, it boggles my mind now to consider the care you took of me. Alcohol was something I'd been exposed to all my life, which meant that I had no inclination to overdo it. My father forbade me to drink anything in a bar except Scotch on the theory that, by doing that, I would be protected from bad liquor. You always ordered Dewar's for me. But the most important thing was that you protected me from the mischief of your shipmates, who thought it would be great fun to get your "cheap date" drunk.

To save money (if we weren't going to a movie) we used to walk Manhattan's largely deserted streets. I remember how we would talk and window shop up Lexington Avenue all the way to Times Square, where the Rossoff bar was always warm in winter, and never rowdy. We would talk while we had a drink, and then start back downtown, this time on Madison Avenue. It's surprising how much we found out about each other just by discussing the clothes or jewelry or art objects we gazed at in window displays. We then went on to discuss the subjects suggested by them.

Remember the weekend with your family at your country cabin, how you paddled the canoe under the black lace of over-hanging branches on the river, and held me close on the dock when we got back? Remember how we talked about horses, books, our mutual friends, and the kind of life that would be good?

We always held hands whenever we were within reach of each other. I was ten inches shorter than you, but somehow we always walked in step.

I had an unbreakable curfew, and you never made me overstay it in the almost four years we were together. In the 1940's, it was not a given that all brides were virgins. You made me know that yours would be. Do you remember the night we were coming back from a party near my birthday? The taxi had a moon roof through which I remember the glowing globe of a full moon looking down on us. You said, as the taxi neared my door, "You shouldn't be sixteen without being kissed," and took care of that.

Thank you, Ron, for teaching me so much about how to be honest about feelings without succumbing to them too soon. Thank you for showing me real chivalry so that I was able to know I had a right to expect it, no matter what my friends were saying or doing. Thank you for teaching me something about the necessary selflessness of love.

The last love of my life would give you thanks too, if he could. I told him about you. I know you will have made your wife a happy, lucky woman. I'm late, but I want to thank you from the bottom of my heart.

Cobalt
by Margaret DeAngelis

I LOOK UP when a voice from the television says your name—and when the voice follows with "has died," I drop the glass I have been washing. It shatters at my feet, blue shards and white suds spreading out from my toes as I peer at the screen.

I can see that the man with your name, the man who has died, is not you. He does not have your straight nose nor your curly hair. He is not the college senior who washed glassware in the lab on Sunday nights while I sat on a stool and read aloud from my poetry books. Nor is he the medical student who, five years later, held me close and stroked my long red hair and said good-bye—because his heart had changed.

The man with your name, the man who is not you, is nevertheless about the age you are now, or, rather, he was that age when he died waiting for his HMO to approve an experimental treatment that might have halted his cancer.

I imagine you as you are now, the color and the curls probably gone from your hair, but your hands broad and strong still, turning a pencil over and over with your long agile fingers as you argue on the phone for a patient whose HMO will not trust your judgment.

The newscast moves to a different story. I move too, away from the sink full of soapy water, away from the crumbles of blue glass, dark against the white floor. I move through the dining room to the living room. I make sure my hands are dry, and then I draw down from the fireplace mantel a cobalt glass vase with a ruffled rim and a narrow base, cradling it like an infant.

You brought it filled with daisies for my birthday that summer after we met. My parents went to the movies that night, and we made love in my sister's bed before they came back—and the next morning, too, after they had gone to church.

I took it with me to my first apartment. I put it on the white bookcase you'd drop your bag beside when you came to visit, across from the patchwork couch where we'd sit for our first kisses, the couch where we sat two years later for our last. I took the piece with me then to the next apartment, the one you never came to, and the next, that you never knew about. Finally, I brought it to this house, where I have lived ever since with the one who took your place but did not erase your memory. I put it on the mantel, a spot of color against a white wall.

I filled my house with books and furniture, with children, with laughter. I filled the mantel too with more cobalt glass, piece by piece, until I had a collection, until yours was the smallest, plainest piece, almost unnoticed. I place your cobalt vase back among the others and return to the kitchen, where the broken jelly glass waits. I bend to get the dustpan and when I straighten, there is my daughter, all barefoot girlish energy.

"Careful," I say, "there's glass."

She gasps. "That's not your special blue vase, is it?"

"No," I tell her, "just a jelly glass."

"Well, that's good!" she says. She steps around the little pile of twinkling blue slivers which is also collecting, as I sweep, a broken pony tail holder, a Goldfish cracker, and a Dallas Cowboys magnet. She grabs a piece of string cheese from the refrigerator and an apple from the counter, and I watch her walk away, this luminous child who would not have been born, who would not be who she is, had you not left me, had I not carried a cobalt vase into a life without you.

I don't know where you are tonight. I don't know how you live, whom you love, nor the shape your life has taken. But I hope that you are crazy happy, and that if a word from the television calls me to your mind, you smile.

I Sing of You
by Patricia Boies

I WAS STILL SIXTEEN, a freshman like you, when we met, you who would become my first love, my first lover. I had a crush on you from the start, your thick curly dark hair exploding under the wide brim of your black felt hat, your smooth olive skin that needed no shaving, your crooked front tooth, your long lean body, the battered cane you carried because of your knee operation. I was shy and you were shyer, so even though we spent months hanging out with the gang, my eyes on you as the joint passed and the music played in all those dorm rooms, at all those concerts, even though we hitchhiked from Boston to Ithaca in the middle of winter, huddling close in the phone booth after the state trooper threw us off the highway, it was not until April, spring breaking out all over, that I told your best friend how much I liked you, and he told you, and so it began.

We would walk into the dining hall for breakfast, for lunch, for dinner, and the guys would tease us, it was so obvious what we had been up to, feeding each other in ways beyond what cafeteria food could provide. The narrow dormitory bed seemed vast, it contained multitudes, as we breathed each other in, hearts and bodies humming.

We would hitchhike into Harvard Square and take the MBTA over the Charles River to Park Street, constantly touching, fiddling with the soft braided leather bracelets we had fashioned for each other. We made love under the willow tree in the Public Garden, and on the terrace of the Fine Arts Building in Cambridge, and in dozens of places with no name at all. We marked our territory wherever we could lie down together. I wanted to get to the bottom of you, wanted nothing to be off limits. I told you things I had never told anyone, and you showed me your own scars. But mostly we celebrated the moment, our bodies our bible.

First love has a strong grip.

After our time together, it mattered to me that we stay friends. Years later, when you met the woman who would become your wife, I was glad that I liked her and that she liked me. I changed the day of my departure for India so I would not miss your wedding. As you stood waiting by the altar, I blew you a kiss, and you acknowledged me with a nod.

When my daughter was born in Seattle, I wanted you to meet her, this new love of my life, this new testament to living in the present. After your son was born, and our two families, each with one child, would get together from time to time on one coast or the other, I imagined our children falling in love some day.

When my daughter died suddenly one April, just after her tenth birthday, you flew across the country to come to her celebration. It mattered to me that you came, that you were present at this unimaginable threshold. I stood at the altar and spoke of life with my daughter, and of life without her, and of the song that was still in my heart. You are part of that song, as you have been since I was sixteen, as you always will be.

Firsts
by Mitchell Close

Y OU'VE TOLD ME IT WAS BEAUTIFUL THAT DAY. The sky was clear and the sun was shining bright. Birds were chirping and children were laughing as they played nearby. I don't remember any of that. I only remember the look on your face as we biked through the park, the sound of your laughter as we told jokes back and forth, the way your hair blew back when we picked up speed. Days like those I'll never forget.

After transferring to a new high school in the middle of my senior year, I thought nothing good would come of the change. I had lived for the hustle and bustle of the city—movement. It was poetic to me—everyone was always on the move, always had things to do and people to see. The countryside town we moved to after my parents divorced was the complete opposite. There were only a few trees miles from the town. There was only one market, and it got shipments in once a month. It was…quiet. Everything was new for me.

The first day of any class is always the hardest, and that day was no exception. The school had twenty-three students in my grade. I walked into the senior classroom totally nervous, accustomed to two thousand more people walking the halls with me. The teacher was welcoming, but the class was everything but. Cold stares followed my walk to my desk.

But when I sat down, you were next to me, striking up a conversation immediately. Your wide green eyes were the first thing I saw. You were so different, so…awake, were something I just wasn't—something I couldn't be.

Every day I went to class, less and less to learn, and more just to be with you. I tried to deny my affection for you, but you were intuitive. You caught on right away. And one day, you just asked. The day is a blur, the surroundings gone. But the question...it was so *you*: "Wanna catch a movie tonight?" I was completely caught by surprise. I'm pretty sure my face was red the rest of the day, and that the other twenty-one students knew about us. But I didn't care. All I could think about was that night. We would be together—it was what got me through the day sane.

When you picked me up, we talked right away. I had been on a date before, but it was completely awkward. We had hardly talked, and when we did, it was about the weather.

But with you, everything seemed to fall into place. When you held my hand, it was like two puzzle pieces fitting together, and everything was right in the world. I remember thinking that you were just too perfect, that this couldn't be real. But it was. The night ended too fast.

When we kissed that night, you became the first person I ever kissed—and a couple of weeks later, the first person I ever told "I love you" to.

You were also the first love I ever lost, when you were killed by that drunk driver the following year. You were the first person I had given my heart to, the first person I ever opened up to about my parent's divorce, my stillborn brother, and many other things.

Your funeral was the first I cried at. I died every day after your death. But you taught me so many things before you died. You taught me to be myself. Most importantly, you taught me love, something I didn't think I could give anyone. Every day I am so thankful for the wonderful two years you were in my life.

Frankly My Dear I Do Give a Damn
by Katie Eichele

O
N THE ROLLING HILLSIDE of a small rural community, we sprouted. But all throughout our innocent school years, I believed you to be the plague. Your dark hair, mischief mahogany eyes and the tiniest freckles on your face, to me were contaminated with boy germs and unpleasantries. Yet, growing up, there was hardly a moment when I saw you without a smile. And there was hardly a moment when I donned one

I hid my unlikablities like the ravishing Miss Scarlet O'Hara. I was after something beyond my reach at the time: freedom.

But fate kept drawing us together, for our last names fell in alphabetical order and you were glued to my back every waking school day. As the antagonist, you were the boy who teased me, pulled my hair, tattled on me for saying "go to hell,"cheated off my homework, and poked me in the ribs just to gain my attention. You were brash, bold, and obnoxious. And I haughtily despised and ignored you as I saved myself for the dashing Rhett Butler, pretending to be the untouchable, unscathed Scarlet.

You lacked the gentility and swagger of the ambling Clark Gable. Of course, you were only a pubescent teen back then.

As seniors, we contended for GPA superiority, wanting to best each other. I felt a drive to always outdo you, and never knew why. Some days I got ahead, some days you'd knock me down. And ohhh, I'd want to rattle some cages then.

Still I knew, without you, I'd never have the strength to save my own Tara, or grow the calluses on my ego to withstand the hardships ahead.

We flittered about each other like bumblebees vying for the same flower, never acknowledging, yet always knowing, something special was pollinating, both too shy, oblivious, or stubborn to work together to construct the hive. Our own sweet plantation was just starting to blossom like the buds of young love.

Then there was chemistry: literally, having to work side by side as lab partners setting things ablaze, burning them in flames of blistering blues, gaseous greens, and raging reds. But while we watched the Bunsen burner, everyone else eyed the chemistry igniting between us, flickering white hot. All were assuming after high school, when we'd both become doctors, the day would come when bells and babies would follow.

And surely they almost did. For college was our sweet Savannah time.

We heated up with long, humid walks, hushed, private nights under the crescent moon, me sitting on your lap sharing the pains of my betrayed childhood, removing the masks of troubled angst, abuse and regret inflicted by a love-famished family. I curled up in your arms, and you soothed away my tears with loving kisses and gentle words.

When I thought I was nothing but broken and beaten, you nurtured and healed my wounds with soft strokes to my cheeks and lips, your low, rumbling voice, and the comforts of hospitality and love. You graced my body and soul in ways every young woman desires, without spoiling me for when I was truly ready.

Then, like Miss Scarlet, I lost you in the fog, the mist of distance, separation, and time. You went away and I thought you didn't care. I called to you in my dreams, I cried for you in my heart; I prayed to the moon and the stars to guide you back. But I knew you had a path to follow and I knew mine was just beginning. No matter how much I ran and chased after you, I knew if we were going to have that epic love tale, we'd have to have our own adventures, and somehow they'd weave together in the end.

So I found another.

But without your openness and patience to help me find myself worthy of love, to help me gain my freedom and independence, I'd never be as blessed as I am now. For you cultivated my heart, readying it for joy. And I thank you.

"Frankly, my dear, I do give a damn." For tomorrow is another day to love.

Your Memory More Real
by Judah Raine

*T*HE WAY WAS HARD, SOMETIMES. And so often you would thank me—for little things, like toast and honey, and a pen that wouldn't run dry when you had to write lying down. You said I'd touched your life, and you were glad you had found me. But looking back, as I sift through the memories and trace their textured colours, I see now that it wasn't that way at all.

I could be strong, because your strength was so much greater. I could have faith, because your faith was so much simpler. I could endure, because your courage was so much deeper. Somehow, you filled the space you were in—not with words or demands, or even obligations—just filled it gently, then over-flowed, and gave, and gave, and gave. I knew from the start that I would always share you with the world. There just was too much of you for one heart to hold. But that was okay, because somehow the more you gave, the more you had to give.

Our time was so short, and now our "together-dreams" are gone. But we had so much. We *lived* so much. And I had the most precious gift of all. I had the chance to walk with you, even just for a little while, to share the moments of pain and to comfort you, in the moments of fear, and to hold you, the moments of peace and the moments of joy, and to be touched by your humility and your courage.

I was able to walk with you, and then to watch as you "walked" on out of sight to a place where I cannot follow until another time. But, though the space in my heart is as great as the space you filled, knowing that at last you are free, I am at peace with your going, as you were. I am at peace because, through all those long, dark hours, it wasn't I who prepared you for the leaving, but you who prepared me for the staying behind.

It's the courage of your dying that keeps me strong, keeps me holding on through the dying of all that I was with you. And all the wisdom in your waiting to die taught me so much—of life, of love, of hope and of acceptance. I learned to see myself through your eyes, learned to touch the simple things that make the deepest memories. I learned to laugh, and to cry, to immerse myself in those moments where silence can be beautiful and darkness kind. I learned to love without reservation, without fear, without hesitation. I learned to trust and to dream. I learned how to say goodbye. And I learned how to go on.

I can't pretend I don't think of you. When I wake, alone, in the grey light of dawn. When things get too much and I don't know where to turn. When I see a special beauty, or hear a phrase, or catch a scent of rain on its way. And sometimes I wish that you could hold me, enfold me in the beating of your heart or simply touch me with your smile. You will always be there, larger than life itself. And sometimes your memory seems more real than I, softly, in the silence within.

Yes, the way was hard, sometimes. And so often you would thank me for the little things. And you would tell me you were so glad you had found me and that I had touched your life. But, looking back, I see that if I did, in some small way, touch your life, it was because you loved me. And, in giving me the joy of loving you, my life was touched, and healed, and changed. Though the ache in my heart is as great as the space you filled, still I can be content. Because, for just a little while, I held in my hand the most precious gift of all, and I know, in a place much deeper than the sadness, that if I'd known what was to come, I'd have done it anyway.

Love Is Never a Coincidence
by Jerry Gaube

*B*EFORE YOU EVEN SAID THE WORD, I knew I had seen you before, in a different country, in a different life.

"Do you speak English?" I ventured. My Spanish had shipwrecked drunkenly on the cacophonous shores of the waning fiesta. In that moment, the Festival de San Isidro had become synonymous with the day I regained faith—the day I pulled myself from the wreckage.

"A leettal," lilted bashfully between us. Your chin down, your hair in strands, you tried to veil your eyes. "I spent a year in upstate New York, in high school. A very small town. You wouldn't know it."

"Try me," I responded. Two words like a wax seal over the folded pages of a story already written, only unread. "I come from a small town there."

I had first seen you, all those foggy years before, hair veiling your speckled brown eyes, ambling languidly up the aisle of the school bus, mumbling something to your equally dark and long-haired brother that sounded sarcastic in a language I could not penetrate. Then, more than a decade later, I somehow fell in love with that girl, a girl who I'd never met, but had seen every day in my neighborhood in a far off country, in a far off existence, when things were smaller, and I was more, or less, impressionable.

A coincidence is a commonality that is unknowingly shared—like a supermarket meeting between old friends. Or a shared birthday. Love is never a coincidence. Love is a journey written on a promise, a declared secret that words can only approximate—the opening of a door and crossing of a threshold, daring to trust the other not to leave you in the new unknown.

I remember the day I told you. In late October, on my balcony, the morning sun caressing our necks and shoulders, I cradled you on my lap and the fat brown leaves danced over the plaza in a violent grace that lives only in Spain. It was the day we turned the clocks back. A leaf lazily fell across our laps. I picked it up and you ran your tiny finger over the veins. I nuzzled my forehead into the soft pillow between your neck and shoulder and said, "I love you."

You were older than me, an accomplished professional embarking on an odyssey of opportunity in the height of affluence. I was an outsider, a boy, a wanderer. Spain was the playing field for the last great game of adolescence, the championship, the final test of my youth.

I spoke to you in a foreign tongue. I thought about you in non-native syllables, touched you in a savage wilderness. You held my hand and refused to let me be content with the present, to laze about my potential. You were a muse who challenged me to explore everything at my disposal, to create, to trust—to push the boundary of where my heart could go and, if it could, penetrate and become yours.

In the end I failed—not in the greatest challenge you set me. Yes, my heart, my intellect, my vital energies were your heart, intellect and vitality. But I failed the challenge of trusting myself to embrace the fundamental of existence: that nothing stays the same. Everything must change. Do you trust yourself to have faith in the face of time? To love because you have no other choice?

The moment would inevitably come, we both knew. I knelt before you and took your hand to my mouth, looked up at your swollen eyes and puckered lips. I intended to ask your life for me. But the words did not come. I rolled onto my side, crying.

Now, in the bitter dregs of winter, after the Spanish autumn has laid bare the branches and the gitanos in the plaza have returned to their clandestine caves, I remember you. I remember the mountains we trekked, the beaches we conquered, the operas we invented dances to, the poems we composed and left on park benches, the shoulders we offered each other. But memories are like the spring: you love them more as you wait for their impossible return.

Apparition
by Karen Paul-Stern

YOU APPEARED IN MY DREAM last night, your annual visit. I always feel a bit off kilter the day after, as if the world had stopped on its axis while my eyes were closed.

The dream reminded me of the cold sore that developed on my mouth the day you first asked me out. I had spent several hours in the sun that afternoon, willing it to shrink and disappear. It didn't, and as we sat at the cabaret table that night, I rested my hand over my mouth as much as possible, trying to hide my flaw. When we walked home, it no longer mattered, and you took me in your arms and kissed the life force out of me. I was so dizzy I could barely walk back to the dorm.

No one has ever kissed me like that again.

If we had both better understood how to plumb our hearts and listen to each other's stories when we were nineteen, we might have been more seaworthy. Initially, it felt like possibility existed in every particle, that there was so much more to follow.

I loved you deeply, fiercely, as I never believed I could love. But I doubted you as well. I needed someone, something, to replace my mother, who had left me. And you burrowed into my adolescent soul, promising me that you could.

I counted my life in coffee spoons; I couldn't stop thinking about the future. I worried that you would leave me, that your love would stop. Taking the bus each weekend to visit, I would lie in your dorm bed and dream only of the following weekend, of seeing you again. But still I needed more—I thought there was more. So I left to find it; I left first, to stave off greater damage.

I wounded your heart and your head and your fingers and your toes. I tossed you out like sour milk. Immediately regretful, I followed you around the world after graduation. Each time I arrived, you punished me by making love to me and then telling me to leave. I kept following.

My mother came back, and listened when I told her that you were the hole in my heart. I wanted you to come back. I had wanted her to come back. She encouraged me to find you. She, who knew about leaving and returning — she came back. But you never did.

I didn't know at nineteen that, except for the occasional spark of a dream lighting up your sky, life demands to be made up of ordinary moments: sitting in traffic on your way home from work; worrying about the dog that has been inside all day; watching the moonlight dance over your children's closed lids at night while they sleep; eating bread across the table from your beloved, your fortune is now a daily shadow dropping crumbs that will need to be swept up.

You are no longer a flesh and blood human being, but the paradigm of love. You are not the patter of relationship building, not the quotidian life I have learned to be patient around, and embrace and shape to fit my damaged destiny, but the one who was supposed to be my Galahad.

I am glad you are happy. You followed the path to professional satisfaction, marriage and family, a life well lived. I sometimes dream that you and I will find each other again in old age. But I fear that I will never reach old age, that the world I have built is unsteady, and will come crashing down around me. I keep water bottles and food and emergency supplies in my basement, but I know they won't shield me from the fallout of loss.

I hope you will continue to be the spark in my dreams.

A Letter to Penny
by Luke Beling

*P*ENNY, I THOUGHT OF YOU TODAY as I listened to our favorite song play over the radio. I was rolling stones to cover your father's grave when the stereo waves stirred my memories with a haunting melody.

Do you remember when we buried your father? When we thought our days were old? His death was as sudden as first frost, his absence as costly as the cold. The gravel above his head comes loose once in a while when the cattle cross to feed in the southern pasture. He wanted it that way, you know: to be in the earth, surrounded by his years of labor.

The day he left us was a day I'll never forget. You held my hand over your heart and reminded me of my pledge to keep you safe. Although you were frightened, your beating pulse was consistent, like a grandfather clock. I knew you trusted me then. The words you spoke are still near, like your photo in my wallet. If only I had cared more then about your heart than the fields and animals of what had become our farm, perhaps you'd still be with me.

This morning, when I was cleaning the chicken coop, the cattle sang. It was my first time to hear them. I confess, I never did believe in the sounds you heard. A farm is a factory of noise, noises that are impossible to identify. But I know now that what you said is true: "Listen with ears of the city and you will hear concrete, cars, and murder. Listen with ears of the country and you will hear animals sing, rivers dash, and the life that is constantly giving birth."

On the day you left, record rainfall saturated our farm. I have no doubt that you felt it, curving "Meyers Bend," as surely as the tires of the old Bantum did. I prayed for you, and asked God to keep you out of harm's way, while feeling guilty for allowing those smooth tires to stay on so long. The screaming water on your windshield did not convince you to turn around. Even it could not wash away your fury and heartache. I am still haunted by the irony of that day, but with it came perspective and revelation. Our love, or lack of it, was hardly about the prosperity in our barns. You left, and the rain rescued our farm, and the rain drowned my heart.

Would it serve me well to tell you that I have changed? I disagree with the impersonal taste of clichés, but it's all I know to write. I have become a man of substance. When you knew me, I was the scarecrow in our cornfields. Today, I am the feed in my hand for our animals at first light.

Do the bright city lights cover the darkness? Do the busy streets and noisy engines silence the voices of regret? I stumble in the daylight, and I live with a backwards clock. Our farm is sunless without you, and disappointment is laced into the wild dandelions that grow on lonely meadows. Neighbors frequently ask where I hide the light that was once in my eyes. Unfortunately, I do not hide it; the light has disappeared. The green in my pocket does not hold it. The blue in my heart stole it.

Penny, I will not bother to write you promises that fade in the sun. Words are only words, when held by paper. I have written you more letters than I can count. I have held more tears than the Atlantic holds salt. My love for you will cease only when my heart is buried deep below the earth.

If these words find you well, then pardon them. If they find even a small space in your heart that keeps my face or memory, then welcome them. In the night, I will continue to keep the front light on, and in the morning I will pour two cups of tea, as I always have, one with honey, one without.

When We Were We
Anonymous

*L*AST NIGHT, I dreamed of a wedding.

I don't make a habit of fantasizing about these things. I've never been one of those girls who buys bridal magazines so she can cut out the pictures of her favorite dresses. And floral arrangements have never held much interest for me. Theoretically, I want to get married someday, but I'm not particularly anxious.

Yet, last night, I found myself marrying you.

I'm not an idiot. I know what that means. I'm lonely. I want to be loved. And I miss you.

I don't want to admit it, though.

We haven't been "we" since eighth grade. That makes all this sound crazy, doesn't it? In eighth grade, half the class hasn't even hit puberty yet. In eighth grade, kids still want to be astronauts. Kids are still kids in eighth grade. But kids can still catch beautiful moments, and they can still make mistakes they'll regret forever.

You asked me to the movies less than a week after my last boyfriend kissed one of my best friends. I hadn't particularly cared about him. My dates with him had been few and awkward, chauffeured by parents making stilted conversation, and our conversations had mostly taken place on AIM. Still, when I'd found out about the kiss, I'd known I was supposed to be furious, and so I had been. More than being angry at what he'd done, though, I was scared for what it meant about me.

So when you asked me to the movies, I felt the warm blushing pleasure of being wanted. And so soon after what had happened! Besides, everyone liked you. You were a little goofy, in the smart classes, but not too smart. You had short blonde-brown curls and you were still tan from the summer.

I said yes.

For almost three months, we were "we." We weren't very good at flirting, and there was a lot of loud joking and playful fighting, and cutely stubborn refusals. But our awkward practicing still spread my lips into an irrepressible grin. And there was the touch of your arm, warm against mine...the fine golden-brown hairs shining against that summer tan.

The trouble came when I started to remember, and started to think. The last boyfriend had left. He had left, and I had been hurt, and it was a stupid waste of pain because I hadn't even liked him that much. What if you left? What if I was hurt, and I didn't even like you that much?

So I decided to break up with you, because I didn't know if I really liked you that much. And I didn't know when you would do it, if I didn't.

You cried a little, and my friends who weren't your friends laughed. I felt terrible. As soon as I had done it it I knew it was cowardly. Self-destructive. Sad. The first boyfriend had bent me, but what broke me was you — what I did to you. I haven't had anything as good as our "we" ever since. I've been cowardly; self-destructive; and mostly, sad.

The wedding I dreamed last night was not perfect. Everything was going wrong: my best friend was on a flight from France that had gotten delayed; the gift bags were missing; and I don't even think I was wearing a dress, let alone the frilly white meringue of little-girl dreams. As we were waiting, I said to my friends, "It's okay. You're not supposed to enjoy your own wedding. Your job is to make it nice for everyone else."

They looked at me like believing this was the strangest thing in the world. But I knew I was right. Because even though I was frantic and worried, all of that was just ruffled caps on the surface of a deep, serene happiness. I looked over at you — haphazardly stuffing gift bags — and smiled. They could have today. We had forever.

This wasn't a bad dream. It was a good one.

Dear Mr. Katinsky
by Geraldyne R. Weiser

*D*EAR MR. KATINSKY,
Sunday's New York Times carried the story of your daughter's wedding. Congratulations! They seem to be a lovely young couple.

I readily confess my addiction to the wedding pages, savoring announcements that command an entire column about where and how the couple met and decided to merge. But my response to your daughter's announcement was completely different. You see, it is **your** name, not hers, that caught my attention.

Aren't you the Kenneth Katinsky, currently from one of the trendy Long Island suburbs, who attended P.S. 36 in St. Albans a very long time ago? There are only a few kids I remember from then: Norman Hudson, whose father died when we were in third grade, Marilyn Bergman, whose mother let her wear a bra when mine insisted I still had to wear a Carter's undershirt, and you, on whom I had a major crush.

I remember that no one ever called you Ken or Kenny but always Kenneth, that your birthday is exactly three weeks before mine, that your parents owned The Jean Shop, and that your mother saw me make your lip bleed when I pushed your face into the park drinking fountain. Does any of this sound familiar to you?

I'm curious about something relative to your daughter's wedding announcement. I've come to expect the Times notice to include a line or two about the accomplishments of each of the couple's parents. Generally, every parent seems to have raised an extraordinary offspring while managing his or her own career as a Nobel Prize-winning doctor specializing in an obscure disease, a lawyer dealing with precedent-setting cases, or at the very least, a captain of industry. As I recall, your daughter's announcement said nothing about your resume, or your wife's. Did I simply overlook it? Given that we lost contact when my family moved to Philadelphia, I was particularly eager to know what you've been doing all these years.

In case you're wondering, I graduated from Penn with a degree in Spanish and French, married a nice Jewish doctor, raised four great kids—three sons and a daughter—all of whom have professional degrees and similarly credentialed spouses. Later, I acquired an MSW degree, divorced the doctor who turned out to be not-so-nice, and moved to Israel, where I lived for six years. When I returned to the US, I settled in Washington, DC.

You might be suspicious of my motive for being in touch after all these years. Here's the thing, Mr. Katinsky. Kenneth? The reason I am contacting you is that, in retirement, I've become the writer I had always wanted to be. I've been working on a memoir that my grandchildren may want to read some day, and I hope you might be able to fill in some gaps. Although it might seem too trivial to obsess about, I can't remember our second grade teacher's name. Can you? She was the one with dyed red hair and a very long nose.

I've reread this letter and admit that the last paragraph doesn't ring quite true. I suppose I should confess that there may be another motive for my contacting you, one that is quite embarrassing to acknowledge. Whenever I read about people who liked one another in grade school or high school, but then went their separate ways, only to meet again at a 50th school reunion, where their long-dormant spark was rekindled, I get goose bumps. Don't you just love those stories? When your name leapt out at me from last Sunday's Times, I couldn't help but wonder what would have happened if...

Again, *mazal tov* to you on your daughter's marriage. I eagerly wait for a reply that tells me about your life...and about your memories of P.S.36. Oh, and of course, please extend my best wishes to your wife.

Sincerely,

Geri (Penn) Weiss

Temporary Juliet
by Daniela LaRosa Schirripa

SHORTLY AFTER MOVING to a small town, I would take walks alone just to think. One walk lead me straight to you. But the first time we met wasn't love at first sight. You were sweet—but not my type. You were funny—but not for me. You were handsome—but not the kind of guy I would date.

But we became friends, great friends, spending so much time together that it was as if we were a couple, but dating other people. We shared our darkest secrets. You accepted me for me, and I didn't have to pretend to be someone else. I shared stories with you about me that made you cry, and at those times I would picture you there rescuing me. I started falling for you. But your family didn't like me and it was for the best to stay as we were. We hung out with other people, tried to hide our attraction for each other, but it was too apparent.

I had realized that this particular small town wasn't for me, and we had often talked about me leaving. I saw the grim look on your face, and how you tried to hide what your heart was feeling. It hurt me also, but I knew that I could not make my life here. I decided that shortly after my nineteenth birthday I would try living on my own back home.

And then that fateful night came; we had gone out with all of our friends for a New Year's Eve party. Shortly after midnight, you asked me to step outside. You needed to ask me something important. You took my hands and held me close and said, "After all this time of being friends, you and I both know how much we care for one another. And I can't go on another day thinking that you may leave, and you will never have been mine, just mine."

The moment had come when we had to give a voice to our feelings, when things had to finally be put into words. I told you that I did care for you—but you already knew that. I just wanted you to understand that no matter what happened in our relationship in my few remaining months, I would eventually be leaving. I didn't want to hurt you, nor did I want you to hate me when I did leave. I just wanted to make the terms clear. And you accepted.

Now it was my turn to accept your terms. You asked me to be "yours" and yours only, in a time when dating two or three people at once was normal. I would need to put aside the fact that I would be leaving and almost pretend it would never occur. You even asked me to avoid talking about it, if possible. You asked me just to love you as much as I could, and you would do the same. And I accepted.

From that night, we never left each other's side. You made me feel more special than anyone had in a long time. Not many people were happy about us being together, but it just made us stronger. We lived for each other, we lived for those moments, we lived for the limited time that we had together, and made the most out of it.

The time to leave came, as we knew it would. As much as I loved you, and as much as it hurt me to leave you, I had promised myself that I had to at least try—try to make it out on my own. No one could change my mind. We had spent night and day with one another just to not miss anything or any thought that the other would have. Then, on the very last night, we held each other and tried to stay up all night. It was as if we were trying to stop time and make that night last forever.

You accompanied me to the airport that morning and waited with me until I boarded. You said that you hoped I would make it, and that I would find what I was looking for. You also told me that if I ever came back you would not be there for me, since once that plane took off, you would be closing a chapter in your life. It hurt to hear, but I understood. Our love was intense…too intense to let it go and then pick it back up again as if nothing happened.

But I never did go back. Could be because I was too afraid of seeing you again, and the thought of you not wanting me was too painful. I guess I'll never know.

Thank you though, for loving me—even if it was for a short time.

Maybe...
by Thuy Hua

I WAS ONLY THREE AND A HALF YEARS OLD when I came to the states, when I entered the foreign world that birthed and nurtured you, yet was so new and bizarre to me. The streets were wider, with cars in place of motorcycles; stores replaced street vendors, and your cool California air replaced my thick humid Vietnamese air. Yes, we came from different worlds.

It wasn't until two years later, when our mothers became best friends in their sewing class, that our paths became entwined. When your mother was at work, you started to come to my home regularly, and we would spend the majority of the day together, crammed into a two-room apartment. All we did was fight, and then when my dad separated us, we would eyeball each other anxiously from across the room. I hated how you always hid my dolls behind the couch, took my father's attention away from me, and made my home your own. But if one day you didn't ring the doorbell, there was an emptiness, a deafening silence.

As the years passed and we entered our teens, you grew from my best friend to my boyfriend. Of course, to everyone else, our relationship seemed platonic. And for the most part, it was one of innocence. The extent of our physical interactions were hugs and kisses on the cheek that tended to find their way down to our nude pink lips. However, my fondest memory was of us on my dirty black couch, snuggled into each other's arms, watching and re-watching *Titanic*.

Titanic—the epic love story—you always believed in those. "Imagine a love that defies everything, even thousands of miles apart," you said. And even though neither of us wanted to admit it, in the silence I understood it clearly.

We would cuddle each other until the day you departed. The chill of your lips kissing my warm neck, the way you saw the sunrise, our walks around my neighborhood—it was heart wrenching to know I would soon miss all this. Your father had found a better job in Vietnam, and you would have to leave me. We were about to switch worlds, but this time, you were entering the one I had left behind.

A day before you went, you whispered in my ear that if I wanted you to stay, you would. But I couldn't do that to you, because I knew how much you loved your family. Your decision then would ruin you later, so I had to let you go, no matter how much I wanted to force you to stay—be selfish, and only think of myself.

From you I learned that loving someone is not about waiting to feel their love before expressing our own, but to choose to show love enduringly, forcefully, and without question. You were always the first one to grab my hand tightly and hold it like a trophy, kiss me on my virgin lips, and hold me until I felt only your existence.

I was too afraid to ask you to stay. To hold you.

Our relationship has dwindled, first to a few phone calls a day, to some Facebook posts, to silence. Distance has made our love wane. But there is always the *maybe* hovering around my head.

People say that when they are with the one they love, nothing else matters. But to me, everything in the world mattered, only because you existed next to me.

Maybe...maybe...

Karma Is a Funny Thing
by Drury Fisher

I CAN'T SAY I REMEMBER the date we first met. I was in sixth grade and you were in fifth. You were the skinny little blonde girl with pig tails and freckles, from across the street. As most boys that age are, I was too dense or uninterested to respond when your best friend approached me and said: "My friend Julie loves you."

My senior year of high school became the year I fell in love with you forever. You were the most beautiful creature to have ever walked the earth. I attempted to flirt with you and often I would catch you giggling in my presence, although I was still unsure of exactly what that meant. You asked me to the "Women Pay All" dance. My search for true love had ended. We were inseparable for the rest of the school year and into the summer.

In college, we learned the joys of sex, the wonder of one another's bodies. We were together for two years before the hundreds of gentleman callers turned your head. I was terrified I would lose you. I panicked and talked marriage. It blindsided you. We would spend the rest of our college days apart, but would always send one another a Valentine's Day card. And we would always see one another at Christmastime, attending church together on Christmas Eve and kissing lightly as the congregation was asked to greet the person next to them.

Upon your college graduation, ironically you were hired to work at the same company where I was employed, making working conditions awkward and yet karmic. I asked you to lunch, then you asked me to a concert. The next day you called to say that you couldn't get the tickets. Was it over…again? I was afraid of getting my heart smashed to pieces. When you left the company, I was sure I would never see you again.

Five years later, I was going to LA frequently for work. We spoke by phone, and you told me to feel free to stay at your apartment when I was in LA the next time. It happened that I would be there the following week. When I walked in the door and you greeted me, my knees went weak. You were magnificent, your blonde hair stylishly cut to your shoulder, your bright blue eyes piercing my soul as they had when we were in love. I knew nothing could come of it. I was seeing a woman off and on, and you were seeing a wealthy socialite, going out that night with him to a big gala.

I retired to your bed late that night and would awake to the sound of running water in your bathroom. You'd come home very early that morning, before sunup. When you entered the room, I was almost embarrassed, frightened. You slipped under the covers with me and it was like returning home. You were crying, kissing me, holding me. I didn't ask why the tears. I was happy to hold you, if just for one night.

We would not see one another again for ten long years. I called you to cry on your shoulder about my pending divorce. You were going to be in town for the next holiday weekend. "We should have dinner," you said. You were involved with another wealthy man at the time, but once we were in one another's presence for a couple of hours, love blossomed again. Your one day stay turned into five. We were inseparable for weeks after. "I love you. I want to get married and have your babies," you said. I was blindsided by that, and my hesitation hurt you deeply, I know. I didn't want to hurt you. But I knew I couldn't lose you again.

And so, we agreed to be lifelong friends, as we had been before. And I have thought of you every day since that day, fifteen years ago.

It has been almost thirty-five years since I fell in love with you the first time and truly, I have never fallen out of love with you. Karma truly is a funny thing, isn't it?

You
by Matukio OleAfrika Aranyande Chuma

MINUTES, HOURS, DAYS HAVE GONE; years have passed. Still, when I remember you, I smile. In such early ages of my growth as a man, when I knew nothing that this world has to offer, when I saw you the very first day, the very first moment, I needed nothing from the world but the sight of you (the beautiful you).

Too shy to light up, too soon to have even words to go about speaking, when I saw you, all I could give is a smile, an innocent one, not one of passion to cuddle you in my arms and have you next to me every morning by sunshine, every evening to oversee the sunset. (You, the beautiful creature I cherished whenever I saw you from afar, but very shy whenever you came and greet me, my love.)

Even now that I am writing this story, and all my memory comes afresh like only yesterday when we first met, guess what? I am smiling. All those years gone, all that past memory and the fact of unknown distance kept between us (you my first love, you a cute girl I had fallen in love with).

Though not knowing where now you are, though not the same feelings that you are remembering, wherever you now are (you my sweet little girl that I remember, you that I had at that innocent age thought marriage was our together destination, only later to realize life is not as easy as we imagine) wherever you are right now, I wish nothing but blessings, success and your true happiness (you, my first, my innocent, cute, beautiful, ever-smiling, yes, you—my one and only, my first love).

Yours once in that untold innocence called love...

A HINT OF
WHAT IS TO COME

From an early age, girls and boys conspire to create unspoken "rules of engagement" that allow them to comfortably coexist. But eventually a day comes when one of them reaches out and ignores those "rules." They then experience a hint of the enchantment that will become a major part of their lives as adolescents, and beyond.

Like a Princess
by Daphne Rice

*T*ALL FIRS REACH toward summer's sapphire sky. Something moves, and I sense someone near. Turning toward the cooler, shadowed drive, I whirl back again with an "Aha!" to catch his wide-eyed stare and surprised open mouth.

Almost fifty years ago, I met Johnny. We'd moved to the forested lot next to Grandma's house, far from our trolley-stop home in Milwaukee. I was four, he was five. Closing my eyes on this hot August day, I can still smell hot dirt and fir sap, feel a cool breeze sneak past at the edge of the heat. I see sparkly blue eyes and blond cropped hair sticking up in the back where he has a cowlick.

My summer of love. Isn't that silly? How can a four year old think she's in love? Where does a child get such an idea? I'll tell you:

Mamma reads fairy tales to me. Princesses always fall in love with handsome princes. My mamma married the most handsome man in the world. When I tell her I'm going to marry Daddy when I grow up, she smiles and gently strokes my hair. "No, little one, you must find your own handsome prince."

So, Johnny. He is the man of my dreams. We become fast friends. By week's end, he shows me the hiding place beneath the weeping willow and introduces me to his seven siblings. We play with his dog. I learn where scotch broom for stamping down into forts is best. We pick juicy, ripe blackberries, coming home with stained fingers, purple mouths, and darn few berries in the bottom of a tin can for our mothers.

We are inseparable for a year. He teaches me to fish in mud puddles with a safety pin, a stick, and a piece of string. We search for agates on our gravel road. With spit, Johnny makes the dullest rock shine like a gem.

On his first day of first grade, Johnny waves from the end of the gravel road, then again from far across the scotch broom field. I have to stay home. My heart is hurting.

I ask Mamma what time it is all through the day. When Johnny trudges up the hill in the hot afternoon sun, little dust clouds puffing from beneath his sneakers, I run down the road to greet him.

"How was school? Do you love it?" I ask, out of breath.

Johnny smiles, "Oh, yes! I have a girlfriend and her name is June! She has long, beautiful hair, just like a princess!"

My pixie cut, which I thought made me look like Audrey Hepburn, is no longer magical, and my heart breaks right in half.

When I retired this June, photos from my childhood, from college, from the past thirty years of classes, adorned the gym walls. In every picture my hair is long, past my shoulders, like a princess.

Has Anyone Seen Ronnie Kramer?
by Taryn Henry-Latham

JUST AS I PUSHED OPEN THE BIG HEAVY DOOR of our tan Oldsmobile, the one with the red stripe down the sides, the curtains at Ronnie Kramer's house slammed shut.

I could hear his feet thunder as he bolted for the front door, announcing, with his usual enthusiasm, "Tary Henry's here! Tary Henry's here! Tary Henry's here!" His welcome always made me feel I was in the right place at the right time.

Ronnie and I played better together than any other kids on the block. Our moms were best friends and we were the youngest in each of our families.

If we were lucky enough, we got to sit next to each other for Sunday church. But most of the time, we got separated for giggling way too much. Some things were just too funny for us to exercise any control at all, like big Pearl Tatum's arms swinging back and forth to the beat of "Bringing in the Sheaves" or hearing the overly exuberant Elanore Hardy hit a wrong note really loud on her trumpet.

How the grown-ups kept from laughing, we never knew. But one thing was for sure. Ronnie Kramer's smile would light up a room—it packed more teeth than anyone I knew. Proof of this was the fact that he held the blue ribbon from the Easter Contest in the park, "Boy with the most teeth, age five category." Actually, I think the judges created that category because they didn't have a ribbon which said, "Boy with the most exuberance, enthusiasm and unconditional love." That was the spirit behind all those smiling teeth.

Has anyone seen Ronnie Kramer?

Whether he was offering me the very last bite of his velvety smooth avocado sandwich, or letting me take the first try on his new bike without training wheels, it seemed that Ronnie thought more about me than he did about himself.

Me. The ribbon on my lapel read, "Girl with the bluest eyes, age six category." The one with the straight-across bangs and the Mary Jane shoes with the sox folded exactly the same on each side.

We didn't know anything then about unconditional love—we were just best friends.

Has anyone seen Ronnie Kramer?

Ronnie and I explored everything together. We knew then that we had a lot of choices to make every day. We would discuss them, but we never argued about what to do next. Whether it was trading stickers down at Wade Thornton's, exploring sand dunes on our bikes, or playing "pants down," choices were never an issue. We just seemed to know how to follow our hearts—and each other's.

"Pants down," we called it—looking at each other's nakedness was our innocent and androgynous way of celebrating our differences, and was part of our natural progression of knowing each other, just as were avocado sandwiches, climbing trees and racing to the dunes. Sometimes "pants down" would make our top three list of things to do, and sometimes not at all. But when it did, it was always clear whose choice it was.

"Ronnie, do you want to play 'pants down' or ride bikes to the dunes?"

"Pants down!" was his reply.

"I'd like to go to the dunes," I'd say.

"Okay, let's go to the dunes," he'd say.

There was never a question about unconditional love; we didn't know then that we had it, but it sure felt right.

Has anyone seen Ronnie Kramer?

A Specific Wind
by A. L. M.

I KNOW I MUST HAVE LAUGHED many times before, but the first time that I can remember, I was sitting in my best friend's room. I had lived next to Charlie ever since I had moved to Massachusetts in the first grade, and that night I was nine years old — and in love. Of course, I did not know about being "in love" for many years.

At the time, all I knew about was his blue eyes, which, while we sat in his warm room, were suddenly more vivid than I had ever seen them. (Michigan lakes, I think now — his eyes are the color that a huge, pacified body of water must be.) I was moving my arms in some wild, dancing gesture, trying to fully convey a story that my small self was not equipped to tell.

I remember him smiling. Every freckle on his newly tanned face and each auburn eyelash converged like a constellation, an entire myth of stars, to form that smile. My heart fluttered weakly in my chest: I could feel it — a glass bottle turning and turning in water, bobbing momentarily before it sank. If I felt that feeling now, I would call it trouble. Back then, I didn't have a word for it — could barely make enough room in my body for it.

I laughed and laughed that night, until I felt my entire body flushed and glowing. Both of us grabbed the end of a joke and pulled until the whole thing had been wrung dry, every last giddy drop squeezed from our lips. What I felt was a more complete happiness than I had ever known — a peace best felt obliquely, like a very specific wind, or a time of day.

As the last laugh subsided, a definite sobriety pooled around us. Every thought and idea that, only a second ago, was casually floating through the air, suddenly felt the pull of a thread anchoring it back to our bodies. The air in the room was thin. I saw his eyes, which still echoed with our words, and in that moment, I loved his innocence and his goodness.

I wish I had kissed him then. Young as I was, I wish I had attempted some action to bring us closer than we became, to tie some sort of knot, to celebrate the moment. But neither of us moved, and the moment slipped past, almost audibly leaving the room on the way out.

I moved to New Jersey shortly thereafter. For years, I talked about all the people I had known in that town—they stayed with me in my writing, in my conversations, in my day-to-day living. But I never really spoke to any of them again. Everyone I knew fell away, petering out like a weak flame.

Nine years later, I couldn't sleep. I was applying to college, and there were many nights I stayed awake, listening to the vibrations of insects in the dark, tracing strands of poetry until I could tie down a line, a verse. It was on one of these nights, while I wandered absently online, that it occurred to me to use the Internet to try to find some of the people who had passed out of my life. Charlie was the first.

I half-jokingly typed his name into a search engine, barely expecting to find anything. Half a dozen results popped up. Within minutes, I found out that he was attending a school close to where we had grown up. Photos of his nineteen-year-old self sprang up, unbidden. Each discovery was full of guilt and voyeurism, but I was quickly falling back into the step of the nine-year-old girl, outsmarted by the joy of sitting in silence with a boy.

In that moment, I told myself that I would apply to the same school he was enrolled in, move back to the same town, and make up for lost time. But it never happened.

I wasn't accepted to that school, never made it back to that town. and now—only occasionally, only when a memory seeds itself in my chest and insists on growing—only then do I find his face, his current face, his childhood face, in a life far away from my own.

A Moment Never Shared
by Laura Grace Weldon

*H*IS NAME WAS VINCENT. He may have entered Pine Elementary School when we were both in fifth grade, or may have been in my classes all along. But that spring he moved directly to the center of my awareness. He had silky black hair that fell low over astonishingly blue eyes. Unlike other grubby, snickering elementary school boys, he was quiet and attentive.

It was probably no coincidence that I fell for Vincent soon after getting Don McLean's *American Pie* album. A song about Vincent Van Gogh on the album captivated me. The lyrics told of a misunderstood visionary, a man with "eyes of China blue" whose soul was too beautiful for an uncaring world. Although I'd never really paid attention to boys before, somehow I merged the intensity of those words with a look I was sure I saw in Vincent's eyes, and I loved him for it. My girlfriends claimed to have crushes all the time over celebrities, the symptoms of their crushes including shrieking and silliness. I had none of these signs.

Once, as the teacher told us to line up at the door for music class, I found myself standing behind Vincent. I was sure he was aware of my presence. There could be no other explanation for the sudden frisson between us. Surely his skin prickled and his breath deepened, as mine did. I wanted to touch his dark hair. I wanted him to turn and smile at me with casual ease even though I knew that was not possible at school. The boys' loud obliviousness and the girls' sharp watchfulness kept any such thing from happening.

Boys and girls were friends only in books, where together they wandered moors or solved crimes or dreamed up new inventions. They talked openly and sometimes held hands. I wanted that with a longing more intense than I'd ever known.

Vincent kept me awake at night. His reserved nature made it easy to develop idealized concepts about him. I decided that he was smart and kind. I imagined that he was secretly drawn to me, but too shy to look my way. As I lay in bed, sleepless, I felt the injustice of being eleven years old. Too young to have love taken seriously, too young for anything.

Strangely, I felt old. Sorrows I'd carried for years became more intense because I'd lost the childhood distraction of play. I was on the verge of adolescence without sports or hobbies to keep me busy. All I had was this secret love for a boy named Vincent.

Over summer vacation I painted my toenails, tried to write poetry and wondered if God existed. What kept me awake now was worry over how I might make myself pretty enough for Vincent. But I was also dreading the prospect that he might reveal himself to be something less than the person I'd imagined.

Vincent didn't come back to school for sixth grade. No one knew where he'd gone. That made him, in my mind, more mysteriously alluring than ever. Sometimes at night I opened my bedroom window to breathe in the night air and look at stars. I hoped he might be at his own window. I no longer ached to hold his hand; I only wanted him to be happy.

I can still easily picture Vincent's face, even if I've forgotten his last name. My secret love for him taught me the first gentle lesson in becoming a woman. Unrequited love isn't always painful. Sometimes it's as tender as a moment never shared with a beautiful blue-eyed boy.

My First Paradigm Shift
by Juli E. Ocean

O<small>N MY BLOCK, AROUND TWO CORNERS,</small> stood a white two-story clapboard house. Two towering pine trees guarded the house like silent green giants. Inside lived Jeff, the first love of my life. He had straight dark hair and freckles. I don't remember meeting Jeff so much as just becoming aware of him and his kind heart. He was good and fair. He and his sister Cindy used to ride one bike together, even though she was older and could have had her own. They acted like best friends.

While we were walking to school one cloudy fall day, I gave Jeff some cherry licorice. We each bit the ends off a piece and blew through them, making whistling sounds. When we tired of that and they grew a little soggy from being in our mouths, we ate them.

A few blocks later, a boy named James joined us. Jeff was "walking friends" with James, but I didn't like him. He was a trouble maker who was in my class. James didn't like me either. When Jeff wasn't around, James teased me.

Jeff gave James his last piece of licorice. James eyed me, knowing I would never give him mine. But he gladly accepted Jeff's offering, and just as he was about to bite it, I yelled, "You can't do that!" James froze.

"Why not?" Jeff asked.

"I gave that to you."

"I know, but doesn't that make it mine?"

"Yes."

"If it's mine, then I can share it with my friend if a want to." His "want to" came out "wonna."

"But..."

James shoved the entire length of candy in his mouth, before Jeff could change his mind. He looked at me, na-na-na boo-boo in his eyes. Until then, I had never thought of myself as selfish or controlling. I couldn't get over Jeff's willful sharing, or his lack of expectation that I would replace what he had given. In fact, Jeff seemed to care less about the candy.

When we hit school, my boyfriend went to his kindergarten class and I went to mine. Before five minutes had passed, James was in trouble, and our teacher, Miss Mary, stood him in the corner. I went to the coat room to get a cough drop and discovered someone, Linda, backing away from one of the coats. She'd found my Luden's cherry cough drops and stuffed her mouth nearly full. No one had ever stolen from me before. Linda stood glued to the floor, looking horrified at having been caught.

Following Jeff's lead, I offered her more. She declined. I pushed one into her lips. She looked confused. I left the coat room.

For the rest of the day, Linda apologized and wanted to be my friend. Test-driving generosity, I discovered, felt good.

Over the summer, Jeff moved away, disappearing from our neighborhood, but not my heart. I'll always remember that he gave me my first paradigm shift.

Johnny Forever
by VonQuisha Ann Russell

OH, YOU KNOW HOW WE LEARN LOVE. My foundation formed in relationships with my Mama, my Papa, and my brother. Do you believe it is true that however love turns out, we begin with something like that: our family making the way for who becomes our first sweetheart?

My first sweetheart was Johnny Hernandez. I vividly remember him coming to my house on his bike, always stopping exactly the same place between our grass and the tarred road. Right there!

He would stand astride his bike to gaze over our grassy yard, waiting for me to come out. He always wore a grownup style black-rimmed hat. His shadowed eyes warmly glistened, even when shaded. Johnny also wore a badge-like shiny clip around one black-trousered leg. He stood ready to wait or to peddle away on his bare-chained bicycle. I liked Johnny to stand at my house that way. It seemed important. He was important.

I liked going to his home too, especially in the summer. It was an adventure to walk down hot Ashland Avenue and to trot, or tarry, on the Calumet River Bridge. On the other side of the bridge, I gladly entered the forest preserve. Then I went back into bright sunlight and onto a forgotten dirt road to sneak past Franky Popp's abandoned farm. Finally, I traipsed down shining, blistering railroad tracks to go to the end where Johnny lived.

It was a relief, and I was semi-blinded when I climbed into their welcoming home, out of the hot glaring sun. It all smelled good, the newly washed white things and something cooking in a darkish corner. These impressions mixed with mysterious passions going on in the home among this extended family.

Johnny's home thrilled me. Outdoors, Mrs. Hernandez hand-washed the perfectly white cotton shirts the boys always wore. Water came from a spigoted pipe down the track, and I enjoyed carrying buckets of water for her. They lived in a roomy box car, where dim, glaring light shifted on windowless newspapered walls, readable walls. It was exciting when stark shadows of someone moving past the open doorway would suddenly leap, blocking out all the words on the paper. All was fascinating.

A silent affection attracted my heart to Johnny, who in my mind seemed to yearn toward me. I loved being with serious Johnny, and with Frankie, his exuberant brother. Johnny, Frankie, and I played by those railroad tracks or on my street where the rest of kids also gathered to play—tag, baseball, hide and seek, or races, war, cowboys and Indians, hockey or marbles—until we had to go home.

I had a child's sense of the human quest going on, the universal drive for survival and happiness, ancient human existence, families coming from far away. I was aware that mine, too, came from far away and ancient times. Johnny meant all of that to me, and more.

When I grew up, I married a man who looked at me with poignant loving gazes that might be just like Johnny's gazes at my house from the road. My husband told me he was enthralled by his childhood sweetheart to whom he had never declared his love feelings. She fills his heart to this very moment. That sometimes makes me wonder if Johnny remembers me, and what could be his memory of the eager girl who loved to be with him.

That first romantic relationship stays perfect in my soul. I use the memory for sorting life and as a reminder to cherish the dear ones. Sometimes I use it just to remember back to when my mother brushed and then braided white taffeta ribbons into my auburn hair before I went out to play with Johnny or the other kids.

Beneath a Pink Umbrella
by Michael Keyton

*H*E WAS STILL BEING FOLLOWED. He fingered the Lugar. His lips tightened. If all else failed, there remained the cyanide capsule lodged behind a back tooth. *Don't look round.*

He crossed the road barely in time, swerving left to run beside the truck that had so nearly run him over, and swerved again—right this time—down the alleyway running parallel to Warbreck Moor. His eyes scanned the desolate lane. Not even a cat moved. Some ways in the distance, a row of bins. Cover.

His pace quickened. There were footsteps behind him. Remorseless and fast. Oberführer Gessler. He dived behind the nearest bin, sending the others crashing along the ground. His Lugar was out now, the capsule resting between two teeth, waiting to be crushed. He thought of Gabrielle and glanced longingly behind him at an alley that seemed to stretch forever. So close.

"Mike, do you think you've passed?"

"Hope so." I slipped the pencil-case into my pocket, swallowed the mint.

"Me too," said Tony.

It was unlikely, but still I hoped. The 11 plus—Britain's own "Sorting Hat"—the exam your parents wanted you to pass. Gabrielle Moffat would pass and go to a different school and I would never see her again.

I had been in love with her from when I first saw her standing in the rain beneath a pink umbrella. She wore a blue plastic raincoat and an innocent smile. Her eyes were blue, hair yellow, and she smelled of sweet pastry. I was eight and had fallen in love. I hadn't told her—assumed that she knew.

The bell was ringing as I burst into the classroom. I sat beside her for the very last time. The feeling was strong.

Mr. Fylde walked into the room. He was wearing a new tweed jacket. Grey. And he stared down the room until there was silence. It began with a cough, followed by the names of those who had passed. Gabrielle smiled. I punched her gently.

"Well done."

Mr. Fyled frowned, and I stared at the desk. *Should I tell her…?*

Her knee brushed against mine. I think it was sympathy.

Mr. Fylde stopped and looked up from the list. "Those whose names I haven't called out may take an early break."

Gabrielle would go to Grammar School, be given a bike, wear a smart uniform, and carry her work in a glossy leather satchel. She'd go to University and she'd become more beautiful, and I would never see her again. We whose names were not called would stay where we were and become mechanics or plumbers —or, perhaps, secret agents.

Love, the Most Stingy Person
by Nhan Ho

GRANDPA SAID, when you look at a boy's eyes, and spontaneously you see a vivid light, that you have to immediately avoid. And when your hands accidentally touch his, the feeling of improbability makes you want to run away. But you are still standing there, challenging anybody making you move, for that's the only thing you are wanting to do. You know you look very silly, and you are. You act funnily and try to get every single attention from that one and only person while yourself paying every bit of yours to him. You feel itchy, and your heart beats so vigorously, angrily and then poignantly when seeing the boy talking to other girls and giving them his smiles. You become so controlling. You cry for no reason. You feel yourself standing in a different world of vibrations. You are in the no-no-world, or the love-so-distracting world.

I felt nothing like that, honestly to say, when my palm slapped your jaw as you told me I was fat. I really wouldn't have done that on purpose if you hadn't made the bet that I didn't dare do that. That gamble of destiny brought us to be enemies like forever, since we were six. I wouldn't care that much if you didn't tell my mom I had failed in my language art test. And certainly, after that I paid you back by showing your dad your love letters. Trust me, it was fun seeing his countenance.

Those were the days following you to fights, to your soccer games, to be your biggest anti-fan. Those were the days you went disturbing my elementary tutoring class. Those were the days you laughed like bizarre seeing me doing exercises in my PE class, and I giggled watching you being panicked with algebra.

Once you rode me to school on your bike, the day my leg was twisted, and the everyday street turned out to be so fresh. The smell of the zephyrs cooling down the heat of the city made me see you much more attractive as your "No" answers were given whenever I asked whether you were tired, although you were sweating like taking a shower. Since that day I had never gone to school in a different means of transport.

And I noticed it was you who told your teammates to shut their mouths when they tried to pick on me. Then we both went to our favorite noodle restaurant, your mom's, in which you rudely made me wash the dishes to pay for the food. It was you also who abruptly hold my hands and told me that everything would turn out right when I was anxious about my exams. You and your teddy bear were ugly enough to do the very "chick-flick" mission of cheering me up. I laughed and warned you about telling your friends. I wished I had told them.

The boy next door, you, corrupted me by teasing me to play truant, which turned out to be my hobby. On your bike, we wandered around every street, lake, café in the city we both love. I feel like flying. I feel myself delicate.

I fled away. I decided to go abroad for studying. I chose going against my instinct, without telling you. I was weak, and having not the same determination when I stayed beside you that I only wanted to be held. I was so in need of being protected by you, and I didn't want myself to depend on that.

Five months after, I called home, and my heart stopped beating, hearing that you were in a crash.

Grandpa also said, "Love is the most stingy person." I have never told you, "I love you." You didn't even have the chance to say that, and I bet you wouldn't do that to me. I don't deserve thinking about that. It has been three years since the day you left me to be the loneliest person in the world. Your image stays so clearly in my recollections. Memories won't re-happen, I know. I am now by myself on that crowded hot street. Forgive me, would you?

R.I.P.

The Magenta Crayon
by Monica A. Andermann

I WASN'T SURE WHAT IT WAS that made me like Tommy. Maybe it was the cowlick that popped up at the back of his crown or the cleft in his chin. Or maybe it was the urgent koosh, koosh of his brown corduroy pants as he ran down the hallway of our elementary school, late for class every morning. Looking back now, I see it was none of those things. It was the crayons.

Nothing thrilled the students of Mrs. Cohen's first grade class more than coloring time. On Tuesday and Friday afternoons, we closed our workbooks, put down our pencils and pink rubber erasers, and spent the last twenty minutes of the afternoon expressing our artistic selves. When Mrs. Cohen announced, "Coloring time!" a stampede would erupt between the rows of neatly placed desks, ending at the back table where the two large coffee cans filled with crayons sat waiting.

Twenty-five sets of small hands rummaged through the cans for the perfect shades. Blues, greens, and even an odd color with the strange name of "ochre," were grabbed quickly—yet none as fast as the bright magenta crayon I needed to complete my drawing of a summer bouquet. That color was a particular favorite of all the girls, and I just wasn't quick enough to grab it before them. Whoever snared the prize crayon first would invariably raise it to the sky and cry out, "It's mine!" But never me.

One day there was a discontented rumbling around the coffee cans. Where was the magenta crayon? Had it rolled under the radiator and melted? Or worse, had it fallen under the table only to be swept up and disposed of by the nighttime custodian? Who could have been so careless as to have lost the magenta crayon? Fingers pointed in all directions. As I watched the witch hunt unfold, Tommy came up behind me and laid his balled-up fist on my desk. While the others searched, he opened his fingers to reveal the magenta crayon. I batted my eyelashes in adoration and, for the first time ever, noticed the cute way his mouth curled when he smiled. Week after week, Tommy would hand me the magenta crayon in our secret little way. Soon he began to bring me other colors, too. I needed only ask.

He may have been quick, but Tommy wasn't very good at math. If he began to stammer when called upon by Mrs. Cohen, I would hold up my fingers indicating the correct answer. So, from the sharing of our individual talents, a beautiful friendship unfolded. I often drew little flowers for him on pieces of scrap paper and then watched as he smiled and pushed the papers into the back of his desk. Proudly, he showed me the improving scores on his math tests and I kept a running list of the grades.

Then came the last day of school. As we all cleaned out our desks, I envisioned warm weather visits and play dates with Tommy. From behind me, I heard some chuckling and a grumble. As Tommy pulled out the stack of my hand-drawn flowers, the other boys began to tease him.

"Do you like her?" one asked, pointing toward me. Tommy's face went expressionless. Even the cleft in his chin seemed to disappear. He shrugged his shoulders and with the same palm he had used to hand me the magenta crayon, he scrunched all my drawings together and promptly threw them in the trash.,

There, at the age of six, I learned an important lesson: the difference between boys and girls isn't contained solely in their shorts, but slightly higher, too, in their hearts. In that moment, I discovered also that love and heartbreak go hand in hand and sometimes, pride is stronger than love.

Most importantly though, my little friend taught me never to open my heart too quickly to any man offering the magenta crayon of love, no matter how cute his smile may be.

Young Friendship Love
by Julia Jacques

I REMEMBER THIS BOY as if our story happened yesterday. On my first day in class, I found out there was a new kid. This gorgeous boy with twinkling blue eyes walked in and sat in the desk next to me. We were both in second grade, but he was one and half years older than me.

I tried talking to him, only to find out he spoke very little English and had just been adopted from Russia. Since he sat by me, the teacher let me help him in class. We talked more and more, and became very close.

He couldn't read English, so when we started working on reading in class, I became his tutor. I spent hours teaching him how to read. Imagine a seven year old girl teaching an eight year old boy to read. We had a connection—I understood him and he understood me.

We were in school together for the next three years. After I moved away, we still talked on the phone and even sent each other letters through the mail. Although we were at that age where kids don't say certain stuff because it's not "cool," we still talked. We talked about everything. We were best friends, and we loved each other in a special way.

Last summer, I tried calling him and found out that he had moved out of his parents' house. They wouldn't tell me where he went. But he's too young to be in his own house.

I'm confused about where he is. From the way his parents talked to me, it sounded as if he had passed away. But I have no clue.

He meant so much to me. He taught me to be nicer and care more about people. He also showed me how to be a better friend and to just be myself. I will always love him, even if I never see him again

So Sergei, if you are out there, try to get in touch with me!

A TIME TO DREAM

During our junior high and high school years, we often feel rather bewildered: those who were once barely tolerated are now infused with a mysterious attraction. We begin to notice, and respond to, the presence of a certain girl or boy, the "other," in a new way. This transition, often clumsy, always confusing, is undeniably exciting.

Ah, adolescence.

Let us be especially kind to our younger selves, reaching for the stars, hoping, faltering, and then reaching again—dreaming the possible and the impossible with equal fervor.

We'll Always Have Chicago
by Kelsey Hanson

I WAS ABOUT THIRTEEN years old when my classmates labeled me a nerd. I didn't mind. I liked my personality, and my nerd status never stopped me from making friends. I had braces. I had glasses. I liked to read. In my mind, yes, I was a nerd. As strange as it sounds, there's something sort of romantic about being a social outcast. I liked sticking out from the crowd, even if it came with some negative feedback.

I never thought I would fall in love. I didn't really think that any boy would look twice at me. I was pretty, but in a bookish way. I was friendly, but in a shy way. Love seemed out of my reach. It was never something that I could understand. I hated Valentine's Day and all the sappy poetry and love songs that came with it. I despised romantic comedies. They seemed so peppy and annoyingly unrealistic. I never could get into them. *I am a nerd*, I thought to myself, and nerds don't have boyfriends. I was wrong.

I think most of my peers had written me off as one of those people who will be single forever. That was probably why, when I finally did find a guy, people found it startling. Heck, it was downright scandalous!

We didn't have a romantic start. I didn't meet his eyes across a crowded room. The world didn't stop when he shook my hand. Instead, I sat on his foot during a school assembly. I apologized and he simply smiled and shrugged, "That's okay, I have big feet." His name was Eric. He was about my age even though he was a grade ahead of me. He was young for his class and I was old for mine. He had glasses. He had braces. He liked to read. It seemed too good to be true.

We were friends for several years before we actually became an "item." That happened on a class trip to Chicago. Both of us had been flirting. Everyone on the bus knew it. Everyone was watching us as if we were some sort of telenovela. We finally made it official during the trip.

We were quite the pair that day. From our ankles up, we both looked pretty good. He was wearing a dress shirt and tie. I was wearing a designer shirt and slacks. But both of us had insisted on wearing comfortable (and incredibly worn out) tennis shoes with our lovely outfits. There was no way I was running up and down The Magnificent Mile in stilettos.

After a night at the theatre, we went to Navy Pier. We started out with a group of about six. Then, the rest of my friends conveniently disappeared, leaving Eric and me alone. We spent the rest of the day walking up and down the dock watching the sunset. It was then that we decided to give it a shot.

I was truly in love with Eric. In his eyes, I wasn't weird. I could talk about *Lord of the Rings* and classical music around him. He wouldn't laugh. In fact, he was genuinely interested. We'd argue about which was better, the book or the movie, and he would send me Josh Groban songs over the internet. It felt so good to be considered normal. Not weird. Not a nerd. He told me all the time that I was perfect, and I believed him. I felt perfect.

Unfortunately, he was a senior. He graduated that year and went off to college. I left him a romantic love note in his year book that said, "P.S. We'll always have Chicago." We spent one final summer together before he had to go away. In the fall, Eric went to school in another state. I was heartbroken, but determined to make it work.

It didn't. Eventually, the distance proved too much and we broke up, but I'll always remember Eric. He proved to me that even a cynical, nerdy person like myself can fall in love. For a moment, I was perfect in someone else's eyes. Someday, I believe I'll find a man who will always think I'm perfect. Until then, I'll always have Chicago.

Electrically Imprinted
by Lori Stott

NOT TOO LONG AGO, I came across a Dear Abby headline that caught my eye: "Happily Married Woman Still Misses Lover Who Never Was." The letter was signed, "Needs Closure".

Needs closure. That's me. My past love, the one I can't shake entirely, was my high school sweetheart, my first true love. Upon graduation, we attempted to carry on our relationship despite the fact that we lived two thousand miles apart.

At forty-five, I am truly happily married to a man whom I adore. We have created a family and a life together that is built on trust and love and grace. But I still think of my first love. I feel that he—or the we that was—will always have a place in my heart of hearts. Our relationship, which to tell you the truth, ended badly, holds a sacred place in my being. It is but a memory, a precious but tumultuous snapshot of a youthful time, passionate love-making on a blanket in the field behind my parent's house, tender hand-holding in the local movie theatre.

I know so few people who are walking around on the planet who don't wonder about a past love, or think about that time of life when that particular love was alive. Mine is named Darren. I have friends of all ages and backgrounds who have told me theirs: Kenny, John, Gayle, Derek, Colleen. My mother recently went to her fiftieth college reunion, and had those old feelings come up after spotting her first boyfriend, a man she had not stood next to in over five decades! This "wondering" seems to be a universal condition.

It is not so much the "what if's" that get ahold of me (*what if* we went to college in the same state, *what if* we had managed to stay faithful, etc.) but more like the feeling in my body that won't let go of the memory of him, of the us that used to be. So when I read this Dear Abby's explanation that past loves are actually "imprinted" in our electrical circuitry, it just seemed right. Ah ha! Our relationship is literally "in" me, still, just as I have suspected now for almost thirty years.

I have seen Darren at two high school reunions. At our tenth, we were still both single and I am sure the thought of "what if?" wandered across both our minds. But nothing happened, and I know now that this is for the best. It was at that reunion gathering, after years of silence and despair (and after making formal amends to him years prior, for essentially screwing things up between us) that I felt I was able to look him in the eye and thank him for the gifts he had given me. You see, Darren had opened up my world to the joys of backpacking in the Rockies. He showed me awe and wonder for the grandeur of nature, while at the same time an appreciation of the small things, even good socks or the right camping hat. I told Darren that, to this day, when I go hiking, the memory of him is with me, in my feet and in my heart. I was able to share my gratitude for the time we had together.

At our twentieth high school reunion, we simply had a good time, exchanging stories and laughter about our present lives, enjoying the fact that we still both shared a love of adventure, travel and the outdoors. He and my husband Jay hit if off so naturally (no surprise there, they are a lot alike!) that former classmates were compelled to ask if we were all buddies.

Through the years there has been healing and self-forgiveness for the pain and loss of that early love relationship. Still...every now and then, Darren pops into my mind or shows up in a dream. But I no longer wonder why. I just think, "Oh there he is again." And I know that he is "electrically imprinted" in me and shall forever be. And that is as it should be. Abby said so.

Shimmer
by Suzanna Freerksen

*I*T'S STILL THERE, a memory of a memory. I was with my high school boyfriend, Jacob, my first love. He was kind—and tall. At just under five feet, I always stared up at his six foot height. We made it work, because the alternatives were unthinkable.

We talked about the deep things that teenagers talk about, but it was in our kisses that we communicated most eloquently. Being with Jacob awakened in me a need I didn't know I had—for unconditional love from a peer. His big calloused hands engulfed mine in a way that always defined safety and comfort. Sometimes, I would flee my tumultuous life at home into his welcoming bed.

It was the summer before going off to college. It was not our last summer together, but we thought that it was. The June night was surprisingly cool, but my recent graduation from high school and acceptance to an honors college had made me bold. I think it was even I who suggested that we go swimming in his parents' backyard pool—without the suits.

There was a full moon, and the water was cold. After doing all the silly, sybaritic, and ultimately forgettable things that young teenagers do while naked in a pool, I felt cold. I hugged Jacob close for warmth. Since I was buoyed up by the water, I was able to look over his smooth shoulder, instead of at it. His head and clavicle framed a perfectly round, yellow moon. His skin was cold on the surface, but radiated heat from underneath. I held him like that for a minute.

For those sixty seconds, the universe was totally complete. I was exactly where I needed to be. I felt calm and content, as if all my life up until then I had been treading water. For that moment,

I had stopped struggling, immersed in the water, to have a religious experience.

I could have died happy at that moment. Perhaps something in me did. That might have been its magic. There was no reason to suddenly and inexplicably feel as if I belonged right there in that pool, with that man, looking at that moon.

It is something I long for even now that we have gone our separate ways. Jacob has a two year old son and I look forward to a new future with my own true love.

But I will always remember my first love, and the way it shimmered that one night in the pool.

More Than Pocket Change
by Abigail MacKenzie Sprague

*A*s I WRITE THIS, I realize that I am still eighteen years old. My past love was not that long ago, but that sanctuary we created together, using only our crossed fingers and rapidly beating hearts, feels like a lifetime ago.

Jack. Even his name sounds like an adventure, at least to me. I met him when I was still sixteen years old, innocent as ever, completely the opposite of this brilliantly blue-eyed, brown-haired, weed-smoking boy who reeled me in by making me laugh. Not just a small giggle, but a laugh that starts deep down in your soul and keeps you smiling long after the joke is over, long after the person has left.

There were a lot of things wrong with our relationship, some of which I am only recognizing now. There was the disrespect, the lying, the cheating, and the overall downfall of our relationship. But after our junior year in high school, and before the long summer days began to grow shorter, there was a love that we swore would never die.

Every once in a while I try to bring back a memory in my mind, just to remind myself that yes, I did feel that free, that happy, that loved, once upon a time. Lately however, with my first year of college only three weeks away, the memories have become hazy. They've become harder to bring back—that is, all except this one.

Jack showed up at my front door unannounced that humid afternoon in May, smiling and confident as usual. Upon entering my kitchen, he asked my mother's permission for me to drive down the Cape with his family to meet his grandparents. It was a school night and I had a history test the next day, but even my mother could not refuse those ocean blue eyes. As soon as we knew it was a definite yes, I ran upstairs to put on nicer clothes. He mentioned cashing in change at his bank, so we began collecting a shoebox full of coins we found scattered about my room.

His maroon-colored Saab with the sub speakers and tinted windows pulled up to the bank just before the rain came. I placed the shoebox on the roof of his car and we stood there smiling at each other.

"Oh man, do you smell that rain?" he asked, just as I shouted, "I love the smell of rain!"

He grabbed my hand and kissed me in that moment and we ran inside to turn our coins into dollar bills.

On the ride to his grandparents' house we held hands.

We had a homemade Italian dinner with his family, and his grandmother instantly fell in love with me. I remember feeling at home at the kitchen table, as if I belonged there—I could have spent the rest of my life eating dinner with his family on hazy afternoons.

On the car ride home, we fell asleep, our fingers entwined like the rest of our lives were supposed to be, or so we promised.

I know there is nothing spectacular about that story. No fireworks, no passionate kisses under the stars, no heartbreaking moment that makes you run for the tissue box. I could have told you about our watermelon-flavored first kiss, the time he cried because he realized he had fallen in love with me, or the harsh ending to our love story. I could even have told you about the week I almost won him back again, how he wasn't at graduation, or how I'm starting a new life while he's staying in this town forever, though I believe he will do something great with his life…someday.

No, instead I decided to tell you about a simple day in our story. I'm realizing those are the moments that come back to me, as clear as crystal. You see, Jack gave me more than a way to turn my change into cash. He gave me a way to turn my fears into dreams, my dreams into reality. He gave me love, a love as pure and simple as that day in May.

As If by Accident
by Albert W. Caron, Jr.

WHILE RUMMAGING through a dust-covered box in a storage area in my home, I spied an oversized manila envelope, faded with age. As I opened it, I could almost hear the voice of Rod Serling telling me that I was coming up to a signpost in the road ahead. In spite of the "Twilight Zone" music in my head, I decided to proceed.

I opened the rusted metal clasp and pulled out some photos, taken long ago. My senses suddenly went into overdrive as the past came alive. One color photograph triggered my mind back to a wonderful time in my youth. A smile came to my lips, my eyes squinted, searching to find small details of a bygone era, and my nose could even smell her perfume.

The picture was taken when Linda asked me to go to her junior prom. That was an easy decision. Linda was a pleasant young lady with a winning smile to go along with her outgoing personality. Her distinctive features were gorgeous brown eyes and soft, sensuous lips.

I felt comfortable with her and she with me. We enjoyed each other's company and knew each other's parents. I even thought someday we might go steady, get engaged, and possibly get married. Those were the dreams of my first love, long ago.

I remember our first "date" as if it was yesterday.

One afternoon I took over a sixty-customer newspaper route for a friend. Delivering the papers was easy, since the houses were duplexes or even triple deckers, close to one another. With my Schwinn bicycle I could finish the route in about an hour. And I was paid fifty cents.

I decided that this day was going to be special. I would have money in my pocket, enough for a "date." I told Linda that if she wanted, I would "take" her for a soda at the corner drugstore, where they had old-fashioned marble-top counters with stools cemented and bolted to a step in front of the fountain. I also told her I couldn't stay long because I had to do a paper route. After all, there are priorities in life, and I had to make sure that those newspapers were delivered on time! Linda accepted my clumsy attempt at a date.

Let me explain "take" her on a date. It meant that I would meet her near the drugstore, as if by accident. Then we would go in together and sit next to one another at the fountain. We both ordered a soda. She ordered a plain Coke and I had my usual, a vanilla Coke. I needed that "extra kick." I gave Linda money for the Coke under a napkin, very quietly, without anyone seeing us. I let her pay for the soda herself, so that if anyone saw us sitting together at the counter, they would be none the wiser. It would be one boy and one girl, sitting at the counter, talking and each having a soda. My friends could never tease me about dating Linda. I was only thirteen at the time, and one could not date "officially" until the end of the eighth grade.

We had several similar "dates," where I gave her the money outside before we got inside the drugstore. Then, over the next few years, we went out on a few real dates to drive-in movies, bowling, dances, and even a prom while we were in high school. But as college drew near, we began to drift apart. After high school, she moved to New Jersey and out of my life, but not my memory.

That furtive "date" was an awkward, but necessary, first step in the early 1960's. It was nothing more than an icy cold drink and a quiet conversation at a real soda fountain with a girl— Linda— my first love.

My Hero
by Ariella Nasuti

*I*NTER-RACIAL DATING was not common forty years ago in the small town where I grew up—at least not for twelve year olds. In those days, there were two African-Americans in our school, Joe and Larry Prince. Joe was a star athlete who sprinted his way across the minefield that is junior high, silencing his critics with the sheer scope of his talent. His brother, Larry, had the lanky build of a dreamer and the hands of an artist. Instead of the muscled t-shirts favored by most boys, Larry wore flannel shirts and baggy jeans. He wasn't blessed with the ability to run fast or jump high, but he could make people laugh. His sense of humor set Larry apart. He was convinced it could also bring the world closer—that even the most ignorant kids would see in time that laughing with him was more fun than hitting him. And it was, but not as much fun as kissing him.

Larry and I first kissed in a darkened hallway lined with floor to ceiling lockers. I mention the setting only because the feel of louvered metal pressing into my upper back, as Larry took me in his arms, isn't something I've easily forgotten. Still, it was worth it. That the kiss was tentative, chaste, brief and somewhat awkward goes without saying—we were in seventh grade, after all. And seventh graders in my day weren't as sophisticated as they are today—a point of both pride and shame for my generation.

The morning after "the kiss," I received a missive from Larry, one passed to me in a crowded hallway between classes. Expecting a declaration of undying love, I glanced down to see instead a hand-made comic book. Every few days after that, I received a new installment in the saga of *The Captain*, a crime-fighting superhero born of Larry's imagination. After school, he'd read the comics aloud to me, bringing the painted images and printed dialogue to life. We'd sit on the grassy playground behind the gym, knees touching and heads bent over Larry's handiwork. As he spoke, I'd stare into his chocolate brown eyes, seeing a hero more real to me than any superhero could ever be.

As The Captain battled injustice with his fists, Larry fought racism with words, disarming his enemies one joke at a time. Some mistook his gentle manner for weakness, but I knew better. Larry taught me that although punching a bully may stop him, it doesn't make him think. Larry's method did.

In time, he won over all but the most hard-core racists. Larry no longer needed *The Captain* for guidance and inspiration, so he stopped writing the comics. The superhero he'd created slipped into the shadows of my mind, resurfacing only in dreams and scraps of memory that flit through my thoughts at odd moments. When that happens, I remember the lesson of those comics: that good always vanquishes evil. That's what Larry believed, or at least it was the way he wanted life to be.

During our hectic high school years, as sports and work moved center stage, Larry and I drifted apart. Like all teenagers, our gaze shifted from the security of what we knew toward the promise of distant horizons. Part of me regrets that we lost touch, for I never knew the man Larry became. But, another part will always celebrate the gentle, funny, imaginative boy he was. In countering racism with humor, bitterness with optimism, and ugly words with barbed jokes, Larry walked a path few do. And because he welcomed me—a white girl—into his heart, he didn't do it alone.

First Love Is Never Forgotten
by Dorothy Baughman

I WAS IN THE EIGHTH GRADE when true love entered my life. Oh, I'd had crushes from first grade on, but this was the real thing.

Don was new to our school, and I caught his eye across the room when we were being divided up for home room. Yep, sure enough, he was in my home room and most of my classes. He was a band student, which was my utmost wish, but my parents couldn't afford that.

I loved this boy with a passion for three years, which is a long time for a school crush. He had dark hair and green eyes, a curl always hung forward, and I loved the way he pushed it back. We never dated, never went out, all we had was school. And by tenth grade, we had the football games. He played trombone and I sat as close to the trombone section as I could get when the band was performing from the bleachers. Not even my closest friends really noticed that Don and I went out of our way to be next to each other. However, somehow the band director knew. He put Don on the end of the line of trombones so I got to turn the pages of his music.

That Christmas he gave me a blue scarf and bangle bracelets, and I wore his band bracelet with our school's name written on it. Near the end of tenth grade, he pulled me aside and told me the most awful news: he was changing schools because the band director wouldn't let him play football. I found out quickly about the engrained sports gene in a male.

So off he went the next year, but I never forgot him. I went on to marry and have three children. I did keep up with him through his sister, who runs a daycare in my town.

I saw him again when I was working at a local hospital as an EKG tech. I went to do a cardiogram; the man turned out to be Don's step-dad, and there stood Don. You always want to look your best when you meet an old beau, not be in a white uniform and pregnant to boot. He was sweet and complimentary, and we said goodbye again.

Years later, I was helping classmates organize a class reunion when we came up with the idea of inviting not just the actual graduates but also other kids who either moved or went into the service. Don's name came up and we sent an invitation.

I had shown his school picture to my youngest daughter, Toni, and she always thought his curl was cute. Toni went to the reunion with me that year, and had gone to the car to get something. When she returned, she walked in with Don. I was stunned. I smiled; he smiled and gave me a hug.

"Your daughter looks like you, he said.

I gave Toni a quizzical look. "How did you know...?"

She pointed to "the curl" in the middle of his forehead, gray now, but still there.

"Yeah, Mama, he's been telling me what a hoot you were in school."

We all had a good time. Don's wife was cute and smart. Both of them had college degrees and they had moved back home from California.

I would not change my life, but I often wonder what would have happened to us if Don had not wanted to change schools. I still think about him every now and then. I can't help it; he was my very first love and one does not forget their first "true love."

Torn Threads
by Roberta M. Guzman

M<small>Y</small> BUILDING ANGER JUST EXPLODED when Ronnie crowed, "Here's my girl!" He set me down after carrying me up to the high school, which was perched nearly at the top of the mountain. The other high school kids had been draped along the three sets of stairs, chanting, "Moose!, Moose!" the way they did at football games. Throwing me over his shoulder, he had carried me up as if I were a sack of potatoes.

Earlier, he had so courteously given me a ride in his home-made truck, and now he was acting as if I were his possession. He was not even winded or sweaty, his six-foot-six frame bulging with muscles. His little exhibition should have melted me. But, red-faced and embarrassed, I didn't bother to thank him.

And wasn't it enough that he had dropped me on the floor at the senior prom on Saturday night? I'd been all gussied up in a new red satin formal, and adorned with a prized Navaho squash blossom turquoise and silver necklace, earrings, and matching bracelet. To think he had dropped me on that sawdust-covered floor, my dress flying up in the air, with only murmured apologies. I thought I had forgiven him for that—but now this?

I forgot all about the sweet kisses night after night, nuzzling each other, him standing on the ground, me standing on the top porch landing.

In a fit of anger, I screamed, "I am not your girl. I am not anyone's girl. I am not a commodity. I am not your possession, just because you gave me a ride to the school in your old pickup!"

Moose's face was a case study in dismay and lack of under-standing. At that moment, I knew our relationship had ended. I was thinking he was downright ugly, and why had I even gone to the dance with him? Was it because he was captain of the football team?

And did I want to leave him because of his church? Or because of my sailor friend, who was faithfully writing to me from his ship?

That moment of rage erased two years of puppy love filled with dances, movies, games, and his proposal of marriage after graduation. My parents would be glad, as he was of a different faith, and they'd planned that I go to college. But in the end, I turned away from him.

What do you know? Years later, Ronnie and I met by chance, and I invited him and his wife over. I showed them the lovely jewelry box and monogrammed leather belt he'd made, which I treasured. Coincidentally, we each had five children. Both he and my husband (not the sailor) had the same profession. Yet, without notice, Ronnie and his wife soon moved away. I sold the jewelry box, gave away the belt.

But removing the keepsakes did not eliminate the sweet, sad memories that make up the tapestry of my life. There are torn threads in the cloth.

Love's Young Dream
by Mary Ann Savage

I WAS IN LOVE. Jamie's hair, eyes and face were different shades of the same golden brown. He was smart, and daring. We liked to talk, sometimes right through parties and dances..

Unfortunately, Jamie did not love me. He was dating Cynthia. So I hid my feelings, wrote them out in a diary. I loved him. He laughed a lot, and teased me. Sometimes I felt straight-on desire that confused and embarrassed me.

I was a virgin. Most of us were in those days. All that longing. Nowhere to go with it.

I was completely vulnerable. I hid my diary.

My friends and I could emerge from the back seat looking rumpled and satisfied, but we didn't go all the way. And despite loosened blouses and belts, we didn't know how to proceed with Real Sex. Get undressed in front of him? Ooh. Maybe if you were really in love...

Jamie and I talked a lot, but only kissed twice. He stayed with Cynthia. I pretended an interest in Bill, but Jamie knew. His laugh drew me in and threw me away. I shivered when I thought of him.

Jamie went to college when I was a senior. I wrote him. He wrote back and he often mentioned fabled lovers—Paolo and Francesca, Orpheus and Eurydice, Cupid and Psyche. He knew I was picturing the two of us. Was he?

That Christmas, the boys who'd gone away to school came back models of sophistication, College Men. Dick and Billy drank a lot. Paul sat around and brooded. Jamie loaded his speech with sexual innuendo. I acted as if I knew all about sex. Jamie smiled as if he knew a secret. He kept dating Cynthia, and I tried to look and talk like her.

"There are two kinds of girl" he told our crowd one night.

I made a big yawn. "Good girls and bad girls. Hope you learned more than that in college."

"Two kinds of girl," He repeated. "Nice girls and good girls." He smiled, leered. "Which kind are you"

I knew exactly what he meant. "I'm a good girl," I bragged, lying.

He gave me that look that melted me. "Maybe I'll let you show me how good."

I was blushing now, but I came back. "*Maybe* sometime I'll want to show you."

That conversation was the trigger. We started looking for each other. Our eyes would meet, he would look speculative. I would catch his eye and try to look provocative, without showing confusion, or the electric shock his look brought me.

Then that fall, we were both at university. We had no classes together, but he would turn up where I was, and we kept having charged conversations. We talked about books that had lots of sex in them. We talked about traveling together—to a science fiction convention, to be freedom riders, to explore the Amazon. We were finally in love. Time away from Jamie was null time. I could think only of him.

Soon the whole thing broke loose. We lay together on his rebel flag in the little meadow above the cemetery. He turned to me, and I almost felt safe. I trembled with excitement but somehow, I couldn't get to the point of undressing

"Come on," said Jamie, "be Cleopatra. We can go up in flames." But I still couldn't. I was cold. It was late.

Finally, "Not tonight"

"So you aren't a good girl after all," he almost sneered. We walked back to the dorm in silence. Without holding hands. Jamie didn't kiss me. We had had our last kiss.

"So long, Nice Girl," he said.

It was six weeks before I saw him. Oh, how I wanted to try again. I cried, I dreamed. But when we finally met, he never mentioned the night on the meadow. I couldn't mention it. I looked away from his stiff face. He ignored me when I said, "Let's go somewhere and talk." Not lovers, not even friends.

And I dreamed about him, cried, had my first real grown-up regrets.

Sunfish
by Deborah Finkelstein

I MET JOEY the first day of camp, and we hit it off immediately. It wasn't long before our friends began whispering to each other, mine asking his how he felt, his asking mine. They had relayed that I liked him, and the story was that he would ask me out. But you never know if you can trust such gossip.

The sun was on its way to sleep as my peers and I arrived at the cerulean lake. Counselors instructed us to get in groups of two to four to sail in Sunfish, tiny sailboats. I knew this was it. Joey and I would sail out on the lake, he would ask me out, and we would kiss. What could be more romantic than sunset on a lake?

Joey and I did end up together in a Sunfish, but with our friend Steve. I was upset that Steve's presence was ruining my plans, but decided to enjoy the ride anyway. The lake was calm, and the sky was just beginning to turn pink. We told stories and laughed.

As we approached the shore, Steve jumped into the water and began to swim. No one had ever done this before; the lake was filled with slimy seaweed in this area. Everyone on the other boats began to laugh and point at Steve. No one was watching as Joey took my hand and asked me out. I said yes, and we kissed on the boat with the purple sky behind us.

My heightened sense of surprise and the spontaneous feel made it even more romantic. Later, I found out that Joey and Steve had planned it. Joey had been too afraid of taking me on the boat and me saying no, and then having to be stuck sailing with a girl who did not like him. So he had dragged Steve along. Steve, who was always playing class clown, loved the idea of jumping in the water and making everyone laugh. The plan was perfect.

The memory is of the youthful magic of young love: a sudden awareness of everything around me. Sunfish, sunset, sailing, smiles, surprise, kisses.

FIRST KISSES

Just those words, "first kiss," have a certain magic. And why not? They often define the precise moment of a rich and evocative crossing of one of life's thresholds.

At last we have surrendered to our desire to bestow this mysterious seal on our budding relationship. And, having experienced what earlier may have felt too risky or foolish, we are, perhaps, tempted to prolong our celebration of that moment, wanting to put off washing our face.

The Nose Fits!
by Sam Turner

"SAMMY, WE FORGOT the ice cream mixer. Will you and Ruthie drive back and get it?" my father asked innocently.

"Sure," I gulped.

There was a twinkle in his eyes.

There was jubilation in my heart!

Our families had been visiting a friend's home deep in the Kaibab forest. Ruth would be alone with me for a round trip of ten miles. I had never sat this close to any girl, let alone sparkling, thrilling Ruthie! Her crinoline skirt crunched against my leg. Concentration on my solo drive was difficult.

It was dusk when we loaded the mixer into the trunk of the '49 Chevy. Ruthie slid in on my side, requiring me to crowd next to her. She may have been younger, but Ruthie proved more experienced than I.

The winding curves forced me to move the wheel so that my right arm continually brushed against her soft sweater. Right curves were best! She leaned against me.

I searched the wall of ponderosas for the break indicating a turnout. Once parked, I worried how this thing would happen. What should I do first? Do I lean over and peck her on the cheek?

Ruthie took charge and firmly planted her lips on mine. I heard buzzing. My eyes were closed, yet I saw lights of silver and gold flashing. Was that my heart—or hers—beating against my chest? I removed my glasses.

"Don't lose those, Sam, or we'll never get back!"

The second kiss was less frantic. This time, I could feel the softness of her face next to mine.

"What do you know? The nose fits!" I blurted. Now, she would surely know that I was a beginner.

"Of course. See?" And once again our lips touched. I couldn't let go. But, as if on a signal, we broke apart. She sat up and, somehow, I found my glasses.

She snuggled next to me as I drove. One stop wasn't going to be enough. We parked outside the gathering. The kiss was long and sweet. Again, there were bells, buzzing, and fireworks. Taking a tissue, I wiped off any traces of lipstick. We carried the ice cream mixer in together.

I took the first servings out to the guests. Everyone smiled at me. Ruthie smiled with a blush. People knew something I didn't. I looked at my maroon shirt. It was covered with fuzz from Ruth's white Angora sweater!

Retreating to the kitchen, I brushed the telltale evidence off. Putting his arm around my shoulder, my father said, "I wouldn't brush it all off, Sammy. You can wear it with pride. She's a fine young lady."

I gave him an embarrassed smile and continued brushing. But I saved the fuzz in my pocket. The strains of "My Buddy" came from the living room. But I heard a different tune playing in my heart: one that sang of love and the thrill of my first kiss.

How Love Goes
by Grace Hobbs

W HEN SHE FIRST TASTED LOVE, she was barely eleven.
With pony-tailed gravitas, she passed him a note of the most
seriously romantic nature, borrowing heavily from the country
and western music she had been exposed to (*I think this is how love
goes: check yes or no*), and waited some hours for his reply. It was
the first time she stood at the precipice of losing everything.

He was slender, slim-hipped and fine-boned, with skin like
caramel and hands as soft as butter. His fingers were long and
dexterous, fingernails rounded in perfect ovals He played the
violin, was not the kind to go outdoors, never went barefoot, and
remained in social situations somewhat aloof, apart from every
crowd.

His name was Philip, which meant lover of horses, something
she had always found incongruous. A horse was all wildness, all
heaving muscles and gleaming flanks and sinewy, bestial power.
A horse was not something that this boy, in his immaculate self-
control, could love. He did not heave. He moved quietly, more
like a cat than a horse. He was her emperor of secrets.

Her name was Grace, and in her searching grace-light, everything was revealed. She wanted to know him and answer his
questions and to embrace, with their mismatched names, each
other's darkened places. She wanted to spend years with him, to
examine him microscopically and to go marking his body, pencil
in hand, slowly charting the veins in his skin.

She was shaking when he brought her his reply. *Do you love
me?* she had asked, earnestly, stupidly, already hopelessly lost to
him. He wrote, in scrawling black ballpoint, *Do you really have to
know?* And then smaller, as if he too might be nervous, might be
afraid of what this meant: *Yes.*

Seven hundred sixty-one days into their relationship, by a fishpond near a greenhouse at sunset, they looked at each other, slowly, and moved closer. She wanted to drown in his brown eyes, to blanket herself in the soft fringe of his lashes—be subsumed in him, become a part of him, part of his magic words and caramel skin. He placed his hands on her waist, staid and unsure. His fingertips asked her, *is this okay?* And her lips answered, *yes*.

His mouth tasted like summer, dust and strawberries, and perhaps the last embers of a dying sun. She was intensely aware of the way he felt: the soft cotton of his shirt, his hand on the small of her back; the way he smelled: like a caravan, like a spice train of honey and myrrh. She wanted it to last forever. She wanted *him* to last forever, to stand like a monolith in the passage of time saying, *I Was Here And That Is Enough*. She wanted his kiss to last forever, to keep the pink-gold feeling of his lips on hers til the last possible moment when they would separate in a twilit haze and stare at each other in amazement, marveling at the cataclysmic *event* of it, the way suddenly they had set the world on fire only to open their eyes and discover it intact.

They stopped, and there was a moment of unspeakable reverence, each realizing the magnitude of what they'd done. They stood still, regarding each other in light of their knowledge, observing the way the hair pricked up on each other's arms under their gaze. It was as if all the world was silent in the wake of their earthquake, waiting for the last rocks to tumble and the first birds to sing.

They left that place silently, pond and greenhouse and creaking wooden bench. He passed her a letter and a book, looking as if nothing had happened and knowing that everything had.

She felt full—swollen, newly aware of her not-quite-womanly shape, her small breasts and boyish hips. She clung to the fact that somehow this boy saw fit to love her. She wanted to cry. She wanted to sing. She was burning in the places his fingers had touched and wanted to pass out of existence—to grow lighter and lighter until finally she walked into the sky.

Rashiniqua
by Dickens Ihegboroh

I SPENT UNUSUALLY MORE TIME drying the last plate than I'd done its now spanking-clean brothers, which sparkled with the Palmolive's green apple freshness where I'd arrayed them on the dish rack. My hands worked dexterously. It was more of a polishing than drying—a sacrosanct practice, in other words. I handled it with a delicacy and fondness that would "rub the other plates the wrong way," so to say. Gleaming now, golden-buttery, for that is its color, I wrapped it gently in a soft cloth...as a mother wraps its newborn.

Made of ivory, and by at least five years older than the rest of the dishes in my kitchen, the plate may not have been of any use in my kitchen. Yet I value it more than every one of my other culinary items. It is a reminiscent of my first kiss...a vestige of Rashiniqua.

Selecting the shelf farthest from the sink—its sanctuary—I slowly, with a greater cautiousness than I'd done the others, stowed it away. I hung the towel on its rail, and the next moment, I was a twenty-one-year-old again. I was taken seven years back. It wasn't this same house, much less this same kitchen; but it'd been at this juncture, and that very ivory plate had peculiarly been the last she washed and the last I dried. Having hung the towel over its rail, I'd turned to...I couldn't remember what I'd turned to do but, whatever it was, I didn't just do it.

She was waiting for me to turn. It wasn't brisk, yet it was quick enough that I didn't see it coming: my first kiss. Instantly my lips opened, and my eyes instinctively closed. Our lips, in their utmost sensitivities and hers in full succulence, as wet as the ivory plate had been a few minutes ago, glided irrepressibly and inseparably for what seemed like eternity.

What can I say of Rashiniqua? How do you describe color to the blind? Beauty, strength of character, and intelligence are the attributes men usually look for in women. I don't know what I'd looked for in her—if actually I'd ever looked for anything—but what I found transcended all those.

"It's because she was your first date," Kay, my closest friend, suggests. But does being my first date explain why dishwashing, and cooking too—which until I met her were things I detested to do—gradually became things I passionately love to do?

Whenever Rashiniqua was mentioned, people usually wondered what the sudden brief silence engendered in me concealed. Anybody who walks into my kitchen, seeing the conspicuously empty space meant for a dishwasher, will wonder why I don't have one, or why I had the inescapable "KITCHEN: THE HEART OF THE HOME" inscribed on its wall. These, however, are only inanimate, destructible reminiscences of Rashiniqua.

But my heart, forever, is where she ineffaceably exists.

First Kiss
by Betsy McPhee

*F*RECKLES SPILLED ACROSS HIS FACE like spattered coffee. Poppy red hair obscured the top rim of his rectangular black glasses. We sat near one another in seventh grade social studies class, where we passed notes folded into paper footballs when the teacher's back was turned. Between geography and civics lessons, I learned that Ethan Guttman liked the Beatles and Simon and Garfunkel, and that he could make me laugh.

One afternoon he called me on the phone! The white cord snaked from the wall in the kitchen, around the corner to the dining room, as I tried to escape my mother's ears. Sometimes I "forgot" our homework assignment and had to call him, but more often I anticipated his calls, the phone's ring inspiring a Pavlovian response of butterflies in my stomach, just in case it was Ethan.

In one of these phone calls we talked about movies, and he invited me to a matinee on Saturday. Immediately I began to prepare. Four days was not too long to decide what to wear. By Saturday morning a pile of rejected clothing dripped off the chair in my room and spread across the floor. I finally selected the least wrinkled candidates from the bottom of the heap: a pair of mulberry hip-hugger corduroys, matching turtleneck, and macramé belt. A dab of Peachy Frost lip gloss, a dash of Lilac Dew eyeshadow, and I was ready—at 9:30 a.m. I had three hours yet. I wiped off the Lilac Dew eye shadow and tried Blue Mist instead.

By the time I spied Ethan's wood-sided station wagon, I had chewed off the Peachy Frost lip gloss as well as all of my finger-nails. Though ready to bolt for the car, I waited—just as my mother instructed—for the doorbell to ring. Then I perched quietly on the front seat as Ethan's father drove us to the movie theater. We bought a bucket of popcorn and settled in to watch *2001: A Space Odyssey* about space travel, which we understood, having seen the moon landing on television the summer before last, and a computer, which was something straight out of science fiction. A freckled hand slid over mine on the armrest between us. I was afraid to move, to breathe. Could the audience hear the sound of my heart beating?

I had discussed Ethan on the phone with my girl friends. Boys were an enigma to us. What did Boys think? What did Boys want? What did it mean if a Boy held your hand?

Nearly every Saturday after that we would hike with my dachshund in the Arboretum, rake leaves, then make Apian Way pizza from a box. As autumn leaves faded from brilliant reds and golds into crisp brown shreds, we wrote plays together, played dominoes, and listened to records, enjoying this new experience of friendship coupled with the sheer physical thrill of being near someone of the opposite sex.

Snowflakes tumbled, diamond dust glittering in the halo of a streetlight, as Ethan and I trudged up the long hill from the campus theater where we had seen a musical. Hand-in-hand we watched the snowflakes dance like fireflies, the only sound the crunching of our boots in the powdery snow. Before we reached the hedge by my house, we paused to disentangle our cold enmeshed fingers so that my mother, who might have been watching from the front window, would not see us holding hands. Ethan suddenly brushed my lips with his own, as gently as the melting of a snowflake on my skin.

"Oh! I didn't know you were going to do that!" I blurted. We grinned at one another shyly, wonder and surprise lighting our smiles. Even now, years later, the glimmer of magic in that first kiss lingers, bringing with it a nostalgic wistfulness.

First love was a large, red helium balloon, glorious and playful, tethered lightly. But like the balloon, it withered, slowly sinking in on itself, lower and smaller every day. Yet the image I hold in my heart is not one of regret, but of possibilities floating lighter than air, bobbing unexpectedly above my head, as weightless and fleeting as a first kiss.

Sock Hops and Cornfields
by Jill Koenigsdorf

*E*VEN THOUGH IT WAS 1972, my girls' school was putting on a sock hop. At sixteen, I was neither cheerleader nor nerd, but off on the outskirts somewhere, writing poetry, playing my guitar and singing along with Joni Mitchell. I went all out on my costume: red lipstick, bobby socks, a poodle skirt, saddle shoes. I was the classic "sweet sixteen and never been kissed." Although I maintained a certain bravado in my writing and when relaxed around my friends, I was shy around boys.

I saw about six of the senior boys walk through the door in full Fifties glory: duck-tailed hair, bolo ties, saddle shoes, cigarettes rolled up in the sleeves of white tee shirts. They moved about the room as if they had just seen "The Wild Bunch" and were trying to imitate the lead characters.

"Wanna cut the rug?" a voice said from behind me. When I whipped around I saw "Ray," a senior I had never said two words to before.

"Sure!" I answered.

He dipped and turned me until I was sweaty and breathless. It was fantastic to move like that with someone who seemed to be having as much fun as I was.

Ray phoned a few days later and asked me out for that Friday. We stepped out into the driveway and he opened the passenger door to his incredibly cool forest green Volkswagen Bug.

"Wanna go bowling?" he asked. And when he shifted gears, his hand brushed my knee.

Bowling? How perfect a first date was *that*? And from the minute we pulled out of the driveway, the fun started—and it didn't stop for a full month. He taught me how to drive a stick shift. He took me to dark Italian restaurants where we ate toasted raviolis and laughed behind giant leather-bound menus. He never got me home before two in the morning. And best of all, my first kiss was one for the books.

"Wanna go on a drive out into the country?" he asked on our second date. "I have to warn you though, this spot we're going… it's haunted."

"You mean like…ghosts?"

"It's by some old railroad tracks. They say you can hear the train whistle even though the trains haven't run for a long time, and there's this ghost, the conductor maybe, who people see all the time walking up and down the tracks." Then he added, dramatically, "Sometimes, he grabs people."

There was a half moon and we had no flashlight, but Ray seemed to know the way. He had brought a blanket and after we had walked in the darkness through the dry swish of the summer corn, his shirt smelling like fresh hay, he took my hand and said, "Now just stay close if you get scared."

We lay on our sides on the blanket and talked about music and college, and he just drew me to him and we kissed. Then I heard strange moaning and hoped that it wasn't coming from me.

"Do you hear something," I whispered.

"It's the ghost," he hissed, hugging me closer.

Just as I had a group of four girlfriends so close they called us The Four Musketeers, he too had a gang of four tight buddies. Unbeknownst to me, he had arranged for them to hide out in the dark and make noises, standing in for the rumored "conductor."

When his friends got too hammy and came out of the bushes, I at first felt embarrassed that they had seen us kissing. But then we all headed off to a diner, and I got to sit with four handsome seniors, holding hands with Ray, already in love for the first time. And even though he moved on and inevitably broke my heart when he did, he was the most sheer *fun* I had with a man then or since. I was like an eager puppy with him, game for all the adventures he planned for us on each date. And he taught me that such spirit was wonderful, pleasing, and could even be reciprocated.

Sweet Twenty-Five
by Nadine C. Keels

"Sᴡᴇᴇᴛ Sɪxᴛᴇᴇɴ and never been kissed." Is that classification a stigma, or a badge of honor? Well. Try being sweet *quarter of a century.*

I never would have envisioned myself falling in love with a man like him. He was too daring, too controversial, and perhaps, I thought, too cool for his own good. Moreover, too many girls liked him, and I wasn't exactly a bandwagon rider. Nor was I moved by the latest male pop icons or movie stars. I never could keep up with what was hip or hot, and I figured that if anyone was cool or popular, chances were that he would never know I existed, on any intimate level.

Besides, I was coming close to that quarter of a century mark, and I hadn't liked any guy since I was a teenager. I'd had a thousand crushes from kindergarten to high school. But after continually crushing on boys who never crushed on me back, I was all crushed out. Obscurely desirable, and crushed out.

Then, I met him. A couple of people who'd known him far longer than I had were saying there was something different about the way he liked me—different from the way he'd liked girls in the past. I wasn't buying it. This apparently hip and hot dreamboat could have his pick of a plethora of chicks, so what would he want with a goody-two-shoed little lady like me? And even if he was, perchance, developing romantic feelings for me, could I ever like him back? After all, I no longer had a knack for all of that "liking" business at my ripe, ancient age of twenty-five.

Strange as it was, however, he did enjoy talking with me. Whenever we were out with a group, he'd seek out my company. Hardly a day went by when he wouldn't contact me. He'd pick me up from my house and take me places (on purely companionable terms, of course.) He said that I was smart, pretty, spectacular, sexy, and a whole host of things that no man had ever told me before.

I took it all in stride, until I realized that I was starting to like him back—but not because of his alleged hipness or hotness. He was, simply, precious. Bashful at times. Profoundly brilliant. Deceptively strong. Refreshingly funny. And his peals of boyish, ebullient laughter would melt my all-crushed-out heart.

He asked me to be his Valentine. I'd never been asked before. Our official date on Valentines Day was the very first date I'd ever been on. And the essence of Sweet Twenty-Five hit me with a wave of delightful force, about a month later, when he stalled for an entire evening before he finally cradled my face in his hands and warmly graced me with my first kiss. After all my years of waiting, I was evidently quite ready; in light of my amorous response, he could hardly believe that I'd never been kissed before.

Yet, as it happens in life, he and I had to go our separate ways. Nevertheless, I believe that we loved each other as much as we could. When I think of him now, I still can't help but smile, even if wistfully, at the memory of the spring and summer we had, the experience of which had been so fresh and full of jubilant sunshine to me. I'd never completely believed I would personally see that tender brand of sunshine, in real life.

I'll always treasure the memory of the precious, brilliant man who, all hipness and hotness aside, had brought my obscure desirability into reality to me, adding such sweetness to my first quarter century.

WHEN PARENTS INTERVENE

Believing they are doing the right thing, parents sometimes meddle in the romantic lives of their children. That interference is often disastrous for the young sweethearts. They are left with a legacy of resentment and questions that cannot be answered: What might have happened if my parents hadn't interfered? Could this have worked if I had been allowed to make my own choice?

Young Love, Old Rules
by Samantha Ducloux Waltz

*T*HE WARMTH OF teen-age love infused my body as I clasped my hands behind Mel's neck and we swayed to the strains of "Blowin' In the Wind." We had discovered each other at the Encampment for Citizenship, a six-week summer program for high school graduates held in Berkeley, California. 1963 was a time of social rumblings across America, and students from all over the country had come to learn how we could make a difference.

Heady with idealism, I noticed Mel, an African American from Chicago, the first evening we Encampers gathered for orientation in the multi-purpose room of our dormitory. He was the tallest student there, his yellow sport shirt stunning against his ebony skin, his big smile inviting.

Within days we were inseparable. We sat next to each other in morning classes, held hands afternoons as we walked the streets of Berkeley with surveys on employment practices, and evenings sang "We Shall Overcome" with our new friends. I still have the heart-shaped redwood pendant necklace Mel gave me on our EFC field trip to the Redwoods. He called me Princess, and treated me with more tenderness and respect than I'd ever known. It seemed we had a fairy-tale romance.

If people raised an eyebrow at the young black man and white girl as we passed, I stood a bit taller. We were part of a changing society where I believed we could ultimately be accepted as a couple.

"Please come to Pasadena and meet my parents," I begged when EFC ended. "They'll love you too." I'd written them about Mel, and they'd raised no objections. Mother was a member of NAACP and had a dear black friend who visited in our home. Although we were active Mormons, she was adamant that the Church policy at that time— denying blacks the priesthood—was wrong. Dad held the same values. I imagined they were proud of me for living the liberal values they espoused.

Mel was hesitant, but finally agreed to come. He would stay with another Encamper who lived near me.

My first afternoon home, I counted the seconds until he came to my house. Finally, the doorbell rang. My parents and I arrived at the front door at the same time. There on the porch stood my sweet, handsome boyfriend, holding a bouquet of pink carnations for me, or perhaps for my mother. When I looked into his face my breath caught. "Mother, Dad, this is Mel," I said proudly.

Mother's breath caught too. "He's so dark," she moaned as she took a step back from the door. "My heart," she said, her hand clutching her chest as she slumped to the living room carpet.

"Probably an angina attack. I'll get her pills," I said as my father knelt beside her. Mel stood watching, concern written in every line of his face.

Worry and anger mixed in me. Mother had suffered with angina since rheumatic fever had weakened her heart when she was just seven years old. What a welcome for my wonderful boyfriend!

When I returned, Mother was conscious and my father and I helped her into their bedroom. Although I invited Mel into the living room, he waited on the porch.

With Mother settled in bed, I went to Mel and reached up to put my arms around his neck. He caught both my hands, kissed them, then pressed them against his cheek. "Good-bye Princess," he said.

"Won't I see you tomorrow? I'll meet you anywhere." Tears burned my eyes.

He shook his head. He was ready to take on the disapproving frowns of strangers when we went out together, but he wasn't ready to take on Mother's "heart condition."

Decades later, I am still troubled by what happened. But I understand that societal rules taught to Mother as a child, and forces still at work in 1963, were far stronger than the liberal ideas she'd developed as an adult. Today, society has different rules. A black man is our president. In many cities, a couple like Mel and me might be able to enjoy a happy ending to their fairy tale romance. I wish it could have been us.

Why Didn't You Write?
by Ann DesLauriers

*T*OMMY AND I were high school sweethearts. We lived in Small Town, USA, in the Fifties, when rock 'n' roll was the coolest. The boys tried to look like Elvis, and the girls wore crinolines and ponytails. Young love was sweet in those days. I wore Tommy's class ring on a chain around my neck. We were "going steady."

We could hardly wait to get to school each morning to meet at our lockers, hearts pounding, for just a brief touch before we were off to class. The anticipation of meeting for lunch kept us going. It was all so normal and innocent. But my mother didn't see it that way—she kept us apart as much as she could and didn't allow many dates.

When he could get his dad's car, we'd go to the movies, where we shared popcorn and held hands. We weren't supposed to go to the drive-in, but once in a while we did anyway. Little did my mother know how we steamed up the windows of that car! In those days, only bad girls went "all the way," and Tommy and I were still virgins when we graduated.

In senior year, my parents dropped the bomb. We were moving across the country after graduation. "I won't go," I told them. My best friend and I were going to college together in the fall, and Tommy and I were going to get engaged as soon as we were eighteen.

But no—my mother was having none of that. First it was the guilt trip: "You wouldn't hurt me that way, would you?" That didn't work, so she delivered the ultimatum: "If you stay here, we will not pay for your college."

Tommy and I were devastated. There had to be a way for us, but we weren't eighteen yet and, in those days, kids did what their parents told them. We had pledged our undying love and promise for the future. And three days after graduation, I moved away.

I wrote letters faithfully all that summer, but never received a response. My heart was broken. I could not believe Tommy hadn't meant all those sweet words we shared. In the fall, I went to a business school and I presumed that he went to college.

Twenty-five years later, we got in touch and spent a wonderful day together. One of the first questions we both asked was, "Why didn't you write?" We soon figured out that one or both mothers had either not mailed the letters, or hadn't given the received ones to us.

We saw each other for about a year, but it was too late. Between us, there were three marriages and divorces and four children, not to mention that we were working toward pensions on opposite ends of the country.

Our teenage love was pure and intense. Who knows how it might have turned out if circumstances had been different? One thing is for certain: we both will always remember our first love.

Times Have Changed, but Not This Boy
by Sean Burnside Quigley

MODERN WISDOM holds that every man has ex-girlfriends, that every man has felt the pain that accompanies the loss of his better half. True, some may take the first stages harder than others. But in the end (always the end!) we are all better off and more complete—only those who were once miserable can genuinely understand what it means to be blessed.

But to this very day, exactly two years after Ashley persuaded me that we needed to separate "temporarily" before we each began our undergraduate education, I still wake each morning possessed of a mind whose attention is distracted. Possessed, too, of a spirit who cannot see itself because the one that gave it sight has parted, and of a boyish desire to rekindle and live happily ever after.

Ashley gave me far more than certainty in my weekend plans. Though, to be sure, for a boy whose weekend plans were perennially under question, her presence was convenient as well as ebullient. Besides being a stable romantic friend on whose shoulder I could lay my weary head, she infused purpose and passion into my life. She gave me reason to ponder the many unconventional modes of existence that I had always stowed safely away in the deep recesses of my stable New England person. She allowed me to be, embraced my soul and its never-ending assortment of schemes and pretensions.

Oh, without exception, she told me that I was crazy—as my parents and brother always did. But there was always just a little bit of disingenuousness, just enough, to make me know that, secretly, she really did love my quirkiness. And perhaps this quirkiness was precisely why she did love me. I knew that though she may poke fun at my anti-modernity disposition and rhetoric, she would follow me anywhere, as I would her.

We were destined to be ancients living in a world of modernists who, with each other, would guffaw at interstates and e-mail. She, being a nature-loving future veterinarian, would have the village dogs and horses to whom she could give care, and I would have my pen. We assumed that one day I might get a typewriter.

Then came our breakup. But do not worry, for it was only our first breakup, to be quickly followed by our first makeup. To spoil the ending, only one of the two was repeated, and I trust that you know which.

University always loomed over the horizon, waiting to slice back open the raw breakup wounds and permanently scar both of us. It was always on my mind, but not in a melancholic sense. I eagerly awaited the day when the "scheduled" (and temporary) breakup would happen, because I knew that our love would triumph. There were train stations near to both of our universities; we, not being airplane folk, felt our love was seemingly fated by the gods. Save the suicide part and the inter-familial enmity, she was my Juliet and I her Romeo, for neither set of parents liked or respected the union.

"The boy and girl are too serious, especially that idealistic boy who always talks about marriage, who wears a promise ring from his girlfriend that looks suspiciously like a wedding band. And, wait! Is he wearing it on his left hand? That maniac!"

In the end, as one can only write of these things after a fair amount of time has intervened, she dumped me. I will be frank. I was dumped by the one girl whom I had loved, and had allowed to love me. She will probably still claim that it really was her decision to end our relationship, but I know better.

I know, as I painfully knew then, that her parents, being conventionally modern, would never sanction a young marriage with that hopelessly romantic, traditionalist boy. "Doesn't he know that times have changed?"

No, apparently he doesn't.

Two years later, in reflecting on that relationship, I still clutch my promise ring and my ideals passionately, but am now realistic enough to type on a laptop.

Praying the World Soon Heals
by Molly O' Day

IN 1963, WHEN I WAS THIRTEEN, I'd skate up and down the old cracked sidewalk, never straying too far. My low-income neighborhood could be a dangerous place. Wanting something more challenging, I took apart my skates and made my first skateboard. It didn't work too well, objecting to every tree root and pebble.

My old elementary school was abandoned, but still open to the outside. The hallways were paved with smooth cement, and I soon saw that space in a new light. I'd found a new sanctuary. And, within a day, I'd found my true love.

Avery was sixteen, training his dog, a mutt named "Puppy." It must have been hard to find a place to hang out if you were a boy who wanted to stay out of trouble. I liked him instantly. Soon, we found ourselves talking about everything. I quoted books, and he'd know just what I was talking about. I knew we'd never run out of things to say.

One day, a young girl stopped and looked at us as we sat on the grass, deep in conversation. She asked, in a sarcastic way, what he was doing there with a "white girl." That was the first time I noticed he wasn't white. He looked Hispanic, but I remembered he had told me his mother was from Oklahoma, and his dad from the Philippines. I then noticed the girl was black. I looked puzzled.

He said, "Just talking," and looked a bit defensive.

This confused me even more. Finally, I said, "I don't understand. According to all I've learned, we are all from the same God."

Her eyes wide, she opened her mouth to say something, but quickly closed it and left. He looked at me, eyes full of admiration; he grinned, ever so slightly, and then shyly looked away.

We talked like this for over two years. I felt mature, wise, safe and respected with Avery. I could be myself, my best self. We looked like complete opposites, but we both knew what kindred souls we were and what a safe, trusting haven we'd discovered in our friendship.

Avery had a soft Motown singing voice that he rarely shared with others. One day, when I was sixteen, he sang "My Girl" to me, and I was so touched, I kissed him. He looked surprised, his eyes filled with tears and he kissed me back with all the feelings he'd held back for years. I actually felt physical chills run up my spine and explode into my heart. We decided to start dating, without really talking about it.

My parents were appalled. When Avery came to pick me up for our date, my father told him to have me home early, that he didn't want to see any 'black babies' running around later. I was shocked and angry, and about to explode. Avery was quiet, respectful and whispered, "She's not that kind of woman," as he urged me towards the door. I apologized all that night, but Avery had dealt with prejudice all his life, and expected it.

The pressure from my parents to stop seeing him was unrelenting. I finally threatened to run away, and called Avery. He tried to be mature and talk me out of it. But when he saw I was determined, he asked me to marry him. I said 'Yes!" But my mother said she'd call the police, and I caved, breaking Avery's heart again—and my own.

I saw Avery again, when I was thirty-four. He was with a buddy and they happened to stop in where I worked. After seeing our exchanged looks, his buddy asked us if we'd known each other long. Avery started to say something. His eyes were filled with pain and love, but he said nothing. I mumbled something about us "going way back."

I heard sometime later that he died from a heart attack. Anger at the destructiveness of prejudice filled me, and with tears of love and grief, I prayed the world would soon heal.

Forced to Say Goodbye
by Meagan Brooks

*F*EELINGS FOR YOUR FIRST LOVE never go away. They always remain perfect—probably because the relationship ends before it really takes flight. But in that moment between the beginning and the end, something magical happens.

I met mine the summer I turned sixteen. I had just moved from the city to a town that, in my mind, barely existed. As far as I was concerned, my life had ended with the move. And the first time I met him, nothing happened—no sparks, no music, no cartoonish hearts above my head. He was just a boy—a tall, gangly, strange boy.

When school started, I joined a running club, an attempt to keep my sanity. He joined the club too. For months we ran together, through cornfields, down unpaved streets, and on the dusty outskirts of town. As the days passed, our relationship grew. We became friends. He was like a pocket of sunshine in my otherwise cloudy existence. He always had a smile, and he always had a joke, made my life fun. Our conversations were light, our time together easy. I didn't realize I was falling in love. It seemed too simple.

It wasn't until the next summer that I realized I loved him. Once, during that summer, he had been gone for three days. To me, it felt like an eternity. And when he came back and told me of the other girls he had been around, I grew jealous. Those girls had no right to be around him; he was my friend. The realization that I loved him took me by surprise.

Then it was winter. One dark, snowy night, I ran past his house, and he came outside. We had promised each other a hug. I could have stayed in his arms forever, but eventually, we let go.

After that night, things changed between us. We had declared our feelings, and in doing so had formed an unbreakable bond. Our love was innocent, but it ran deep and satisfied our souls. We were always holding each other; perhaps we knew the end was near.

There are many reasons a first love doesn't work out. Mine was a matter of religion. Our Christian faiths were just different enough that my parents disapproved of the match. Like Romeo and Juliet before us, we tried to keep our love hidden, but this didn't work. When he was around, I couldn't hide my smile; I couldn't stop the excited glow from seeping into my eyes. When we were together, life was blissful. When we were apart, my family's pressure was intense and adamant. My parents worried about the depth of our relationship. And they were right to be worried.

One night, a decision was made. I was never to see him again.

In agony, I wrote him a letter—a last good bye. How do you tell your soul mate that you can't be with him? How do you tell him that he is everything to you, and yet, still not enough? Somehow, I did, all the while feeling cruel and spineless and desperate.

When he wrote me back, he told me he only wished for my happiness, and that someday I'd find someone else. The ache of that letter burned like fire—leaving a scorch that has never left.

The pain of losing him matched every heavenly joy of having him. It was just as intense, and just as consuming. I was miserable without him, and the minute I was able to leave town, I did

But I have always looked back. I can't help it. His presence in my life changed me. He taught me to be happy; he taught me to smile. He showed me simple joy in the midst of the nightmare that life sometimes is.

What would have happened if I had stood up to my family? In my heart, I know the truth. In my dreams, I've seen us to-gether. Or maybe the memory of a perfect summer love is better than the reality of what a life together would have provided. Maybe it was meant to end before it began. And maybe this is the beauty of a first love.

I Loved You Once
by Kathryn Hackett Bales

"*I* LOVED YOU ONCE, that love perchance might yet remain," Alexander Pushkin wrote in 1825. These words are as true today as they were almost two hundred years ago, for who among us has not at some time secretly yearned for a lost love?

I still envision a sandy blonde flat top, his blue eyes dancing as he folded his six foot frame into a tiny Morris Minor sedan. My mother hated him, said he was too old. But he was my first love and, it would seem, a true love. He instilled in me a lifelong passion for British sports cars and sports car racing. To this day, I can close my eyes and smell burning Castrol, can hear finely tuned engines scream as they are thrown through the gears.

My mother solved her immediate problem with her rebel daughter by banishing me to the family ranch in Idaho. While there, I was expected to learn to cook and clean, and in general become a suitable candidate for marriage to a young man who befit my station. Instead, I learned to doctor animals and dismantle and reassemble engines. I fine-tuned my driving skills on elderly farm trucks with transmissions that fought every gear change. When I bought my first sports car, Mother just threw up her hands in disgust, wondering where she had gone wrong.

After I bought the MG, I spent the next ten years attending every British car show and vintage race within driving distance, but I never saw him again.

About twenty years ago, I was on my way home from Reserve duty at Whidbey Island, Washington. I decided to spend the night in Portland before continuing on to Eugene. I phoned some old friends and dredged up some memories. While thumbing through the phone book, my curiosity got the best of me and I looked for his name.

It was near dusk as I drove down a dead end street in a newer subdivision. What was obviously a married person's home sat two doors down a side street. At the end of the cul-de-sac, I made a show of studying my map while I smoked a couple of cigarettes. Anyone observing me would, I hoped, think me just a misplaced tourist.

When I finally drove back down the street, he was standing on his front porch, as handsome as ever, hair gleaming in the setting sun. I didn't stop, so I will never know if he was staring at my Morris Minor or at me, resplendent in my dress blues.

I eventually married a good man. Navy issue. My parents would have liked him, even though he and Dick were the same age. I sold the Morris soon after we married, as whenever I looked at it, I always thought of what might have been.

My husband and I had fifteen good years together before he passed away. His last gift to me was a shiny white Chrysler convertible in the model he knew I had admired since it was first produced. It will always have a home in my garage, alongside the little red MG that first stole my heart.

I still sometimes wonder what life would have been like if Dick and I had not been forced apart. Would we have had a long and happy life together racing our sports cars? Was I really too young for a permanent relationship? Would he have decided that he wanted someone more feminine?

I will never know, and perhaps it's best that I don't. That element of mystery lends a nostalgic air to my thoughts as I drift back through the years. So many questions that will never be answered. So many memories, both good and bad. Perhaps one of the advantages of growing old is the ability to retain the good memories and relegate the bad ones to the nether regions of our brain.

BEYOND THE MALE STEREOTYPE

Men are sometimes stereotyped as making self-serving choices when it comes to their relationships with women. But some men, maybe more than we realize, are willing to put their own interests aside in order to support a woman as she moves along her path. A man may do that even if the woman's path will not continue to include him. Here, we navigate the fog-bound waters between stereotype and essence—the best of what a man can be.

Inside Out
by JoAnne Potter

I SAW HIM today. Yes, I tell you, it was him, swirling up through an eddy of 6 a.m. airline passengers at SEATAC like a fleck of gold. He's changed during the last twenty-five years, but I knew him. Oh, I knew him.

He wore a beat-up baseball cap that could have been the same one he wore to the race track in the 80's. It looked that old. And he still wore the silver-rimmed aviators he always liked, though they have bifocals now. But you'd expect that, wouldn't you? His denim shirt buttoned over a blooming belly he never had then. But when he leaned down to take his granddaughter's hand, he looked at her with the same blue twinkle he had once turned on me. He drew her up on his lap, right hand circling her shoulders, his left under knees in a quick, practiced arc. Don't you remember how he used to do that?

But it was his intensity that convinced me, the way he focused his attention until the child filled his entire horizon as she told him her tiny troubles. He absorbed her little cries, bearing them tenderly next to his own, offering himself as a willing haven for her sweet worries, protector of long practice. He'd done that for me, too.

To a stranger, he would probably look old, hiding whatever sinewy youth he once wore beneath age's crepey cover, stretched too thin. To anyone else, he would probably look like an un-remarkable old man, kind and harmless. There, sitting in an orange plastic chair in an airport coffee shop with a six-year-old, he revealed none of his ripe, tight-coiled strength, his taut, purple-veined attention, his broad, deep-muscled vitality. How could he? Only shared memory carries these, resurrecting them for my private use without apology.

Time tries to commit slow thieving, but he still lives in the fullness of long-spent days, remaining ever young to my eyes, full-fruited and bursting.

It was him, all right, even through the aged camouflage long years have dealt. For me, he carries the best of himself hidden from casual view. He still wears the same shining boldness, but as skin rather than armor, now distilled over gentle years. Maybe you, like the rest of the world, see only what you must, but I know him inside out.

Until the Twelfth of Never
Anonymous

*I*N A SMALL MILL-VILLAGE TOWN, about the only place to hang out was the corner drugstore. And that's where I was when I met Howard. Having led a rather sheltered life as the daughter of a minister, I was surprised that anyone could be interested in me. To think he chose me, even though I was not as pretty as the girl I was with. Imagine that!

His intense blue eyes held a depth of surprise that I'd never seen before, and I knew he liked what he saw in me. There was an immediate connection. As fate would have it, his brother was with him. That meant my friend Susan and I could double date (which was the only way I would be able to go out with him). In retrospect, I think we were dazzled by men in uniforms. They were Marines, and handsome, to boot!

That summer night began a whirlwind romance that changed my life. He was experienced, older than I, but very respectful and intuitive. He recognized my immaturity and naivety. I knew he wanted me, but he never pushed the envelope. Why, I'd been taught that having sex with anyone before marriage was the "unpardonable sin." I didn't dare, but I experienced feelings I'd never had before.

The summer wore on, and I supposed those days and nights were going to be endless. He hadn't told me that he was going to be sent out of the states in just a few weeks. When I looked in the mirror, I saw a wonderfully happy seventeen-year-old girl who knew the meaning of "desire" for the first time in her life. Howard made me feel alive and beautiful.

In the weeks preceding his departure to Puerto Rico, we played in the pool, hiked near a local reservoir, shared peanut butter and banana sandwiches, and I told him every thought I'd ever had. (He was a good listener.) Being an amateur photographer, he also took dozens of pictures of me, which I still have. Some memories were made to be kept forever. I think I loved him, but I had reserved the right to say "I love you" for the man who'd eventually want to marry me.

On a balmy, autumn Sunday afternoon, which would be the ending of a chapter in an unfinished book, he told me he was leaving. While I sat in his lap, I cried, as the 45-RPM repeated itself over and over, and the words to "The Twelfth of Never" ingrained themselves in my memory.

He shipped out the following morning, my virginity still intact. I never saw him again. I'm married now, have been for forty-six years, to a minister who reaped the rewards Howard sacrificed.

But "until the twelfth of never," I'll remember my past love, and in some ways regret that I can't add the "r."

As the Sun May Rise
by Alexandra Foxx

*T*HAT SUMMER, I LIVED IN THE WEST WING of the monastery in a long room filled with scarcely occupied beds. The men lived in the east wing—the crumbling wing with cold rusty water and old pipes that groaned when used at night. Between the wings were the nuns' quarters, their ears trained to hear the soft footsteps of a teenager against worn carpet.

His name was Kyle, and we met at the beginning of camp. We were in a huge group, talking, getting to know each other, when he asked, "So is anyone going running tomorrow?"

I paused, waiting for someone else to answer first, and then said, "I love to run." That was the first time he smiled at me, one side of his mouth crinkling up higher than the other, creating a lopsided dimple. I fell in love with that dimple first.

We had the surrounding lands to ourselves on dew-filled mornings. We met every day at four to watch the sunrise as we climbed over a swollen hill, into the orchard. We climbed high into the trees to watch the hues of pink, red, orange, and yellow all melt against the greenness in the distance.

After the sun rose high enough to peek between the trees, we would run. Trails wound through the woods, twisting past old decaying murals and eroding stone pulpits. We ran until we couldn't breathe, until our worlds grew light and our legs heavy.

Then we would lie in the grass, cheek to cheek, and just listen to the world going on around us. Kyle would press his face close to mine and whisper jokes that made me laugh until birds, disturbed by our thunderous sound, beat their wings against loose tree leaves, hushing us. Other times he just held me, and we let the quiet say what was between us.

But once the breakfast bell rang—a foreign sound that tore down the illusion of Eden—we hurried back to the dining hall, apart.

Through the weeks we became best friends and then something more. We made excuses to see each other during the day, and we always had our early morning wanderings. Soon enough, all I could think about was him. At noon we'd steal away to the orchard again, hiding from passing interlopers in the giant pear trees, quietly singing Bob Dylan. It was there I told him about all the little hurts, and the great hurts, in my life. He was the first person I ever told about the reason I couldn't sleep at night, the reason I cried. He was the first person to tell me it was all going to be okay—and I believed him. He was worth believing.

But the season came to an end, tearing down the summer leaves in streaks of burnt orange. On our last night, Kyle skirted between the wings of the monastery to say goodbye in private before we all left the next morning. I'll never forget how he whispered in French that he loved me.

After that, we sent letters back and forth, murmuring into the paper those dangerous words of love. For years we were best friends, lovers, supporters, confidants, and then, slowly, inexplicably, we faded away from each other the way summer fades to fall.

Years have passed, and there have been new loves, new stories to fill my heart. But Kyle was the first person who made me see how beautiful I was, how beautiful I could be. He was the first person to push away my darkness and let the sun kiss my skin. I couldn't say I thought it would last forever—there were too many problems for that—but I also wouldn't say I regret a moment. Like each individual memory of him, my love for him slipped away a little at a time. But every now and then, especially when I drive by green hills, I still think of him and his lopsided smile. And I can't help but wonder where he is now. I hope his life is as beautiful as mine, as beautiful as we were all those summers ago.

The Debt

Anonymous

*H*E WAS SO UNATTRACTIVE to me, cockiness on adrenaline to brand himself cool his first week of college. I was a senior, his mentor, and without patience for that athletic, partying type that gave girls harsh nicknames based on appearance. One of the largest and most encouraging mysteries of my life is how that boy became a man I loved for all the best reasons.

That year, he drove me insane with his irresponsibility. Then, just as I broke blissfully free of him when I graduated, he began a crash course in real life, falling in love with a girl pregnant with someone else's child.

I began teaching and he rearranged his life to be daddy. Somehow we began emailing and calling, both removed from typical college life. I learned his mother credited me with his change in attitude; he credited my face in apparition keeping him from drinking the previous year.

I watched him nurture an infant. I watched him put himself through college with a factory job. I watched him not care when many on the small Christian campus looked down on him as an unmarried father, instead of seeing him as the hero who took on a responsibility that wasn't his, and then turned even further on him when he broke up with the girl.

Our relationship was complicated with admiration, perhaps latent attraction, and the paradigm shift of a hierarchical relationship shuffling to an equalizing parity. Add that my father was dying, and then did, and we both were dating others, to explain that I didn't recognize how my feelings and regard for him had changed in ways I didn't admit to myself.

When an engagement ring on my finger paralyzed me, I ran to him for perspective. I think part of me wanted him to confess his interest and pose an alternate choice that had never seemed open to me before. Instead, he helped me sort. I didn't trust my feelings about much of anything, but I did trust him—so implicitly that I did what he said was OK. I married my fiancé.

I lost touch with my friend soon after the wedding. But the glaring stare-down between him and my husband at the wedding haunted me when my marriage began to beg for a mercy killing.

Then my husband's job transferred us—to the very city where it was rumored my friend had married and worked as a cop. I both dreaded and hoped to run into him, but never did. Then, with the magic of social networks, we reconnected. Verbose writers, both of us, we apologized, retraced our history and encouraged each other in the past decade's pursuits: kids, jobs, hobbies.

He reopened a door in my soul that had been closed for so long I'd forgotten it. Behind it was a me I'd lost—a me he still thought I was but had ceased to be after years of lacking intimacy with someone who really understood that part of me. As much as I was flattered into bloom, I was terrified. My husband was many things to me, but not the one thing my friend was. I wished he was my brother, so I could continue to thrive in the friendship. I knew it wasn't safe as it was. I knew emotional intimacy leads to affairs. I backed away; then an undercover assignment required he erase himself from social networks.

I had long thought the difference between these two men in my life was obvious: my friend shared my interests; my husband did not. But the truth was deeper. It was about encouragement and feeling valued. I'd never noticed, when dating, how begrudging my husband was with compliments about things I considered my identity—until the absence of my friend's nurture revealed how severe the deficit was.

I'd loved my friend for how he showed love for me—for how he saw me as a talented writer with a big heart, and told me all the time. Being able to finally articulate to my husband what I was missing from him began a new chapter for us. In some strange way, as my marriage transformed into something brighter, I realized our improving marriage owed a debt to this man in my past for what he revealed.

Life Saver
by Samantha Priestley

I DIDN'T REALISE I was leaving my boyfriend when I went to Portugal. I did it under the veiled protection of my parents' plans. I did it without thinking, and without realising that it was the right thing to do. And for the rest of my life, I have been thankful.

Aged nineteen, I had been living with my boyfriend for two years. It wasn't working. We were young and so obviously wrong for each other. But being young, we refused to see that. My boyfriend didn't work, took drugs and, on occasion, had a temper that kicked out and terrified me. But I was stubborn. So my parents planned a trip abroad, asking me to accompany them alone. And, to my own surprise, I jumped at the chance.

It's strange how we sometimes need an outsider to point out the things in our lives we should be able to see, but can't. In Portugal I met a boy who did just that, and so much more, for me.

Drowsy with the day's sun, heavy with holiday laziness when I met him, it was as if I had never encountered a boy before. Everything was new: his smell, the way he talked, his dark eyes and his apparent naivety. I was hooked from our first kiss, and knew there was no going back.

Being with this boy re-instilled in me the self-worth I had lost while living with my boyfriend back at home. Suddenly I felt I deserved this. I deserved to be with someone who told me I was beautiful, held me gently, as if I might break, and placed me at the centre of everything he did and said.

I will never forget the moment when my Portuguese lover confirmed what I was beginning to understand for myself. We were sitting on plastic chairs outside a shuttered juice bar at six in the morning. We had spent our one and only night together in his house while his parents were away. I knew I was falling for this boy, but I still couldn't place this new love in a slot in my life where it seemed to fit. I had a boyfriend back at home whose house I shared, our possessions still mingling in every space like wet clothes in water.

We sat outside the juice bar, still closed in the early morning, and he looked at me over the table. "You must leave him," he said.

It should have been obvious to me, but I still needed the push, like a blessing.

"You shouldn't let him treat you like he does," he went on. "You should have better. Tell me that when you get home you will leave your boyfriend."

I remember looking at him as he sat back in his chair, our faces locked on one another's, seeming to see into each other. The sky was slowly shifting from midnight blue to yellow, the sun rising and the hot day about to begin. And I thought, *this is how it ought to be*. This was love. This sense of caring was what was missing from my relationship back at home.

I left a few days later, vowing to return. I went straight home and moved my things back into my parents' house, away from my boyfriend. It was a decision I would probably have reached on my own eventually, but without so much clarity and surety as I did at that time. And who knows how long it might have taken me to get there?

Long distance relationships are hard. And even though I did go back, and we did try, it was never going to last with my Portuguese boy.

But I will never forget him. He showed me how to love again, not only another person, but myself. He taught me that I was worth it, and I have carried that through my life. When I think of him now, it still feels warm inside. He set me straight. Made me believe in myself again. I have no doubt that he changed my life. He altered things so dramatically for me that, in a way, he saved me.

Came September
by Karen Monroe

A LATE AUGUST MOON filled the darkness of the night sky, casting patterns on the porch as Kim and I lingered over what would be our final embrace, a farewell kiss, a moment to remember, although neither of us knew it yet.

We had spent many days and evenings together that summer after graduation in 1967. But first, I had left with my family for a three week road trip across the US. Kim went with us in spirit. I stayed in touch with him all along the way, sharing highlights from each stop: a post card from Hot Springs, Arkansas; a brochure from the Alamo; a note from Mesa Verde National Park; a Las Vegas silver dollar wrapped in a napkin from Caesar's Palace; and a picture from the photo booth at Wall Drugs in South Dakota. There were notes and post cards from Yosemite National Park, Yellowstone and Mount Rushmore, as well as a sand-filled envelope from the Salt Lake City Beach.

We visited my grandparents on the way home and a stack of letters from him waited, one for each day I was gone. They would not be the last letters I received from Kim, for he had enlisted in the Air Force and would be heading to boot camp before September.

Temperatures were hot and steamy late into July, until the cooling evening breezes arrived in August. We shared refreshing dips at Kensington Beach, walks along the river bridge where men sat catching fish, and we watched double features while making out at the Jolly Rogers Drive-In. We laughed while licking blended drips from the side of a double scoop ice cream cone, mint chocolate chip for him and strawberry for me. There was a trip to the zoo, and foot-long Coney dogs from Daly's while we sat in the front seat of his orange Mustang with the radio blaring the songs of our youth.

It was hard to say goodbye, to let go. I had just watched the tail lights of Kim's Mustang as he barreled down the street, each wheel's rotation screeching a goodbye.

The cold fall winds swept away the secure routine of high school and Kim. I felt the mood shift from the carefree days of youth to the challenges of young adulthood. The Vietnam War raged on, as did the protests. Although already war-worn myself and ready for a drawback, I vowed to support Kim wherever he went. But, weeks into boot camp, and with the reality of what he expected to experience, there was a letter of good-bye.

Our parting in August on the moon-dappled porch had been simple: no tears as we pulled away from a long embrace, no face-to-face agonizing apologies. Now his written words crushed me.

Yet I do believe his reason was to give me the chance to live fully without holding onto him. A year, he thought, would be too long to expect me to wait. He taught me there is goodness in the heart of a soldier, honor in what they do.

Fall brought a new job, and eventually a new man walked into my life. We married, had a child, then went our separate ways. The Vietnam War ended. Memories of the protests, Woodstock, and the romanticism of the hippie culture gave me new-found belief that peace and love could co-exist in a world ever changing.

Then, while skimming through the paper in 1973, my eye caught the obituary, a small and fitting tribute to my first love. My heart ached. Tears exploded. It was not war that took him away, though surely it did from me, but a brain tumor. He had remained in the Air Force, became a nurse, never married.

I have found a lifetime of happiness with a wonderful man. But I still think of Kim on my way to my grandchildren's, when I pass Colleen Court where he lived. And no matter how rich my life, I'll never forget there was something magical about that summer of '67.

Dream Lover, Dream Music
by Lyla Ellzey

*D*OUG. TALL AND DARK. Smooth. A voice like an Italian tenor. He was very popular with the schoolgirls all over our county, since he was a basketball player we had seen play several times in the past couple of years.

I met Doug when the kids from his school traveled to our school to take the Senior Placement Test. Lucky me: Doug was seated across the table from me. He pushed a wavy lock of hair off his forehead, leaned forward across the table, and said, "Hi, I'm Doug."

I had been sitting there in my straight-backed library chair, trying to look as if I was unaffected by his presence. I looked back at him, and could see what all the hoopla was about. He was gorgeous!

I said "Hi, I'm Lily." This drew the attention of the test administrator, who shushed us.

As we listened to a spiel about the test, I bowed my head, concentrating, because I hoped to go to college and knew I would have to do well on this test. I looked up a couple of times during the test and caught Doug looking as if he were appraising me. He would just grin, and bow his head back down to his test. Each time, I smiled at him, musing on the thought that if he didn't soon get around to answering the questions on this test, I would not be seeing him in classrooms or on campus once I got to college.

During the break for lunch, somebody had a radio on in one of the open-windowed classrooms. "Rockin' Robin" was playing.

"He rocks in the tree top all the day long, a-rockin' and a-boppin' and a-singin' my song," Doug sang along in a surprisingly good voice.

I said, "Wow, I didn't know you could sing like that!" He told me that he hoped to sing in his own band one day. I figured he probably could.

He asked me out, and we went to the movies that Saturday night, then parked by the beach. Oh, boy!

The next day I called my girlfriend and told her that if I wasn't in love with Doug Burnham, then I certainly had a good case of the *likes*. She had double-dated with Doug and some girl or other many times, so she knew just what I was talking about.

I was feeling pretty special the night we parked his car by the inlet and smelled the tang of the salt water and old fish that permeated the night air.

Doug looked at me, taking his eyes from where he had been gazing out the windshield. He peered intently into my eyes. Then he surprised the devil out of me by saying, "Lily, don't fall in love with me."

I just stared up at him, wondering what on earth this could mean? Was he somehow warning me about something? Was there something wrong with him? Was he joining up and heading off to Vietnam?

He saw my confusion and said, "I just mean, Lily, that you have your whole life ahead of you. You are going to college. You will make something of yourself. And I won't. I'll probably stay right here the rest of my life and never do anything important. This ain't the kind of life for you, so don't fall in love with me, because I wouldn't be any good for you."

Later I realized that this was a very selfless side of Doug Burnham that likely did not show itself often. I think he actually cared enough about me to not let me make that mistake.

The old Doug that all us girls knew and loved returned with a bravura grin, and started to softly sing "Sixteen Candles." Then he laughed and pulled me close.

Today, Doug is part owner of a restaurant and sings in the house band.

Letting Go
by Barbara Milstead Stanley

*H*E WAS THE FIRST BOY to ask me to "go steady." Tall, dark hair and yes, he was handsome. I loved him and I loved the way he adored me. The year was 1969.

Even though my family moved eighty miles away, he drove up to see me as often as he could afford to. As usual, when teens move away from each other and attend separate schools, the temptation to see other people is very strong. I had started dating a young man who made me question my undying love for Daunette.* Not wanting to give up either one, I just didn't tell either of them about the "other boy." Things went well for a few months, but my mother, sister, and friends badgered me to make a decision. I was told that I wasn't being fair to either boy. I chose the new boy, and now we've been married for thirty-six years.

Before my wedding, Daunette wrote a letter expressing his continued love for me, with assurance that he would always be a phone call away if I should ever need him. I ran into him once when our children were young. He was divorced at the time. We talked for a couple of hours. As we said good-bye, he hugged me close and told me that he still loved me, and would always be there for me. Throughout all the good and bad times in my life, I kept the special knowledge that someone loved me no matter what. I found out a few weeks ago that Daunette had died several years ago in a tragic automobile accident. For me, it was as though he had just died. It was more than the death of a person I once loved and always cared for; it was the total and complete loss of my first real love, and the emptiness of the space he occupied in my life for so long.

Author's note:

Daunette, pronounced "Don'eat," is a French-Canadian or Cajun name. When we were dating, I would put the letter E at the end of his name. I told him it looked sophisticated. He began signing his name that way and eventually changed it legally. He told me later that it was his way of keeping a part of me with him.

TOO CLOSE FOR COMFORT

Some of us, when we are moving toward deeper commitment in an intimate relationship, become aware of a vague sense of discomfort. And we wonder why, because in the beginning the closeness felt so good.

In these stories, we see that something not quite named may have caused a person to just walk away from a relationship that otherwise held promise. That something was likely an unrecognized or unacknowledged fear—the usual suspects being fear of rejection (or being abandoned) and fear of commitment.

But named or not, fear is inherent in deepening intimacy. Couples walk a fine line, both wanting to be close emotionally and holding back to avoid a feeling of being "too close." Even if their fear is not seen for what it is, it can still precipitate action. Sometimes it leads right to the path of least resistance, the nearest exit.

Friday Nights
Anonymous

W E USED TO PACK UP Friday nights after work—sleeping bags, tent, dented cooler, freshly burned CDs and a thermos of black coffee. Remember that twenty-year-old hatchback we called Dusty? You named her that, after one of our long August drives down the cinder highway that cuts across central Oregon.

I miss those days. I miss those nights—heading out of Seattle, east across the mountains, into the great wide open. Just us. No expectations. Somewhere, late in the darkness, we'd stop and set up the tent. Fall asleep to the soothing scent of sage and ponderosa pine as we used to when we were kids, stars falling like lazy rockets.

Saturdays were the best, weren't they? Bliss, I used to say—waking to cool cheeks and hands, craving coffee and pancakes. Fresh water from the river to wash up with.

The last time we talked, you said, " I've never had so much fun with someone doin' nothin.'" Your voice was heavy with sadness. I understood that you knew you cannot get any of that back.

I half-laughed, trying to ease the moment, "You're right. We never really did much, did we?" But silently I remembered playing Frisbee, watching the clouds, tailgate picnics, driving, laughter, listening to Springsteen. It may not sound like much, but it's all I wanted.

In the evening we built a fire, played chess, drank a beer or two. We talked about your step-dad, Mike. What would he say if he could see us now—early thirties, decent jobs, re-united high school sweethearts? I always wondered if he could feel the tension. Mike always knew what was up with us.

Sundays were bittersweet. The mornings were good, basically a continuation of Saturday, without the freedom sprawled out in front of us. We took down the tent, re-packed Dusty and filled up the thermos wherever we got breakfast. We'd go for a hike or swim in the middle of the day. Lunch always tasted fantastic after the exercise. Late afternoon, I crashed inside. Stopping at the last mountain gas station just before closing time to fill the tank, grab a snack and scrub bugs off the windshield—that was when reality hit me, as the sun started to go down. That was the signal it was time to make the push back to the real world.

"I just don't know how to move forward," you'd say, like clockwork, every few months. You were all over the place during those four years. At first you wanted to get married, then six months later you didn't. You were scared. You needed your own place, but still wanted to sleep together every night. After two years of schlepping between apartments, separated by three city blocks, you decided to move in. Our friends, siblings, cousins, co-workers were getting married left and right.

One Christmas, you bought me a diamond necklace, and weeks later, broke down sobbing in the kitchen, "I wanted to buy you a ring, but just couldn't." I stuck around though, hoping you'd get there. But deep down I knew that you suffered from something I could not see; it had been there when we were sixteen, and it was still there at thirty-two. Whatever it was, I knew I couldn't save you.

We returned to the city with the sweet smell of campfire in our clothes. I wanted our life together to be like it was on Friday nights. But you couldn't seize that—said I wanted fireworks. Not every day is the Fourth of July, but secretly I knew it could be.

Then, one day, I accepted where you were. It was like a switch turned off inside me, and I remember thinking, *If he can't do this, fine. Then it's time for me to say yes to my soul.*

It took me nine months to say good-bye, quit my job, pack up my life and buy a plane ticket. If the love of my young life was not working out, I would indulge my Bohemian soul, travel Europe and make my own fireworks.

The Boulevard
by John Day

*I*T WAS WELL AFTER MIDNIGHT when I parked my car. Opening the door and stepping onto the street, I was met by the sounds of the city's symphony: the L train, off in the distance; somewhere, gunshots, interrupted by shouts and the far-off wail of a siren. I stood on the corner and closed my eyes. I was taken back to a different time.

It was the summer of 1961, and the world was filled with the promise of adventure for boys entering seventh grade. Joe, Rich and I were at Ben's Soda Fountain. We each had a vanilla Coke and a Nestle's Crunch bar. I purchased an adventure magazine with a picture of the Loch Ness Monster on the cover.

Rich had a new transistor radio, so small it could fit in your shirt pocket, yet it could tune in to all of Chicago's great AM stations. I heard, coming from that radio, a tune that has haunted me ever since.

We left the soda fountain and walked out into a day filled with sunshine. Trees on the boulevard made a rustling noise as they do only on a summer day. The wide, shiny green parkways of the boulevard stretched out in front of us. We started walking, on our way to no place in particular.

Crossing the boulevard were three girls walking toward us. Everything around me became a blur. The only thing I could see was a girl with brown hair and green eyes. Joe told me she was his cousin. As seventh grade girls will do with seventh grade boys, the girls walked past, barely giving us a glance.

I was smitten. I couldn't get the girl out of my mind. Later that night, sitting on our back porch, my father asked what was troubling me. "Nothing !" I almost shouted.

"I think you're in love," my father said. Then, in his infinite wisdom he added, " Don't worry. Love's like a bellyache. You'll get over it."

And get over it I did...until the following year when I saw her at a nearby roller rink. We skated together and I began walking her home every week after that. I thought this would last forever, but, along came high school and we went our separate ways.

Time moved on. The struggles of school. Dating others. Adventure of some kind or another. We moved from Elvis to the Beatles. I often thought of her. Then we met at a church social, and it started all over again. We began dating.

We went to dances and parties. Had seemingly endless summer days at the beaches on Lake Michigan. Midnight mass on Christmas Eve. Went to the movies when Chicago still had downtown theatres. Walked for miles and miles down the boulevard. Listened to records by the Beatles and the Beach Boys. Spent countless hours sitting on her front porch drinking Coca Cola.

There was talk of the future. Talk of marriage and children. Talk of jobs and a better life. Talk of getting out of a dirty city and a dying, working-class neighborhood.

There was, however, something unsettling in the air. There was no college in the future for kids from our part of the city. There were stories of war in Asia. The army was drafting young men in ever increasing numbers. There weren't many jobs to be had.

Something, and I'm not sure what, had begun to go wrong. Perhaps it was just fear on my part. We went our separate ways.

By the time I realized what I had lost, it was too late to try and go back. She had been the anchor that kept me in school. Kept me from the lure of the streets. Gave me hope. Taught me about love.

Like most of my friends, she got out of the city. Moved on. Only a memory now. For my part, in an odd way, I never left.

I became a cop, and ever since I've worked the streets where I grew up and she and I walked the Boulevard. And each day I confront the ghosts of my past.

Opening my eyes, I whistle an old tune and leave.

Hope for Someday
by Sonja Herbert

I MET GORDON AT A SINGLES DANCE at church. He was tall and handsome, and his sky-blue eyes shone with warmth. Although already in his forties, Gordon had never been married, but he wasn't taken aback when I told him about my three little girls.

We hit it off immediately and soon became good friends. He was loving and patient with my children, and in no time turned into an appreciated part of my family. As I watched him play with the girls, a wave of happiness washed through me. I already felt more for him than friendship, and I knew soon he'd feel the same, too. For years, I'd prayed for just such a gentle man to come along, and now God had answered my prayers.

When Gordon finally asked me to a ball game, just him and me, my heart beat faster. This would be our first real date.

After the game, Gordon invited me to a small Mexican restaurant for supper. At a corner table, a candle flickered in the center, painting the dim room with romance. Gordon told me about his life and his desire to have a family. Somehow, his plans to marry had never quite turned out right.

Maybe I can change that, I thought. My love for him overflowed.

He drove me home, and we sat in his pick-up, talking for another hour. One by one the stars appeared and decorated the sky. In the balmy air, the song of crickets accompanied our talk with soothing sound. I sidled nearer to Gordon and looked into his eyes.

Gordon yawned and said, "It's late. I better get home. I'll come by tomorrow and we'll do something with the kids, okay?"

Suddenly, the night seemed darker. Why did he guard his feelings like that? I felt an undeniable attraction to Gordon, and thought he felt the same. But then I shrugged inwardly. After all, he'd never been married, and getting emotionally involved with a complete family would challenge anyone. I could wait. Things surely would change soon.

Weeks passed. Gordon visited almost daily, playing with the children, talking about his youth, and watching old movies with us. He only asked me out for football games, and never touched me. My initial happiness evaporated, and gloom settled over my dreams.

One day, on my way back from shopping, I stopped at a red light. As I waited for the light to change, I realized Gordon was a lot like this traffic signal. The signal would turn green eventually, but Gordon was stuck in a permanent "don't go" phase. I gripped the steering wheel tighter. He would probably never overcome whatever it was that forbade him to have a mature relationship. The love I wanted from him could not be mine.

As I drove on, I told myself my children and I would be all right alone. By the time I got home, my heart was aching. Nevertheless, I greeted Gordon and gathered my children. "School's out," I said, "and we have nothing to do. Let's go to Colorado and see Grandma."

"Grandma's! Can Gordon go with us?" asked Meagan, my youngest.

"No, Dummy," Marit, the oldest, said. "Gordon isn't married to us."

Gordon smiled at the girls. "I'll be here when you all come back, okay?"

I watched the interchange, biting my lip to keep from crying. The girls were attached to Gordon, and it would break all our hearts when he eventually disappeared from our lives, as was bound to happen. Maybe after our trip, when the pain of my unrequited love had lessened, I'd talk with him about visiting less often.

But when we returned a month later, Gordon announced he was moving to Michigan to be with his ailing mother. My heart broke.

I never saw Gordon again, but I'll never forget him. He had so many of the qualities I wanted in a husband. Knowing Gordon gave me hope that someday I'd meet a man like him, but someone who would not be afraid of commitment. And eventually I did!

Winter With Jasper
by B. G.

*I*T WAS THAT CURL OF BEARD that got me, the way Jasper could never manage to grow any hair on the rest of his face. I loved "scritching" at it, combing it with my fingers, tugging lightly. He had such deep brown eyes, like pools of sweet syrup. They'd crinkle and laugh at me over his strong, high cheeks when I'd play with his beard. I lived for his full-throated laughter when I'd move my fingers down to tickle his neck.

It was the first year of college, when we all want to believe that we've found adulthood. We met in the dining hall when, feeling courageous from this first foray from home, I set my tray next to his. I flooded the awkward silence with absurd babble, telling him silly stories about my life. When I was telling him about the time I was attacked by a flock of geese, Jasper offered me his chicken nuggets for "fowl retaliation," and I fell in love.

I think it's funny for my first adult relationship to have started in a school cafeteria, prompted by chicken nuggets. It makes me think of how young I was, how much I had left to learn.

We spent that winter curled up in Jasper's room, playing Frisbee indoors and making terrible puns. He always got a clever grin on his face when I would laugh at something he said, and I laughed more often because of this.

We had never defined our relationship, comfortable in the liminal world between friendship and something more. I fell asleep on Jasper's bed once, and he told me that I looked beautiful. Because we never spoke our feelings for each other, the compliment hit me hard and made me dizzy. After that, I always pretended to nod off at the end of every late evening with him.

We only kissed once. I had stayed in his room until very late, and we decided to share the rest of the night in his bed. I curled up behind his smooth back and lay awake until morning. When his alarm went off, Jasper rose, turned, and gently kissed my lips. He was out the door before I could open my eyes.

That was when we began to fall apart. That winter with Jasper, in the safe warm room, it was as though we were in a waking hibernation. The relationship did not define itself, but lay dormant around us, soft and sleeping. When spring came, when he kissed me, a thawing began.

Our relationship, I now believe, could only exist in that limbo state. One of us would push us forward, and the other would push us back.

Jasper would smooth my hair out of my eyes, but I would nudge his hand away.

I would sit down in his lap and wrap my arms around his shoulders, but he would stand up suddenly, swinging me around and both of us laughing, forgetting.

But the kiss made me long for the endless push-pull to choose a direction. The limbo world we had constructed around ourselves had grown tiresome, and I wanted to know where I stood.

So I asked Jasper why he had kissed me. He said that he thought I was asleep.

It was then that I realized I had been asleep. We both had been comfortable in our hibernation. But I was ready to wake up.

It was an amicable break-up, though I suspect that's because there was so little left to break. That was eight years ago, and we've never spoken since. He was my first love, and I can't ever erase the memory of the winter we spent together, the warmth and the quiet, the unsettled feeling, like floating.

These days, I am fully awake. My fiancé and I speak regularly about what we expect from each other and where we stand. It's a stability that I pull strength from. I feel like I'm always moving forward, walking on stable ground.

I still find Jasper floating through my mind from time to time. It is then, especially, that I embrace the solid earth I've formed, rejoicing fully in the feel of something sturdy underneath my hands and feet.

Brooklyn Hearts
By Leonard W. Kenyon

A MILLION LOVE STORIES, love songs, and clichés already exist. I must admit I'm tempted to try to reinvent one to make my story easier to convey, to simplify the most complexly wonderful and confusing time in my life, with hopes that it would make it easier to understand—maybe even convince you that what I had is familiar, special and beautiful, yet somehow set apart from anything you've ever experienced. But then, I don't know what you've experienced, and I also know it would be foolish to even try. So I won't.

I'd love to tell that from the moment I saw her, I knew she was "the one," but I won't. If I could, I'd tell you of all the little notes that were passed between us, and of the butterflies she gave me, but I won't do that either. Maybe you'd hear more of her, and I'd start by telling you of the way her hair seemed to snatch the sun right out of the sky and keep it for her own. Maybe I'd tell you of her eyes and how I hoped she would never look at me any other way, but how I never had the courage to look any deeper than the smile in them. But these things have all been done and said by someone else about a countless number of other "hers," and probably better, too.

But then, if love is always butterflies and blushing, maybe I don't know what the hell it is after all. Though I think if you just take a second and look right there, beyond that bathroom mirror, and into the reflection of those two tired brown eyes, my eyes, you might catch a glimpse of what I've been trying to say...

"Babe, will you put a little toothpaste on mine too?"
She was sitting behind me on the toilet, peeing, with her

knees pressed together. I heard the spin of the dispenser, and then I knocked the water off my toothbrush. In the mirror I watched her stand and hike her dress back down. She was beautiful, but I never told her that enough.

She took her toothbrush from me and I left her smiling at my back.

I'm not easy to be with; I'm insecure, moody and prone to physical ailments, which in turn makes me insecure and moody, which raises my stress level and makes me prone to physical ailments.

I know she's going to want to make love.

And I know I'd rather have sex, a smoke, and then go to sleep.

Jesus, am I sixty?

She came from the bathroom hoping for my eyes, but I hid them in the fridge. I asked her if she wanted a glass of water. She didn't. I stood to find her right there, waiting for me, still smiling. I gave her a weak kiss and put my back to her knowing it would sour her face—knowing that if I could get her just angry enough, she'd drop the lovemaking thing and I could go on doing whatever it is I do. She's beautiful, and I'm God's most selfish and ridiculous creature.

I went into the living room and hid my nose in a book. A chapter later, I decided I'd better give up and give in. I found her in the bedroom with her back to me, her face buried in a pillow. I lay down and tried to touch her thighs, suddenly converted to the idea of lovemaking, but my hand was slapped away. I tried again and this time she got out of bed. She took the couch and fell asleep crying.

She always said I never wrote anything nice. She's probably right.

She always told me that I never wrote anything for her. But everything I write, I write for her.

Love Every Chance You Get
by Ariel Sky

*A*FTER A DIVORCE that shattered my self-confidence and self-worth, I never wanted to put myself in a vulnerable situation with a guy again.

About a year had gone by when a man walked into my work life and changed that. His name was Greg, and every woman in the room was instantly aware of his extreme good looks. Greg was well over six feet tall, with tanned skin that showed off his broad shoulders and toned body. He had dark hair and penetrating eyes that looked deep into your soul. And that smile—that smile still makes my heart stop. Greg was exactly what I needed and more than I deserved.

When we were together it was as if no one else existed; I never worried about showing my imperfections, and he never made me feel I had any. Before Greg, I would have been well aware of girls who were prettier, or hid my body because it was quite flawed after the birth of my first two children. It just didn't matter now.

Greg and I talked on the phone until the batteries went dead. I could talk to him about almost anything. He knew all my fears about relationships, but I just couldn't bring myself to tell him how I felt about him, and he never pushed. To be honest, he scared the heck out of me. I knew he had the potential to make my divorce look like a trip to the candy store.

When I would start getting too close to him, I'd try to pawn him off on another girl. He would realize what I was doing and why I was doing it, and fade into the shadows. Months later, I would miss him so much that I'd call his best friend Jeff to chat, and sure enough, every time, they would start coming to town again. I always kept Greg at arm's length, and often talked to him as if I were one of the guys. I always told him he could have any girl he wanted, and he was adamant that I was wrong. I remember one night when we were out with a few of his buddies from his home town, and they wanted him to show them how to pick up girls. I just laughed and told him to show us what he had.

Greg whispered in my ear saying, "So you think I can have any girl I want?"

"Yes," I said in a small voice, a little worried that my heart wouldn't handle it if he proved it to me.

Greg spoke up so his friends could hear and said, "Okay, watch this."

With that, he waltzed up to the bar near three attractive women. Instantly, they were asking him if they could buy him a drink. His friends were in awe; my heart sank. Then he turned around and came up to me and kissed me as I had never been kissed before. The heavens must have opened their doors to let the light shine down on us, because it was completely breathtaking. He looked deep into my eyes and said, "I want you."

I'd love to say that I put my fears aside and put all my trust in him, but I can't. Shortly afterward, I took the coward's way out and pushed him away. I decided to marry a man I wasn't in love with, so I could never get hurt again. Greg called before the wedding telling me not to do it. Without a good reason why I shouldn't, I did. Six years later, I let my husband go to find a love who could love him back.

I learned so much from Greg; he gave my kids their mom back and taught me to love myself again. He showed me what love was supposed to feel like. He also taught me when you give your heart away you never really get it back. My heart will always belong to him.

I lost my best friend that day, but I found myself. So my advice to you is to live without regrets, and love with all your heart every chance you get.

The Girl and the GTO
Anonymous

SHE WAS FIVE YEARS YOUNGER and still in high school, but she was the perfect girl for me. She was very good looking, with a great personality. Everybody liked her. I had a 1967 GTO and when we went out, she would ride beside me, sitting on the very uncomfortable consol.

When we were not together, I was working on cars, running with the guys and drag racing at the local drag strip three nights a week. I was a "guy" and didn't tell her I loved her, or how much she meant to me.

One night, I got a call from one of the guys, and he asked me to go to a strip bar. I thought about it for a minute and told him, "No thanks, maybe next time." When I hung up, I thought about why I had said no. What would SHE think, what would her parents think of me?

It was then that I came up with a plan: to tell her I loved her and that I would ask her to marry me when she graduated from school.

I got a license plate with her name lettered on it. I was going to name my GTO after her, a big deal back then. Everybody in town knew that car. I got a big "I LOVE YOU" card and wrote how much I loved her and would she marry me? I got a ring box and put my class ring in it. The ring had "strings" attached to it. The strings meant she had to graduate from school before she would get the diamond. If she wanted, she also could "go for the gold" and not waste time after graduation. I put these things in a box, wrapped it up in pretty paper and put the surprise in the back seat of the GTO.

I was going to call her on Friday and get a dinner date for any day over the weekend—and give her the "surprise package." No one knew what I was planning. I didn't want anyone to talk me out of this.

I was working on the GTO on Thursday night when one of the guys stopped by and asked me to go to a picnic at his house on Saturday. It was a family thing, and I thought that would also be a great chance to ask my girl to go. I could spring my "surprise" on her in the car. When I said "Let me call 'D' and ask her if she can go too," he gave me a funny look and said "Don't you know she's dating someone else?"

My world ended with those words. Without getting into detail, about three years went by without my seeing her again. I never dated anyone steady again. I had "learned my lesson."

One day I was at a party and one of my friends asked me if I could take someone to another party. She didn't have a date. I said "Sure—who is she?" Out stepped "D."

We went out together three or four times and I was falling in love all over again. One big problem. I felt I couldn't trust her to be there IF I fell in love again. Would she just leave again without saying anything? She acted as if nothing had happened in those three years. And I sure wasn't going to tell her about the "surprise" that I'd had for her.

Every time I went to pick her up, I was so nervous. I was sure someone would meet me at the door and tell me "D's not here. Don't you know she's dating someone else?"

I couldn't take it anymore. I just walked away from the girl I had loved, and went back to the bars. It was safe there. No one was going to hurt me there. I would never let that happen again.

I've never seen her again. That was thirty-seven years ago and I still love her. She was the best and the worst thing that ever happened to me. Even now that I'm married to a very nice lady, I still can't wear a wedding ring. That space was for "her."

THE TASTE OF REGRET

Is there anything that tastes more bitter than regret?

To feel that maybe you should have done something differently, long after it is possible to make it right, creates a special kind of torment. Having hurt someone who loved you, you wish, too late, that you had behaved with more integrity.

Perhaps you were responding to a fear you didn't recognize at the time. But now, with the clarity that time can bring, your past behavior seems thoughtless and cruel.

Without necessarily using the words, "I'm sorry," all of these stories acknowledge having done something hurtful. They express a hope that, even now, giving voice to that regret will help an old wound begin to heal.

November Rain
by Kelley Walker Perry

I REMEMBER THE RESONANCE of soft rain falling on a tin roof. The memory of its sound echoes in my heart as the greatest regret of my life.

The cool November rain that night failed to deter my lover and me; we lounged in the hot tub on our cabin deck, gazing at a spectacular mountain view.

We'd gone on the trip to Tennessee because work stress had gotten the better of me. I could hardly afford such extravagance, so Ralph had sold his truck—an old Ford he'd been tinkering with since he was a teenager. Lost in my own world at the time, I never even acknowledged his sacrifice.

Most of the leaves had turned from vibrant scarlet and gold to late-autumn hues of russet and sienna, and a chill was in the air. All that week, we browsed in Gatlinburg's shops and dined in nice restaurants. Nights, we drifted from the hot tub and the rain to the Jacuzzi and its bubbles, and then sat talking in front of a roaring fire made pungent by carburetor cleaner—his unique idea of lighter fluid. Later, he attempted to chase away my demons with his tender touch, in the best way he knew how.

I typically spurned his advances, explaining that I'd been hurt too many times in the past, that I wasn't ready for a commitment, and that I didn't completely return his feelings. I broke his heart almost daily, but he kept trying.

That particular night, he left me in the hot tub and slid aside the heavy glass doors leading into the cabin. I thought he was refreshing his drink, but he was gone quite a while. When he returned, he shyly led me inside—where he'd filled the Jacuzzi with fragrant bubble bath, lit scented candles and incense, and even popped in a soothing CD. Instead of staying, he simply kissed my cheek and closed the door on strains of Celtic music.

While I wallowed in the bath like a pampered walrus, Ralph sat alone on the deck and wrote a poem for me on a yellow legal pad. After I'd dried off and dressed, he offered me those heartfelt lines—in hopes, I'm sure, that his love for me would finally sink in.

At the time, I was less than grateful. I thought he was being pushy; I needed space. His spelling was incredibly flawed—but thankfully, I held back from noting this last tidbit aloud.

That was the final solitude we'd have for the vacation. My mother and sister brought my kids down; they were on fall break, but I'd left them in Indiana for the first half of the trip. We spent the remainder of the time shopping, visiting Ripley's Aquarium of the Smokies, checking out old cabins at Cade's Cove, and meandering through the local artists' colony. During one excursion Ralph took my son, with whom he was very close, on a secret mission. Later, he presented me with a bottle of Tryst, an expensive perfume I'd especially liked.

My mother's birthday fell during our stay. Ralph happily grilled for us all. He never minded spending time with my family, and in fact seemed glad to be included. I later learned that everyone but me believed we had gone to Tennessee to get married; I'd just scoffed when we passed by a chapel and he tentatively mentioned something to that effect.

Everything that man did, he did for me. He continued struggling, even after we returned home. But I can still see the look on his face the night he began to give up.

Too late, I discovered my true feelings for him. Too late, I learned that some things we do are irrevocable. He left his key to the house on my pillow early the following February, and married another woman that summer.

I ran into him in town the other day; he looks good. Happy.

Yes, I remember the rain. It is the bittersweet sound of the only real love I've ever known, lost forever in the misty mountains of Tennessee.

Lament
by David Galassie

I CAN'T REMEMBER WHEN it first came up, but it's bothered me for a long, long time. And every five years or so, coinciding with each reunion, the same guilt comes around.

She'd never responded to the questionnaires. For all I knew, she was still at that address in the souvenir booklet, living a slow, tortuous existence. I don't have the ego to think that I was the sole reason for her to stay away, but what if I was?

To finally make peace with her (with myself?) after all those years might do me some good. Or it might just irritate old wounds. What good reason do I have, after all those years?

A thin girl with a manly, gravelly voice that belied her fragility, Maggie played the clarinet in the marching band. Her long straight blonde hair accentuated the porcelain texture of her milky skin. She literally looked like a doll, a no-curves, androgynous doll. We made quite a pair.

How it happened, how we came together is pretty hazy now. I don't even remember the exact details. She had a textbook I needed; I drove to her house to buy it and we talked. Could that be where it began?

We had many classes together on the accelerated track for college-bound students. We hung out together at a dance and something clicked as we slow-danced to "Color My World," or was it "Stairway to Heaven?" Leaving the gym, we walked together until she stopped at the phone booth at Third and DePere and called home so her father would know where she was.

Occasionally we walked together from class to class, and I know I walked her to band practice once or twice. We never officially "went together." Then what was I doing? I'm sure Maggie didn't look at it the same way I did. And, of course, meeting Bess, my eventual girlfriend, sealed the deal. I mean, I was head over heels in love with that girl. Poor Maggie didn't fit anywhere in that scenario.

And, in the end, I believe I broke her heart.

We were only friends, officially. But all these years later, I know in my heart that she thought it was more. I know now in my own heart that it was more. And I feel so bad about that. She might have been a lifelong friend if I'd handled it differently. She didn't deserve what I gave her.

The other day, I pulled out my yearbook and read what she'd written in our junior year, her only entry in our four years together. After some drivel about the math class we shared, she wrote, "P.S. I really enjoy our friendship." But I know her words were just a clever ruse to disguise her true feelings. I can't for the life of me remember what I wrote in her book.

I think I kissed her once; I held her hand now and then. I know I never said, "I love you." So why, after thirty-some years, do I have to feel so damned bad?

No One Was Supposed to Fall in Love
by Diana M. Amadeo

I HADN'T THOUGHT OF HIM IN YEARS. I barely remembered his name. But it didn't really matter; no one called him by his given name anyway. Due to his bright, flaming locks, he was known as Red.

The young man who was a few rows ahead of me checking out business shirts was the spitting image of Red. He had the same fair skin, red hair, freckles and dimples that deepened when he smiled. Yes, that guy was a dead ringer for Red. Maybe a relative. I smiled and shook my head.

Red was pure fun. Memories of him were warm and fuzzy. For me, they were just good times; no pain, no angst. We had a lot in common on campus. Both of us had intense schedules and lofty goals, so having someone to hang around with was a godsend in releasing some of the pressures of graduate school. We worked on problem sets, then hit the pub to share a few laughs. He was a good kisser, but he knew I was committed to someone miles away.

He was a year ahead of me and had his life planned out. Even though I was younger, my life was likewise planned. There was no place for change or spontaneity in a tough, uncompromising job market. Neither of our plans included each other—at least that's what Red repeated back to me. After his graduation, we would go our separate ways.

I still remember Red in his black cap and gown, eyes scanning the crowd, looking, looking, looking until he saw me. Then he smiled and settled back in his seat, content.

After graduation, there were lots of pictures; his family insisted that I be in every single one. It troubled me to know that soon I would have to be edited out of them, but I took my place next to him, anyway. It bothered me a little more when Red put his arm around my shoulders, squeezed me tight and whispered, "I love you."

That wasn't part of the plan.

Red had known that I was engaged. I had dangled my ring in front of his nose the first time we met. But to him, the ring was a challenge. Every time I reminded him that his graduation was the end of our relationship, he just grinned. "We'll see about that," he would say.

After Red's graduation, I had another year at the university. His new employment was now three hundred miles away. But he was persistent. He called several times a week until, finally, I refused to answer the phone. He would show up at the dorm, unannounced, with that dimply, goofy smile, and I would be cool and cordial, reminding him of our prior arrangement. His letters, that arrived almost daily, were familiar, kind and endearing. My only response was a brief, "Hey thanks for the memories, but life goes on." Sigh.

No one was supposed to fall in love. We were just supposed to be friends having a good time. Why didn't he stick to the agreement? It took a good six months of cold shoulder treatment for Red to get the message. His last letter was so gut-wrenchingly heartsick that I burned it immediately, lest I be tempted to read it over and act on it. I reasoned my actions were tough love.

My graduation came, with my fiance' and family in attendance. It was wonderful. I married and have had a beautiful life. My life went as planned. Did Red's? He deserved a wonderful life. Is he happy?

I shook my head once more. The man checking out business shirts looked at me in annoyance.

"What is your problem, lady?" he asked. "Why are you staring at me?"

I looked down and watched as tears dropped onto my hands. "Oh God, I'm sorry," I said with another head shake. "I am so, so sorry."

The Last Time I Saw Dennis
by D. S. Schildkraut

CLASSIC STORY: OPPOSITES ATTRACT—underachieving high school rogue dates aloof, class brain—as big a cliché as the story line in any 1950's girl band song. Dennis and I were as different as snowflakes and hailstones. We didn't have one friend in common. The differences fueled our relationship.

It was in drama club that I first noticed Dennis. He swaggered when he walked, and wore his russet hair low over his mischievous green eyes. The way he tossed his hair aside when he smiled made me shiver. And that smile, a little off center with just the left corner turned up, only added to his charm. From the first day I saw him, how I wanted to kiss that crooked smile. Silly me.

My aloofness hid a naive girl too shy to talk to him. Dennis had no such problem, and asked me out the second day of rehearsals. I accepted, staring at my shoes, wary that this was a prank. How could such a boy be interested in me?

But three days later he picked me up for our first date, an evening that involved pizza, a movie, and some kissing. I don't remember the details of the movie or pizza, but the kissing…that I remember. Flirtatious kisses, light and teasing, led to a depth of feeling I had not imagined I possessed. For the next year, his senior and my junior, we learned to enjoy our differences and moved through the months at ease with each other.

Dennis graduated in 1966, and went to work fixing cars at his his brother-in-law's auto repair shop. The Vietnam War was at full throttle. Fearing that he would be drafted, I pleaded with him to go to college. He could have gotten a deferment if he had enrolled. I wanted him safe, to be with me always.

We struggled through my senior year. Even when we weren't arguing, the draft was never far from our minds. It was a dark time—all the sweet kisses could not push away my fear. We ended the relationship a month before I graduated. I had gotten a scholarship to a college three hundred miles away. We were weary, and the break-up inevitable.

Fast-forward to Thanksgiving,1968, my sophomore year in college. I hadn't seen Dennis even once in the fourteen months since we broke up. Home for the first time that semester, I took a walk in the damp afternoon chill, needing to shake off the lethargy from the previous day's feast. I walked a few blocks past familiar places, friends' houses, the convenience store and high school. I turned the corner onto First Street, and there he was, waxing his car. He had a chamois in his hand and was wiping the rain from the white and aqua Olds '88 that had been our chariot and refuge. He was bent over the front fender.

His beautiful hair was gone, shaved to the scalp. I staggered and grabbed a fence for support, dumbfounded to realize he must have been drafted. Trembling, wanting to move forward but unable to face him, I skulked away. I slowed at the corner. Just for a second, I looked back. His head began to rise up from the car. I ran away.

The shame I felt thirty-nine years ago, when I heard of his death in Vietnam, lingers. I fear he saw me that day, and went to the other side of the world knowing I was a coward. I should have walked the half block to his car. I should have smiled at him, hugged him, wished him safe from harm. I should have...

Bittersweet are my memories of Dennis, first love and first regret entwined around my heart. And carried from those days are the lessons that love changes you and there is no turning back. For that I still weep whenever I think of Dennis.

Money Cannot Buy Love
Anonymous

*T*ODAY I SIT BACK AMIDST THE LUXURY in my plush mansion, all alone. The threads of my life have too many self-created knots. Every time I try hard to tie the broken ends of the thread, the knot only grows bigger. The invisible knots of my life pain me each time I touch them. Walking down memory lane, I turn back to the golden pages of my life.

Abhilash Nayyar is the buried truth of my life, the truth I have shared with no one. His love was the blanket which always kept me warm. It all started when we were at H. L. College in Ahmedabad, an ethnic city in Gujarat. That first day, we were introduced by a common friend while sitting at the Red Rose, a small café next to our college. We took an instant liking towards each other. I fell for his deep voice, broad shoulders and tall frame. I had started observing the early morning sunlight that falls on the green leaves. I had started listening to the birds twittering around me, and to my throbbing heart. I had started loving him.

We couldn't wait to get to college just to see each other. We talked at length over the phone daily. I could dial his number even in my sleep. We would listen to Ghazals (short lyric poems in the form of a song) and Hindi movie songs over the phone, and convey our love in different forms. He told me about his past failed relationship and I grew jealous.

We couldn't meet often publicly, so we started writing. We exchanged stories which had characters with different names, but the feelings were purely ours. We held hands for the first time while watching a Hindi movie called *Taal (Beat)*. The touch of the hair on his fingers made my body tingle.

We would often meet in the library, sometimes during break hours and sometimes during class hours. His musk cologne smelt so strong, his crisp blue shirt was always buttoned up with just a bit of his chest hair visible, his jaw so broad and his chin with a cleft were so appealing. His deep husky voice still echoes in my ears. My heart yearns for me to be in his arms.

After class, I would drive in my white car down to his dimly lit and sparsely furnished apartment. He would feed me dhal (lentils cooked with spices) served with rice and potatoes cooked in a south Indian way, his staple diet. To quench my thirst, he would pour chilled cardamom flavoured water into my glass. When I would ask for dessert he would draw me closer and carry me into his bedroom and kiss me all over. We caressed each other and watched movies together lying naked. That was the sweetest dessert I have ever had.

We wrote letters to each other about how we felt. He asked me how was my first kiss, to which I replied, "You tasted of onions and garlic!"

He taught me how to find pleasure in little things. He showed me how small gestures can win someone's heart. I had learnt to experience joy and peace in simple things.

Each time I sit alone in the temple, I ask God why He had snatched away Abhilash from my life. But the sad part is that I cannot blame anyone but myself for losing my love. I had cheated on him while he was away. I was seeing another guy, just because he was earning a million dollars.

In my chase for money and status, I killed our innocent love. The ugly face of guilt reappears every time I look into the mirror. There is a vacuum within me. I feel helpless and insecure. His absence has changed the way I look at the world now. My criteria of judging people based on their status and possessions was so shallow.

Over the years, in the turmoil of saving my two marriages, I had forgotten the essence of love. But what I cannot forget now is that money cannot buy love. My chase for wealth has ended in misery. I took too long to realize that true love is true wealth. Money cannot buy love.

Tears and Regrets
by Connie Berridge

*T*HIS IS A STORY ABOUT JOHN, and maybe a story of regrets. I can't even remember his last name now. I only know that he was a wonderful boy.

I met John at the skating rink. I was seventeen and he was nineteen. But since he wasn't in his uniform, I didn't know he was in the Army.

Every Saturday, a group of friends and I went roller skating. It was our Saturday night ritual. John was skating, and I, not being too careful skating backwards, bumped into him and almost knocked him over. Embarrassed, I said "I'm so sorry. I wasn't watching where I was skating."

He smiled and said "No harm done. I'm John, what's your name?"

"Connie," I replied.

"I've seen you here before and wanted to meet you. You come here every Saturday?"

I told him that usually a group of us met there, skated until closing, then the "gang" would go to the nearest hamburger joint and gorge ourselves on burgers, fries and cherry cokes.

As we talked, I learned that John was a local boy, in the Army, and home on leave. He joined us that night and the following three weeks of his leave. We spent almost every night going skating, to a movie, or just walking. I got to know him quite well and liked him. He was intelligent and interesting to talk with. He said he wanted to go to college on the G.I. Bill after he got out of the service. John was perhaps the nicest person I had ever met at my young age.

After leave, John went back to Korea, and we corresponded

for a few months. In the interim, I had been dating others and became quite interested in a boy I had met.

In the last letter I received from John, he stated he wanted me to become his girl and wait for him. He said he hoped we would go steady, that I had come to mean a lot to him and he wanted to know someone would wait for him. "I want you to meet my parents next time I come home," he wrote.

I didn't have the heart to tell him I had been seriously dating another, so I thought, *I'll wait until he comes home and tell him.* I didn't answer his letter. A month went by, and one Sunday I picked up the paper and saw the terrifying news: John had been killed in action. Stunned, I cried and wished I had answered his last letter.

For months I was tormented by thoughts of this wonderful boy whose letter of love I had not answered. Finally, I couldn't stand it any longer. I looked up his home phone number and called his house. His mother answered.

"Hi," I said. I told her who I was, that I had known her son John. I told her the story about his last letter and about my boyfriend, and that I thought I'd tell John when he returned home. "I'm so sorry now that I didn't answer his letter."

"Don't be dear," she said. "I'm sure John would have understood. He was that sort of boy. Don't feel guilty. We all try to do the right thing and never know what the future holds. He is at peace now."

"I'm so sorry" I repeated. "It has bothered me ever since I read the death notice."

"Be happy. John is with the Lord. It's all right. I'm sure he would forgive you," his mother said, and then, "Goodbye dear, and thank you for calling."

She hung up as I whispered a soft goodbye. It has been over fifty years, and I will always remember John, the handsome young man I met at the rink. And I will never forgive myself for not answering his letter. But most of all, I will never forgive myself for not even remembering his last name.

Forgive Me, Babe
Anonymous

*H*E WAS TOO COOL, without even trying—with his blond afro, sparkling blue eyes and his so-smooth demeanor. Karl partied hard and shamelessly broke the law, didn't go to school. He was definitely trouble, and that made him even more attractive. It was as if I knew I was drowning and didn't even care, as long as he was looking my way.

I was fifteen and a fairly good student, although I was always being told I wasn't living up to my potential. I was pretty boring. I read books and didn't break the rules in any major way, but I wanted to; I ached to break the rules. And I did, starting with making him mine. But there was a price.

He cheated on me, and after we moved in together, he beat me. So I left him.

I went back to him and, against all odds, things were better. *We* were better, started working as a team, as a real couple. We set goals and planned a future together. We supported each other.

Karl believed in me. He saw something in me I was never able to see in myself. He taught me to believe in myself. He told me I could do anything and I believed him. His positive energy rubbed off on me. I soaked in his adventurous spirit. Together we reached for the stars.

Then came the cancer and the fight for his life. I closed down our business to be by his side. I was so proud of him. He fought his disease with a courage and dignity I always believed was under all the cool bullshit. He beat a terminal diagnosis and, along with the hell of cancer came an unexpected gift. We were closer than ever before, committed to each other, in love, appreciating life and determined to live it to the fullest.

We restarted our business, bought property. Even in our early twenties, we were determined to make our mark in the world. We worked hard, long days. Things were good, or so I thought.

Then, a locked briefcase. Why? He said it was an accident.

Locked again. "Why, Babe?"

"Because there are syringes in there."

"Syringes, what do you mean?"

"I'm shooting dope."

It was beyond my comprehension. Anger, confusion, disbelief. Why, after all we'd been through? After all we'd accomplished? His partying had been down to a minimum, or so I thought. I knew he had been abusing his pain meds, but he'd been cut off from those. Like a true addict, he had found something else.

Karl went into rehab. After a short while, he left the program and asked, no, begged me to let him come home. I said, "No, go back to rehab." I was scared—scared that with his drug use the pain of our early years would come back, a lifestyle I was no longer willing to accept.

With us separated, everything spiraled out of control. Events happened that changed our lives forever, things that couldn't be taken back. And it was over.

Years later, I went through rehab myself. And it was only then that I understood the disease of addiction. Karl and I stayed in contact for some time. The last time I talked with him was years ago. I wanted him to know how much I missed him. I wanted to let him know he would always be the special one in my life. I told him that it was not him I rejected, but the lifestyle. He said he knew and he understood.

And now, when I'm faced with a trying situation or a difficult challenge, I hear Karl telling me that I can do anything. I feel his spirit of encouragement and his belief in me. I push forward. I just wish I would have had as much faith in him as he had in me. I wish I had given him a gift as precious as the one he gave me.

Who knew? Who knew that he was such an awesome person—brave strong, smart, and energetic? I knew. I knew and yet somehow I forgot.

I hope you can forgive me, Babe.

I Wish I Had....
by Fred M. Prince

*I*N MY SENIOR YEAR OF COLLEGE, I fell in love. I am eighty years old now, so you can imagine how long ago this happened. Carolyn was beautiful, a breath-taking blonde, and the joy of my life. We were known on campus as a couple, always together, always in the same activities. I wasn't a prize catch, so I still wonder what she saw in me, why she agreed to be my girl.

During my junior year, Carolyn dated a boy I didn't especially like. He was sort of free with his hands in public, and I didn't appreciate the way he put them all over her. She didn't seem to mind, but I did. Between summer and fall semester, something happened, and they quit dating.

I was a speech, drama and music major, and in that fall semester, I directed a girls' nine-voice ensemble. Carolyn was one of the altos, and she just sort of grew on me. Never having had a full-time girlfriend before, I wasn't up to date on courting techniques. But one thing I was sure of. I was not going to do what her previous boyfriend did: put my hands all over her in public.

Our college was a Southern Baptist college, and frowned on any display of public affection. Carolyn and I attended the same church and sponsored a youth group who met in member's homes on Sunday nights. After the fellowship period, Carolyn and I walked all the teenagers home before I returned her to her dormitory. They all knew we were sweethearts, and occasionally teased us. To set an example of virtuous conduct, we would get a stick about six inches long; she would hold one end and I would hold the other, barely touching each other's hands. Then we would walk the kids home, swinging our stick between us—all in great fun.

During that year, we were inseparable. You never saw one of us without the other. Carolyn and I never argued, never got angry at each other.

I lived at home, only two blocks from campus, and Carolyn lived in the girls' dorm. She was a close friend of both my sisters, who were also students at the same college, and she was at my home frequently. Sunday dinner was not complete without her. My whole family adored her; I was one lucky guy.

I just relished my good fortune, and took it for granted. I even sensed jealousy among some of the boys on campus. I overheard one football player say, "What does that pious S.O.B. have that I don't have?"

Then I graduated and flew the coop, leaving home and going to graduate school in Texas. But I wasn't accustomed to not having a sidekick. I missed Carlolyn, wanted her, and wished I had shown and demonstrated more affection. We wrote constantly, but it wasn't as good. Long-distance telephone calls were too expensive for a struggling graduate student, so in desperation, I wrote a letter and asked her to marry me. She turned me down.

That summer, she met an Air Force officer who, one of my sisters said, looked enough like me to be my twin brother. They married, and I never heard from her again.

Ten years later, when my wife and three children were visiting back in Louisiana, my sister told me Carolyn had divorced her husband and moved back with her parents in Shreveport. While visiting relatives there, I decided to go visit her.

My wife threw a fit, and refused to go in. She sat in the car. Carolyn's mother met me at the door and told me she was at work and wouldn't be home until later.

So I never saw her again. She was my first love, and I wonder where she is now.

I Finally Admit I Cared
by Aaron Mosley

*I*N FOURTH GRADE, I adored you; in my memories, I cherish you.
I hope you read this.

When I return to northeast Ohio, one of the places I often try
to pass is your house. Some of my life-long friends say that you
moved. The house, now gray, excites my heart, yet saddens me.
I remember your blue house from when we were children. Blue
awakens one; gray induces fatigue.

I never wafted your hair during a kiss, nor felt your fingers
graze my knuckles. I never listened to your troubles, and I never
discussed my emotional vulnerabilities.

Back then, you gave me a note; it said, "Do you like me?" And
I had to circle either "yes" or "no." I should not have backtracked
by commenting, "You are not my type."

I may or may not have a type, but I still secretly care for your
well-being. Perhaps I end relationships when they seem official
because of a pattern I started with you. I loathe that I hurt your
feelings. Please forgive me. I hope other relationships appeal to
you.

STEPS ALONG THE WAY

While every special love leaves a unique imprint, some change you dramatically. Later in your life, you can look back and see that you experienced a fundamental shift in how you view yourself, your life or just what a relationship can be. In these stories, we are privileged to witness some formative steps along the way.

Windows of the Heart
by Ellen Denton

I HAD MY INFATUATIONS like anyone else. But the one thing that set me aside from my friends, and sometimes made me the kindly butt of their jokes (if not the object of their perplexity), was that at the age of twenty-one, I was still a virgin. I was idealistic, and had never been in love. That was until I looked up one day into the stranger's eyes. I turned away, and then did a double take. I felt as if my heart went BOOM-KA-THUNK. I don't know what it was about David that drew me to him like thirst in a desert draws you toward an oasis, but, in short order, I fell head over heals in love—no, never mind head over heels: I sky-dived with the glad heart of a soaring hawk.

David was a young doctor at a hospital where I worked. We would occasionally meet on the hospital grounds and walk, or sit on the grass together, talking about nothing much. But on those occasions, although nothing overtly romantic was ever said, the attraction was undeniable. It was part physical. It was part spiritual. It was part some "X" factor that I could never really put into words. I knew he was feeling at least some of the same for me, too, because even though he was older than me, and certainly more worldly, his hands would sometimes tremble like a schoolboy's when he was near me. Sometimes it's the song that travels in silence from heart to heart when two people look into each others eyes that speaks louder than any words could.

One day, David caught up with me on the grounds after I got off work. He told me that something had come up. Within a few days, he was going to have to transfer to another hospital in San Francisco—clear across the country! I knew then this wild and utterly exhilarating feeling of love I had would never blossom into the relationship it might have if he stayed. He asked me then if he could kiss me, and he did. We looked at each other for a few moments, with perfect understanding. I then told him I didn't have very much experience with some things. He understood and looked away for a moment, then turned to me and said "That's OK. I do."

That was a night I will always remember and cherish, because it's the one that ended my childhood. We said our final goodbyes early the next morning.

That was a long time ago. David was my first love and I guess you could say that, like some fragile, ephemeral thing, it lasted a day. Bill, my husband, was my second love, and that has lasted a lifetime. David opened a door in my life, and my beloved husband Bill will be the one to eventually close it with me, as age bears us away through time.

I did love David. What I so thrillingly shared with him in that brief time is nowhere near the magnitude of the almost boundless love I have for my husband. But, even to this day, sometimes, and at the oddest times, Dave's image will suddenly appear, in a window of memory, like a midnight rain—hauntingly, and beautifully, between me and the world.

Daybreak
by James Penha

*T*HIS TALE OF PAST LOVE is not an easy story for me to tell. Not because it is a heartbreaking tale of lost love. Death does not intrude, thank God. And although our affair ended when the object of my desire found another to love, there was no bitter break-up. We remained friends; indeed, we remain friends.

The difficulty in relating the tale is my anticipating readers' raised eyebrows or worse, sneers, for my past love story is about the first gay lover in my life. That love, that lover, changed everything in my life as I came bumbling and tumbling out of the closet. What I knew and felt, but had repressed about my sexual orientation, could no longer be denied.

My thirteen-year marriage to a loving woman to whom I had confided, prior to our engagement, my attraction to men and the hurdles that might raise for us, ended, as I think we always knew it would. We had been happy as long as my homosexuality had been fantastic. But the reality of a flesh-and-blood relationship with another man, underscored by the uncontrollable emotion of love, could not be ignored by any of us.

Like all gay men, I had had a series of crushes on friends from elementary through high school. In my university years there were fraternity brothers and fellow theatre arts majors to moon over. But in those days—the pre-Stonewall nineteen sixties—there were few advantages in being publicly gay and many, many reasons to hide. In a syndrome typical for gays growing up at the time, I never dared tell any guy I cared for that I was attracted to him because, odds were, I would lose him even as a platonic friend. (Did some gay friends and I pass like ships in a dark night of terror? Oh yes, no doubt.)

But in the early eighties, times were changing—although not for me, I had assumed, since I was by then a thirty-year-old married man, straight for all the world to see.

I was teaching at a large metropolitan university, not only at its campus, but in its prison outreach program. The administrator of the program was ten years my junior, and I found him beautiful—in face, stature and personality. Never before had anyone literally given me palpitations of the heart. When he would pass—and oh! did I keep hoping he would pass close by or, even better, have something important to discuss face-to-face —I reddened and sweated.

I don't know who else might have noticed my adolescent affect, but Tom did. And so one night, after classes, he invited me to go out for a drink. He drove us to his favorite gay bar without ever mentioning its notoriety or our sexual inclinations, and we spent hours chatting with each other and with dozens of his friends, from the queenliest to the most leather-bound.

There was little to say when we drove to his apartment, and there is little of the rest of that evening I will say here—except that what stays with me, even now, after three decades, was our kiss. It was the first time I had ever kissed a man deeply...romantically. But it wasn't lips or tongue that moved me, like an earthquake, then and forever. It was the brushing and scraping of our five o'clock (in the morning) shadows. I was reminded that we were men. I realized that we were men in love.

Yes
by Sylvia Outley

WHEN YOU ASKED ME if I had ever loved anyone before, I felt the skip in my heartbeat. Our relationship was so young, the ocean of possibilities stretching out way beyond my world and coming back to lap at my feet. I stared at your fingers waiting just next to mine on my knee.

Samuel Fisher was Amish and too old to notice me. When I was seven and he was eleven, I scraped my leg, and he carried me home from the pond on his back with the stride of a hero, laden with my brown, awkward limbs. When I was nine and he was thirteen, his sister Sadie told him about the teenagers that had driven by, yelling things about me that neither of us quite understood. I felt my stomach dance for just a moment when he surprised me with such poorly hidden anger; I felt protected by his disgust. When I was eleven and he was fifteen, I watched him throwing hay bales down to his father and brother from the flatbed cart while the team of sweaty mules waited sleepily. And I loved him.

When I was fourteen, it was the summer of the sheep. Three lambs died of lockjaw and the big ram broke his leg in the fence. Samuel was eighteen.

It was almost two weeks into the summer visit with my grandparents when I finally saw him. He appeared in the milking barn while I talked to Sadie over the rhythmic hissing and clicking of the milking machines. His mother, Annie, never raised her head, moving from one cow to the next. He was wearing a t-shirt and dirty sneakers and no suspenders. He followed her from cow to cow and told her he had made up his mind. They switched between Pennsylvania Dutch and English, low stubborn tones and aggravated shouts. I stared.

He didn't even notice me, the half black girl with Amish grandparents who came from the city and tried to make herself at home in his sister's hand-me-down dresses. He didn't even notice that I was there to adore him for yet another summer, this year with my wild hair tamed and a bra. His mother finally reduced her end of the argument to one simple statement, "You're not going to Florida," and Samuel got frustrated and left.

I came across him as I walked to my grandparent's farm. He was coming through his front yard and he jogged to catch up with me. We walked in silence for a minute before he began asking me questions. He asked about Philadelphia, school, my father, my friends, my church. We went to the pond and stayed for the rest of the afternoon. And I knew that Annie Fisher was wrong; her son was leaving. Before we went our separate ways, I kissed him on the cheek and he didn't look surprised.

When I was eighteen and Samuel was twenty-two, Aaron Blank's buggy was hit by a car. Two days after my stay with my grandparents had ended, Aaron Blank was dead. Two days after that, Samuel was home, back in suspenders and an Amish shirt. When I was twenty, Samuel was married and starting a farm of his own. And I, away at college and not having seen him since the time he wasn't surprised by my kiss, was heart-broken.

Now I wait for you to come home from a war that I can't even imagine beyond my cliché vision of desert and my vision of you, the way you looked when you tried on your body armor while I watched. I remember the time I told you, yes, I had loved someone before. I grew into a woman still clinging to a child's love, and I came away with a dreamer's heart. I remember how I felt with you waiting for the answer and the ocean lapping at my feet.

His Invisible Touch
by Indrani Bhattacharyya

ALMOST A DECADE AGO, I was a student in Calcutta, one of the cosmopolitan cities in India. During that adolescence period, with all its secrets, those stolen moments filled with attentions from the opposite sex and, above all, with an excellent friend circle around, I was high on life. Having been brought up in the hard-core Indian society—which was not so permissive at that time—it used to be an adventurous hide and seek game between teen lovers. Maybe that was why it was more fun.

I was pretty used to this intrigue, but never felt anything serious about anyone before I met him. I was on my way towards home with my friends, and it was just like any other monsoon day. There was no indication anywhere that Cupid would soon start playing his "lovely game" with me. Upon entering the metro station, one of my friends remarked "Wow! Look at him! Handsome!" But we ran to catch the metro, and I didn't pay much heed to her comment until I noticed him when we caught the same bus after the metro. A continuous drizzle seemed like a blessing coming from the gods.

I was pretty shy, so mostly he did the talking. But there was such an intense attraction between us that it didn't take long for him to break my outer shell.

After that, Rahul Kapoor and I used to meet every day after school. We kept talking, sharing ourselves, and became best friends. He exactly knew what I was thinking by just looking at my gestures. I discovered myself as an entirely different identity in his eyes. I was so happy from within as I never was before. I was extremely satisfied with this newly blooming friendship which gave a fresh flavor to my then life.

The day my final exam got over, we met in a park. As he was my only stress reliever, I started giving him all the details of what happened in those exam days. Surprisingly, I noticed after some time that he was totally silent, fully against his nature. I raised my eyebrow in question and he just looked at me. I don't know what was there in his look. All I can say is that it was different—very different. I could feel the adrenaline rush; it felt like everything had come to a standstill, as if a magician had waved his magic wand around us. At this intoxicating moment, he just held me closer and whispered in my ears, "Stupid, can't you see *love is in the air?*"

Neither was I prepared for it, nor had I heard before, that someone calls you stupid while proposing. Well it was his choice to love a "stupid," and we were together.

Time flew by. I left my city for higher studies and eventually went far away from India. He completed engineering from abroad and we really couldn't continue this long-distance relationship. But he taught me the meaning of love. I learned to value my feelings, emotions, as well as those of others, from him. I realized that mutual trust and respect form the foundation of every relationship. Today I am quite settled, and the bond I share with my family has his invisible touch.

Last year, I was in India to attend a wedding, only to find that the bride was Rahul's cousin. Rahul, of course, was there. We looked at each other after ten years; my heart skipped a beat, followed by the very normal and formal conversation you get to hear in a crowd. Inside, the bitter thought killing me was, *It's all dead—past can't be revived and shouldn't be.* I wanted to leave. While I was getting into my car, a kid ran towards me to hand over a paper towel written, "It remains forever—stupid"!

While tears were rolling down my cheeks, and with a smile on my lips, I could smell the fragrance of love in the air.

The Players
by Kaylie Newell

*B*ASEBALL. As a girl of seventeen, I had never played, except for those unfortunate P.E. classes where I would wait, wide-eyed, for the ball to rocket in my direction all the way out in the back forty.

Even though I had never played, and had seldom even watched it on TV, it's safe to say that I became head over heels, hopelessly in love with baseball. Even now, when I think about it, my stomach does that curious little drop as if I were riding a roller coaster at the fair.

The valley where I grew up in Southern Oregon had a farm team for the Oakland A's. It wasn't much, a rundown field and bleachers with crispy, peeling paint, but no one seemed to care. Especially me.

I remember my parents taking me to my first game. I'm sure I did all of the things teenage girls do best, like groaning and enough eye-rolling to last until well past college. But I dutifully got dressed that day (a navy blue polka dot sundress) and put my long hair into a ponytail. I looked all right. I remember thinking that. *You look all right, Kaylie.*

I'd always been skinny, so much so that my poor mother had resorted to giving me chocolate milkshakes in hopes that I'd finally fill out. I did fill out, not a lot, but a little. The day I went to my first baseball game, I wasn't as gangly as I had been, and that was a good thing.

We pulled up to the stadium, our hatchback kicking up dust that settled into a brown film over the windows. It was hot, and my hair stuck to the back of my neck in damp tendrils. A nice old lady in a gigantic green A's cap handed us programs as we walked in. I gave her a wilted smile and immediately began using mine as a fan.

My dad wanted to be as close to the action as possible, so we walked all the way around the back of the bleachers, my sandals making suctioning sounds against the sticky blacktop. Katrina and the Waves blasted from the loud speakers. "Walkin' On Sunshine!" The music thumped in my chest and I felt the excitement of the small crowd around us begin to grow. People clapped and cheered, and as we rounded the corner next to the dugout, the announcer's voice came over the crackly speaker.

"Heeeeere's YOUR Medford A's!"

I turned around just in time to see the team jog leisurely onto the field. My heart fluttered and I felt faint. If I'd been living in the Victorian days, they would have called it a swoon and laid me down on a red velvet couch to recover for the rest of the day.

But there was no recovering. I had just gotten my first glimpse of a team of young men in their stark white home uniforms. Their hats sat low over their eyes, and their skin was brown as copper pennies in the late afternoon sun.

I had just found my heaven.

I settled in between my oblivious parents and gaped at the field. Every hormone in my young body was wired with electricity. *So this is what it's all about*, I remember thinking.

Slowly, and against every rule in the awkward teenage girl handbook, I let my head swivel towards the dugout. I saw, with complete fascination, that a few of the boys were actually looking back. They were looking at me. They didn't care that I'd been skinny and uncoordinated. They didn't care that I'd been picked on in junior high and never felt like I belonged.

At that moment, I realized that all they saw was a girl in a polka dot dress who had her whole life ahead of her.

And so did they.

I've loved baseball ever since.

Every now and then, I'll hear Katrina and the Waves on the radio, and I'll smile. If it's a warm day, I'll roll down the windows, turn up the volume and let it take me back to when I was just a girl, discovering how simple love can be.

Poison and Paper
by Susan White

WES BLAMES OUR DIVORCE on the poison oak. Sure, let the plant take the fall. A natural disaster.

He warned me not to climb the rocky embankment, afraid I'd fall. But I grabbed onto plants that grew between the rocks, while the terrain crumbled and tumbled and lost toeholds. Finally I stood on the ledge, triumphant. He looked up, sunlight bouncing off his glasses. He didn't wave back.

The day before I flew to New Mexico for a six-week session of graduate school, Wes had refused to touch my raised, red skin. Intimacy was not worth risking his future discomfort. He would not believe what I said, that poison oak is spread by leaf, not skin.

Technically, his rejection was the poison. But, to be honest, we both had contaminated our relationship before the rash. I do find it amusing, though, that in the plot line of our tragedy, the poison oak is the peripeteia.

In New Mexico, I studied words, while Wes and I withheld ours from each other. Our phone calls and emails were sparser than the grass on the mesa where I ran each morning, pretending to be free. My skin cleared, and I rubbed it against another's. New Mexico, new me: revitalized, but burdened with a broken seven-year commitment. In our case, the seven-year itch was literal and figurative.

Wes picked me up from the airport. Though we could see each other's faces, the distance remained. The internet brought me closer to my affair, until Wes discovered my notebook of printed infidelity. I tossed the notebook into the rusted dumpster and pronounced all contact with The Other over. I thought a new leaf—so to speak—was that simple to turn.

He did not cry in front of me. Instead, he sat at a desk in our cramped, cinder block apartment and made a giant eye out of construction paper. (The only other art project I had seen him undertake was when we painted bright, intricate designs on our plastic, thrift store headboard. We ditched that headboard when we moved to Georgia and bought a grownup bed.)

The eye, he told me, was there to watch over me. The iris was green, and the lashes were thick, black, and rectangular. The pupil, dilated. He used double-sided tape to stick the eye to the wall above our cherry headboard. It wasn't long before the tape dried out and the eye fell behind our bed. Within three months, our marriage, too, dried out.

Yet, eight years later, he brushes against me like paper eyelashes. The weight of his leg across my lower back. The absurdity of storing a box of sweaters in our oven—that's how much we cooked. Our ATM code that I never changed. I still play the guitar he gave me for my twenty-fifth birthday, despite the high action that hurts my fingers. But he is most alive in my stories. Here's one I like to tell:

We left the beach—were walking toward the road—when an elderly couple stopped us. The woman said, "We so much enjoyed watching you dance."

Wes and I laughed at her error. We had barely danced at our wedding. "You must have watched another couple," I said.

The man said, "No, we watched you dance by the ocean, pick up your backpacks and walk this way." Wes looked around as if we were being filmed. I was delightfully confused.

The woman said, "You were doing some sort of tribal dance." She pointed a shaky finger at me. "You'd hold your arms in the air and bring your knees up high one at a time." She made the motion herself. "And he'd," she nodded toward Wes, "do the same moves back."

The man added, "Looked like a bird mating ritual."

Wes and I figured out the confusion simultaneously. The hacky sack. The couple had not seen the small beanie ball we kicked back and forth, as we held our arms up for balance. While we killed time, keeping count, this elderly couple saw a primitive profession of love.

And from this distance, I can see our evocative dance—but if I'm honest, I recall we were two kids playing a game.

Once Upon a Time
by Jeanne Waite-Follett

As I withdraw the slender book from the box where it has lain for more than four decades, memories arise. I hold quite still as they enfold me in their embrace. In my hands, I hold a cherished part of my life, and I see the two of us in another time, another place. We sit, he and I, side by side on the sofa as he reads from this book.

The volume is less than a hundred pages, its dimensions approximately those of a paperback book. The front cover is gray with white filigree, the title printed in pink inside a design meant to recall the Persian wellspring of its contents. *The Rubaiyat of Omar Khayyam,* rendered into English verse by Edward Fitz-Gerald. I believe this to be FitzGerald's fourth translation of the Persian poet's quatrains, though nothing on the frontispiece verifies that.

He was my love, once upon a time, and was a poet, though I didn't realize it at the time. I didn't know until after many years, when I opened a newspaper and saw his picture and the award-winning ballad he had written.

I should have guessed. All the clues were there: his intelligence, his erudition, his mastery of the language. He recited vast quantities of poetry from memory, and frequently interspersed conversation with poetic allusions. Occasionally, he selected this little volume from the many on my shelves, and I sat beside him in silence as his mellow voice and the enigmatic words of the *Rubaiyat* transported me to the ancient Persian realm of Jamshyd and Kaikobad.

I was quite young then, only twenty-one, and much of the meaning of the verses escaped me. I wanted to ask him to explain them to me, to ask if his beliefs were akin to the passages I did understand, and more. Instead I kept silent, not wanting to break the spell. Then the years passed, as did he, and I no longer had the opportunity to ask.

I hope those weren't his beliefs. Are there words more final than these?

> *Oh threats of Hell and Hopes of Paradise!*
> *One thing at least is certain—This Life flies;*
> *One thing is certain and the rest is Lies;*
> *The Flower that once has blown forever dies.*
> *Strange, is it not? That of the myriads who*
> *Before us pass'd the door of Darkness through,*
> *Not one returns to tell us of the Road,*
> *Which to discover we must travel too?*

I have always hoped that someday we will meet again in a place where age and station and public image are of no matter. Then I will ask the questions I've held to myself all these years.

Then again, with all eternity before us, perhaps I'll just sit beside him and let his voice transport me once again to an ancient Persian realm.

His Only Vice
by Leslie Creek

*H*ESITANT KISSES, modified greeting cards, the odor of onions and cigars—memories of a first love so pure, so spiritual and intense, they might live in me forever.

When Scot joined our church, his family had just moved to the area. When finding a place and a comrade in the youth group proved difficult for him, my best friend and I, out of sympathy, invited him to social events and choir practice. We brought him into the fold and, eventually, fought over him. That friendship suffered as Scot and I grew closer, but we couldn't resist the attraction. In the months we dated, he taught me about sacrificing for love, nurturing a relationship with honesty and humor, and letting go.

All my memories of Scot lead to laughter. His humor went beyond the typical teenaged flavor—he'd already graduated to the old-man-dry-wit category. For Valentine's Day, he bought a card proclaiming "Happy Valentine's Day, Grandson," and modified the message to fit his needs. My artless brain took a few minutes to wrap itself around his cleverness, but in that moment, I understood better what lay inside the skinny, shy boy from church.

He had opened a part of himself that he shared only with people who he trusted. His artistic talents and wicked humor materialized into spontaneous cartoons portraying my Doberman as a man-eating monster guarding me as I wept over having short, chubby legs and a copy of Macbeth. That talent was just a medium to relay the fact that he was paying attention and was concerned about my senior year struggles.

Sometimes, however, his humor landed him in trouble. One night, while I was celebrating with friends at a slumber party, Scot executed a prank, hoping to surprise me. Unfortunately, he locked himself out of his car and interrupted our party to use the phone. The boy no one knew was suddenly a romantic hero to my friends. No other boyfriend dared match his practical joking at the risk of looking uncool. Fortunately, Scot had no cares about being cool.

Scot's values contributed to my affection for him long before I understood the importance of values in a relationship. Honesty, purity, and selflessness all defined his character. He was first to profess love and to share his feelings and shortcomings. No one, including my best girlfriends, were as open with me. He worked endless hours making pizzas at a local restaurant to help with the family finances, while maintaining excellent grades.

Though Scot dedicated himself to schoolwork, job, and his family, his faith preceded all things. His heart belonged to God in a way I'd never seen before, and rarely since. As a result, he kept himself pure, including in his actions with me. What I wanted to do with him he refused. In fact, when he leaned in to kiss me for the first time, he whispered, "Bear with me," as if he might violate something sacred. He did not drink alcohol, take drugs, swear, or lie. His only vice? Smoking cigars, something his mother knew and did not criticize. "He's such a good son in every way," she told me. "What's a couple of cigars?"

Scot and I enjoyed a wonderful relationship right up to the moment he let me go. The end of summer loomed. My plans for the fall included college, while he had to finish high school. At the time, he said breaking up allowed me the freedom to experience this new part of life instead of concerning myself with him. In the end, he might have dumped me for his own benefit...so he didn't have to worry about what I was doing and when I might end the relationship.

Either way, it was the right decision. Our lives took very different paths. I haven't seen him in twenty-five years, and I daresay the only thing we'd have in common now are the memories.

San Timoteo Canyon
by Lanita Andrews

*T*HE NIGHT SKY WAS AN OIL SLICK, no sign yet of the coming dawn. He drove us fast up San Timoteo Canyon, a desolate expanse of road coveted for the seclusion it offered underage drinkers and late-night lovers. We were neither—yet. I wondered why he'd chosen to take the long way home. If he were trying to forestall our parting, we'd still be parked at the abandoned stretch of railroad tracks, continuing a passionate discussion on how we defined ourselves. I could have asked, but I didn't—until he came to a stop.

When he parked to the right of the pavement, a fine dust flittered up from beneath the tires. He opened the door and got out. Seconds later, he was opening my door and reaching for my hand. I couldn't imagine what we were doing, parked in a barren field, in the middle of the night, next to the only street lamp in sight. Nonetheless, I accepted his hand, and followed him to the center of the asphalt.

I was still wearing the beanie he'd insisted on earlier—a semi-successful attempt to stifle the chattering of my teeth. In the fierce Santa Ana winds that were a tell-tale sign of autumn, stray hairs whipped against my face, stinging delicate skin. He pulled me into him so that we touched, the warmth of his body stealing the chill from mine. Everything else remained in the dark, and it was only he and I, alone in the spotlight. I had asked why we were here, and now he answered. "So you never forget the first time I kiss you."

Then his lips were on mine, his tongue tasting me, both a gentle giving and a savage taking that left me fevered with the burn of a memory being seared into my mind forever.

I'd been at the receiving end of first kisses more grandly planned than this one, but they'd been with boys who'd thought too much, who'd feigned their confidence and fumbled their way through wooing me. He was a man. He wore his confidence comfortably, and left no room for thought when kissing me. His easy assuredness encouraged me to reveal myself to him, and in the weeks that followed, I bared my soul in ways I'd done only with God. He became my new religion, and my first faith fell beneath his shadow.

My conviction to restrain my lust, to keep it sacred for the man I would marry, weakened with every breath and word, every touch between us. As my body slowly failed to refuse the beckoning of his, my mind began to accept what my heart had demanded from our first meeting. I was in love—consumed with it, in fact. The child in me was withering, while the woman in me bloomed with my love for him.

The night came when I no longer denied my yearning. We made love—my first time—and that gift could no longer be given to another. It was his, and he accepted, staking his claim, and taking my wanting. Again, in that moment, in every moment with him, everything and everyone else remained in the dark, and it was only he and I, alone in the spotlight.

In the days following, while I reveled in the making and giving of love, I also mourned my loss; I missed God's presence, my spirit remaining hungry in His absence. It would take years to find my way back to the path I'd abandoned that night. My Savior and I would have to reacquaint ourselves with one another, as I would be a different person then—a fully blossomed woman, carrying the weight of a history all my own, having found my way with the courage and humility I'd learned in loving another with complete abandon.

A piece of myself is lost to me, forever sealed to a lover past. But a part of him fills in that empty place, along with the memory of a single streetlamp on San Timoteo Canyon Road.

The Summer I Knew
by Juliana Hill Howard

*A*UGUST OF 1953 changed my life forever. It was my first experience at a canoe-tripping camp for girls. Located in the far North, just below Lake Superior, Camp Widjiwagon prepared women from thirteen to eighteen with all the necessary skills to take extended canoe trips into the Quetico Provincial Park in Canada. This area is forever set aside as wilderness—no motors, roads or buildings will ever be allowed.

It was the summer of my thirteenth birthday, and I was beginning to feel many stirrings in my body and soul. Sexual feelings that I could not express or completely understand began to make themselves known. All my friends were beginning to laugh, giggle and talk incessantly about boys. Everyone had a crush on a boy from school, someone's older brother or the bagger in the local grocery. Why were my feelings so different?

During the first six weeks, while I perfected my "J" stroke, learned to flip a canoe and carry it on my back down portages of a mile or more, and pack a "Duluth Pack" so that it was balanced, the constant conversation among the girls was about Marge, the camp director's daughter. She would be returning shortly from an extended trip into Canada. All the old campers and staff had stories to tell of this extraordinary woman who could paddle all day, carry a canoe for hours and hold a steady course across a lake, no matter how big it was or how hard the wind was blowing.

Finally, the anticipated day arrived. We all stood on the bluff overlooking Basswood Lake and watched her canoe trip arrive. You could hear the voices of the trippers singing all the way across the lake, "Break out the oars, course set for...Widjiwagon." My eyes scanned the horizon. Which one was she? Suddenly, there could be no doubt. She was in the stern of the second canoe, red felt hat set at a rakish angle, blue work shirt tied at the waist and long tanned legs showing at the end of cutoff blue jeans.

My stomach jumped, my heart seemed to flip and time stood still. My legs felt weak. And then I began to realize what was different about my feelings, compared to those of my friends. This woman made me know what all my longings and aching were about—and why I did not know how to express them. It was a woman I was attracted to, and this day charted the course of the rest of my life.

We fell head over heels in love, and it lasted for the next ten years. She lived in Milwaukee and I lived in River City, Iowa. We wrote letters every day for more than six of those years, lived together part of our college years. And then, one day, we let each other go. There were too many other women in her life, and I could not go on in that manner. I knew she loved me, but I needed to be her only love.

Twenty-seven years went by without any contact between us. We finally were reunited in 1990, and she still took by breath away. Although we both have other partners, I cannot help but hold her close in my heart. She was my first love. It was a passion perhaps unlike any I have known since. She helped me understand who I was, and nothing was ever the same again.

Coming to terms with being a lesbian in the late 50's and 60's was a difficult path to tread. Marge showed me the way and helped me know that it would be okay. Those were scary days to be gay, and she gave me the confidence and assurance I needed to go forward with my life.

First Star
by Katherine Johnson

*T*HE FIRST NIGHT we slept side by side, he hooked our sleeping bags together and we held each other near. There was no sex, only the feeling of closeness and comfort—friendship that connected at the soul level. I felt as if we had known each other forever, that we had been friends from childhood, boyfriend and girlfriend in our teens, and lovers in our twenties.

Yet we had known each other only a few weeks. He taught me things that night I'd never dreamt. As we lay down on our backs, cocooned in sleeping bags on the cool earth, he pointed to the open, clear black sky. "There it is—the first star in the night sky!" He kept me up far into the night, talking of so many things, pointing out constellations, and the miraculous shooting stars. Early the next morning, he woke me from a groggy sleep state, "Wake up—there's the first bird flying!" This was a new pre-dawn wonder that embodied the sense of awe he brought to me. I began to see and feel this sense of awe for myself.

After an early morning camp breakfast, he told me, "I have a surprise for you. Meet me down by the river behind the old lodge in fifteen minutes."

I, being a woman who loves surprises, couldn't wait. And as the appointed time approached, I circled around the old chinked log structure and found him waiting for me on the rough-hewn, weathered porch that hung out over the river. There was a dark brown, almost ebony wooden chair with a cracked leather seat that he patted, an indication for me to sit. His blue eyes twinkled in merriment. I noticed several pitchers and bowls on the brown planked floor.

As he poured water from a celadon ceramic pitcher over my hair, I could feel the warmth, and then his hands caressing my scalp. The shampoo must have been an aphrodisiac. Later, when he poured clear water from an old stoneware jug and rinsed the shampoo from my head, I knew that this was the stuff of movies. Something had shifted. It was one of life's magic moments, when friendship turned into love, and playfulness transformed into sensuality. My hair sparkled in the morning sun.

A new awareness filled me, the awareness of beauty all around me. From now on, I would notice the first star of evening, the first bird of morning, and the miracle of life lived fully in each moment.

The Hometown Guy
by Conda V. Douglas

I NEEDED A HERO, someone who would hold me, help me and support my heart and my dreams. And that hero appeared. When he came into my life, magic happened.

For me, it was a time of firsts, glorious and wonderful—and so scary. I was attending my first semester at college. It was my first time in a big city, Seattle. I'd grown up in the big town of Boise, Idaho. All the new experiences made my head spin. And my head spun most with the best of all of my new experiences: my first "real" boyfriend, A.J.

A.J. stood behind me in the cafeteria lunch line day after day. He confessed later that he'd figured out when I'd be in line, and made sure he stood a few people behind. He explained that he didn't want to scare me off. Every time I turned around, he smiled and waved. I always saw him, for at six feet, four inches, he stood above any crowd. I always smiled back, couldn't resist smiling at his handsome, friendly, kind face.

After a week of this, A.J. ended up standing right behind me. By the time I picked up my tray, I had a date.

For our first date, he took me to dinner and a movie, and then for a walk down First Avenue. Back then, First Avenue still was the "rough" area of downtown—and we were walking at mid-night! But as we walked, his arm draped over my shoulder, I realized I wasn't frightened, not a bit. He made sure I was on the inside of the sidewalk, protected. A.J. made me feel safe.

His knowledge of "big city life" impressed me. I knew I was an Idaho hick and asked if he'd been born and raised in Seattle.

"Oh, no," A.J. said, "I was born and raised in Boise, Idaho."

Turned out he knew my brother's best friend quite well, as they had gone to school together.

That was only the beginning. Over the semester, I grew to adore my new love. Though it was rainy Seattle, it seemed to me that the sun shone every day. I sat in my classes, amazed at the bright light that suffused every corner of my being. I wondered that my classmates never remarked on how I carried my own sunshine around with me.

Together, we explored Seattle. A.J. possessed boundless curiosity and enthusiasm for everything in life. He took me beyond the dry, dull content of my classes. He wanted to live in the Sahara desert and then move to Antarctica, to experience the extremes. A.J. wanted to travel other places as well, to experience different cultures, different lives. His rampant enthusiasm was catching, and my grades skyrocketed to A's as he taught me to go beyond what I learned in class, to always ask questions, even those without an answer.

He taught me so much, so fast. He taught me that firsts never truly end. From him I learned that as long as my mind, heart and spirit remained open, I could experience all the juicy, delightful joys of life.

He brought a safe zone for me to retreat to, before I ventured forth again to explore. He brought the forever wonder of endless curiosity and discovery into my life.

And when we parted after that first semester, when he moved from Seattle to another university, he left behind my sad but full heart, a heart I'd learned to keep open and free.

All this, and more, I received as gifts from my hometown guy.

Across the Pond
by Madeleine Beckman

W<small>E</small> <small>STOOD IN THE KITCHEN</small> of the youth hostel in Florence, waiting for water to boil. I was twenty, he was eighteen. He was tan, thin, and his jeans were worn to splitting. His backpack sat on the kitchen chair with a beat-up copy of *Europe on $5 A Day*.

"May I look at your book?" I asked.

"Sure, it's pretty good. I've used it a lot."

I wanted him to continue speaking—about anything—in his chiseled English accent.

The next morning, Ian and I hiked up to Forte di Belvedere where the Henry Moore exhibit surrounded us. There, we shared *sfoglliatelle* and a container of milk for breakfast, and kissed—a lot.

That night, over pasta *putenesca* and Chianti, we decided to go to Venice. Ian had been living on Corfu for two months, and was down to a few British pounds; I was daily counting my lire—so we decided to hitchhike. I'd never hitchhiked before, but fear was the furthest thing from my mind.

In Venice we visited the Peggy Guggenheim Museum and shopped for tomatoes, cheese, bread and red wine for dinner. We hiked to the beach where Ian and I eventually slept—on our clothes and towels.

We couldn't see enough art, talk enough about poets and books, or kiss enough.

The next evening, we were on the road to Germany, where a driver, Rolf, took us to his mother's house in the Black forest. At three a.m. she prepared a table of meats, cheese, breads, and cakes. In the morning, Rolf drove Ian and me to the border, and we headed for England.

I returned to the United States and back into my boyfriend's arms. He was waiting with a dozen red roses for my twenty-first birthday. But I only wanted to be with Ian. He had given me something that felt simultaneously foreign, yet just like home. *Simpatico.*

When Ian wrote that he'd like to visit me in New York, I told my boyfriend. I didn't tell Brian *exactly* who Ian was. But once Ian arrived, Brian knew that he was more than *some guy* I had met in Italy; it didn't go well. Ian left for California. I eventually left Brian.

Over the years, Ian and I wrote to one another about our lives—Ian about his wife Laura and school, me about New York and school. And then the letters stopped.

Years later, after my divorce, I was going through closets to make space for my new life and found Ian's pale blue *par avion* letters—from thirty-seven years ago. Everyone was Googling everyone. What was the worst that could happen?

I wrote an email: *Could you possibly be the Ian I hitchhiked with in Europe in the 70's?*

And I hit "send."

The next morning I received an email: *Good Grief! (as we say in Old Blighty) what an extraordinary thing is the Internet. Indeed I cannot deny that I was that callow youth—thirty-seven years ago. Can you believe it?*

The emails had the same tone and wit as his letters from when we were first starting our lives.

I sent another: *I was going through old papers and what do you know—letters from Ian! Those telltale pale blue parchment pages…* This time, I also sent a photo.

He responded: *Good God woman, what have you been doing all these years? Languishing in a vat of goat's milk while Nubian slaves feed you monkey glands? You don't look a day older than you did when we last met…*

We exchanged photos of islands we'd visited, of our cats and dogs and of artwork (Ian's been collecting). One photo of him, wearing an Indiana Jones hat and standing by a stone wall in the English countryside, stirred me as when we were in the youth hostel in Florence. His beltless khaki trousers hung on his still-thin frame, as his threadbare jeans had, years ago.

Ian asked: *So, what are you reading?*

I told him: *I still have "Cloud of the Unknowing," that you insisted I buy, on my bookshelves. It remains one of my favorite books.*

Our conversations have grown beyond the past into the present—children, houses, work, the economy. We both still love Dylan; his fascination for art has bloomed into an all-out collector's obsession, while I continue to dance, despite my knees.

And our excitement, first felt in Florence, thirty-seven years ago, continues.

MASQUERADE

When you pretend to be someone you are not—or allow yourself to be routinely discounted or diminished, a relationship is on a shaky foundation. Sooner or later it becomes too difficult—and damaging—to maintain the masquerade.

These few cautionary tales illustrate consequences of assuming a persona that is contrary to your true nature. Fortunately, when such pretenses are finally acknowledged and left behind, it is possible to find, with someone else, the joy of loving and being loved as who you truly are.

Life After Lobster
by Anna Seip

ONE LOBSTER OMELET can turn a girl's head.

The breakfast tasted like heaven: fluffy egg, melted cream cheese flecked with scallions, buttery chunks of lobster and tiny rocks of kosher salt. As I heaped praises upon my new boyfriend, he took it in stride. I'd never known a man who knew how to cook, and this guy not only cooked, he was a pastry chef at a French bakery.

I was young, just out of college, and my idea of dinner was a drive-thru and a value menu. He was fifteen years older and subscribed to "Gourmet." I pored through the issues as they arrived at his house, as if those magazines would give me some insight to his soul. My vocabulary grew as I looked up words like coulis, palmier and tapenade.

He took me to restaurants and made me try softshell crabs. And escargot. I cracked the sugar crust of a crème brulee and sighed with joy when he pointed out the black flecks of vanilla. He was the first person I'd met who would order things that weren't even on the menu. "Give me some angel hair, not too much sauce and some mussels mixed in," he'd say to the server.

After a few months, I moved into his place

One night, we went to an Italian restaurant where the lighting was soft and candles flickered on the table. I wore a slinky black dress and ordered chicken Alfredo. He shook his head and ordered something else for me. After the waitress walked away, he said, "My Alfredo sauce is so much better than anything they make here."

So I ate what he thought I should, and it was excellent. Who cared about eating, anyway, when the setting was this romantic?

Another time, we went for lunch at a ski lodge with a small menu. I wanted a BLT. "If you get that," he said, "all the cooks in the back will be laughing at you. A BLT is the simplest thing in the world to make. Nobody orders that in a restaurant."

So, I got a turkey sandwich, but what I wanted was bacon.

Watching him send food back to the kitchen became embarrassing. Or he'd demand a better table—or turn his nose up at a bottle of champagne. Cracks formed in the crust of our relationship. And, he still hadn't made me that Alfredo sauce he'd promised.

I wanted to break up, but my birthday was days away. What girl in her right mind would leave a pastry chef then? I wasn't going to miss out on what could very well be the best cake of my life. So, I told him exactly what I liked: yellow cake from scratch, with homemade chocolate frosting. Maybe it was unsophisticated, but it was my favorite.

On the big day, he sang "Happy Birthday" to me and ceremoniously presented a bowl of strawberries soaked in a creamy liqueur. He was the one who liked fruit and alcohol, not me—which he made abundantly clear by scarfing down the whole bowl. Where the heck was my cake?

As our relationship soured, so did our meals. We spent evenings eating in silence—or apart. Sometimes, like an adulterer, I'd stop at a drive-thru for french fries and not tell him. While he grilled shrimp and splashed it with grape oil, I hid Reese's Pieces in my dresser drawers.

We broke up. I took the "Gourmets."

Then I met someone else, a new guy at my office. We sent goofy e-mails back and forth for months before we spoke. I watched him eat microwave dinners during his breaks. Our first conversation was about catfish: where to buy it, how to cook it, how much we both liked it. And a year later, catfish—pan-seared with bread crumbs—is exactly what we served at our wedding reception. We've been married five years and have two children. Our dinners at home aren't fancy, but you sure can't beat the conversation. Lobster ain't all it's cracked up to be.

Gone with the Tide
by Heather Haldeman

I RECOGNIZED THE HANDWRITING, or rather the print—the same as in all those letters packed away in water-stained cardboard boxes in my garage. It wasn't time for Christmas cards. Why a letter from Bill?

I read the first line. *"Can it really be more than thirty years since we first met?"* He'd been going through boxes in his own garage.

Bill had been Adonis to me. He was tall and muscular, with golden hair and eyes the color of sapphires, framed with thick curly lashes. He was a surfer, an athlete—and had wanted to be a doctor. We started dating when I was a junior in high school. He was a senior. With the first kiss, I was hooked.

"There must be some fifty letters from you that tell the story of our four year relationship."

When Bill left for college in San Diego the fall of his freshman year, I traveled by train from Los Angeles to visit him almost every weekend. High school was not my priority. Then, Bill was.

He loved his new life at the beach, but I was a city girl. The sand was messy, the water scared me. But I hung on, spending cold winter weekend mornings wrapped in a towel, watching him surf. In the afternoon, we listened to The Beach Boys while I watched Bill wax his board and write papers for school.

But I'd noticed that the ocean wasn't the only thing Bill looked at on the beach, and I wasn't about to lose him to some beach chick. So, I lost my pasty, indoor-girl complexion in favor of a tan. I lived on green apples, hamburger patties and cottage cheese to stay thin. I highlighted my hair and ironed it straight. I dressed in Levi's cut-off's and peasant blouses, and wore Japanese bamboo sandals. Bill seemed pleased with this new "beachy" me.

"Quick update in life: My wife Christine and I have had some differences this past year. Mid-life crisis, but, we're fine now…"

After high school, I had enrolled at a Community College in San Diego to be near Bill. Without a car, though, I had to live within walking distance of my school, twenty minutes inland from Bill at UCSD. When Bill wasn't around, out of boredom, I started to study, never missed class. For the first time in my life, I started to get good grades.

But Bill's approval was still number one, so I kept up the tan, sitting in a lawn chair outside the apartment.

"Strange after so many years of marriage to be writing to you, but I suppose when we get older we start to grasp at what was, in an effort to decipher what is."

The second year of junior college, my parents gave me a used car. I moved to the beach, renting a small house with two other girls. Bill was there a lot. Still, he scrutinized my looks; I never measured up. The coxswain on Bill's rowing team had "great legs." No matter how tan I got, I was never that girl Bill admired, who could prance around in a bikini without a care. I was the girl who sat on a towel, adjusted her legs to hide her thighs.

"I work in residential design, fun developer type stuff. I had a fair amount of success in state championships for triathlons. And Christine is still commuting an hour to her work. She still cycles, but has had some trouble with an old knee injury…"

I focused on Bill's chest hair that day twenty-eight years ago, that familiar mole near his collar, not wanting to look at his face. It was over—I was the one to end it. The night before, I'd had my first date with the man who would become my husband. He had given me a tour of my new campus. We'd talked all night about books. The following Monday would be my first day at UCLA.

"Let me know how you have been. Perhaps we can get together…"

I sat down to compose my response.

Dear Bill,

Thank you for your letter. Hank and I just celebrated our twenty-fifth wedding anniversary. I feel so lucky to have him in my life. I adore him.

All the best to you and your family,

Heather

We Came For Toast
by Linda Wisniewski

*T*ODAY I PLAYED A LITTLE GAME: I wrote down the names of my former lovers, all the ones I could remember. Beside each name, I wrote the first word that came to mind. Beside Marty, I wrote Catholic. For Dan, it was Anger. Richard meant Control. Jim meant Health. Dave was Kindness, Pat was Dangerous. And for Phil, there could be only one word: Toasters.

He had over five hundred of the little contraptions in his kitchen and dining room, arranged above the cabinets, in book-shelves and across the deep windowsills of his huge Victorian home. (The many bedrooms came in handy when Phil's old girlfriends came to town.)

He collected toasters at flea markets and antique fairs, many of which I'd attended with Phil and his friends, collectors of other oddities like light bulbs and cowboy boots. It wasn't that I was interested in toasters, or light bulbs, or even antiques. I wanted someone to love me.

His friends were weird, but I didn't care. I would have given myself up for a life with him, indeed gave up two years, but only two, in wasted effort.

We listened to classical music, went to dinner or a movie. He chose the date and activity, I went along. We did not fit. His kids were grown, and I only met them once. He was kind to my son, gave him an old bike and a watch to play with. But he criticized my parenting style. He didn't seem to like kids.

A closeted gay friend got the idea to make Phil jealous by kissing me. We laughed together at our secret. And it worked, but not enough to make us right for each other.

One day, after he and I had split, two colleagues convinced me to knock on his front door on the way to a meeting. They knew I missed him, and our route went right past his house.

"We came for toast," I said when he opened the door. He looked at me, then Helen, then Patty, and smiled his bemused smile. He suggested lunch, looking at Helen again, longer. She said we had no time, and laughed. We scampered back to our car.

Patty said, "Now the ball is in his court. You reached out." He never reached back.

Today, I barely recognize the woman I was then: half woman, half girl, divorced, mother of a difficult child, trying to make a career as a librarian. Searching for love and tired of it, lonely.

"We look at life in different ways," he had said. Because I believed I loved him, I cried when he said he'd never love me. But what I loved was the promise of someone safe, secure, older, with a big house, even if it was full of toasters.

When I ended it, he told me he didn't miss my neediness or anxiety, only "the warm body" in his bed. He asked out my best friend. She wouldn't go, out of loyalty and also because she wasn't interested.

An old rickety toaster at a flea market today brings a smile of recognition, not for Phil, but for the woman I was then, open and loving—too much so. But now I forgive her. I don't blame her for trying.

In a way, I owe Phil for the woman I became, the contented one who knows what she wants, and gets it. Without that one-sided exercise in futility, I might still be trying too hard to please, forgetting myself—forever on the doorstep, knocking.

184

A SUMMER OF LOVE

Shaped as it is by the knowledge that it will be ephemeral, a summer romance can be both sweet and sad. More than likely, come September, distance and ordinary life will intervene. Until then, surrendering to the magic is almost irresistible.

Sometimes, though, only one heart is smitten. Still, when all is said and done, a summer romance is just long enough to be delightful, short enough to avoid complications, and perfect for creating lasting memories.

The Cash Crush
by Carmen Beecher

I WAS TWELVE, going ungracefully on thirteen—that awkward stage in a girl's life where she has one foot in childhood and the other in womanhood. My grandmother and I were spending the summer in Knoxville with my sweet Uncle Ray and my very assertive Aunt Bea, as we did every year.

That was the year the best-looking boy I'd ever seen walked into our house, and my adolescent heart went pitty-pat. He was a senior in high school, and worked at his family grocery store down the road. His name was Cash. To this day, I don't know if it was a nickname or an abbreviated version of some horrible moniker. Maybe his parents loved Johnny Cash.

Brown hair, blue eyes—Cash was tall and perfect. We sure didn't have anyone back in Dundee, Florida, who looked like that. He was perfectly at ease with my family, even my Aunt Bea, who was quite overbearing and had been known to frighten the faint of heart. In my dazzled eyes, he was the epitome of sophistication and style. He could wear blue jeans and a plaid shirt like no one I'd ever seen.

From that moment on, my life pretty much revolved around Cash sightings. I would gladly go to the store to purchase a bag of carrots or a gallon of milk for Aunt Bea. And, of course, I was so enchanting: I was sporting one of Aunt Bea's haircuts (who would dare to tell her no?). It was like a big brown mushroom on top of my skinny body—with its flat chest and twig-like legs. Of course, twig-like legs later became fashionable, but timing is everything, isn't it? I came from Dundee, where wearing *shoes* made a kid overdressed. Even though Knoxville is a city with a small-town feel, to me it was a metropolis, and I felt like a country bumpkin.

I was doing oil paintings then (as now), and Cash was very complimentary about my art—which made me blush and turn all googly-eyed and practically say "aw, shucks." It was difficult for me to respond with a coherent sentence. But in spite of that, he was always very nice. So the summer passed, and I painted, played piano, hung out with my girlfriend, and lived for Cash sightings.

One rainy night, alas, reality knocked. Cash was coming over to see my aunt and uncle for some reason, now forgotten, and my heart leapt when I heard him arrive. He came in from the rain, accompanied by the most gorgeous blonde creature I had ever seen. She was so perfect that I couldn't even pick her apart—or maybe I had not yet learned the ugly female trait of pettiness. Her hair was styled like Marilyn Monroe's; she had on a beige sheath dress of the sort that I would not wear for at least four more years; she was curvaceous and beautiful and wore no shoes. They had run through the rain, and were laughing and happy.

Not only was I horribly jealous, but I felt in that instant that what I wanted in my future was a moment just like that with someone—a giddy, romantic, carefree moment. I knew that my moment was a long way off, and my big crush on Cash became my first inkling of what lost love feels like. I spent a lot of time after that looking at myself in the mirror and wondering if I would ever turn into anything shapely or even passably well-groomed.

Years later, after I married and had children, I was staying in Knoxville for a time. I went into the grocery store and, of course, wondered if I would see Mr. Dreamboat from fifteen years before. When I went to check out, there he was, not quite so handsome, but still pretty cute. I told him who I was. He looked very surprised and gave me that look of appreciation all women recognize, saying, "Wow, you sure are growed up!"

I guess he always talked that way. But who noticed?

Song for an Angel
by Norm Titterington

THE AMAZING THING ABOUT "LOVE" at the age of fifteen is how true and intense it feels, right from the first moment. It is the age of love at first sight, or first conversation at the very least—that idealistic age when the obstacles of reality are invisible and even the most implausible of pairings seem to be within one's grasp.

Such was the case for me in the summer of 1991...a summer filled with wonderful weather, incredible music and a powerful, yet unrequited "love."

It was going to be one of the most exciting nights of my young life—I was attending my first rock concert with a group of my friends...no parents, and no rules. Just me, my friends, two of my favorite bands and the expectation of a very wild time!

Oh...and Heather-Rose.

Love at first sight? Well, maybe more of a young lust at that point, I suppose. As soon as the petite beauty with the reddish-brown hair entered the room, I couldn't take my eyes off her—she was the most attractive girl I'd ever met.

The concert was everything I expected—in fact, far better than I could have anticipated, due to Heather's presence. And the night only got better when some of us—including Heather–decided to stay the night at my friend's house because the concert had ended so late.

It certainly wasn't a "sleepover" as far as Heather and I were concerned. We stayed awake all night, completely engrossed in conversation. As I gazed deeply into her striking green eyes, I fell head-over-heels in love. The fact that she was nineteen to my fifteen didn't seem to matter; we had forged quite a connection that night. I was disappointed that I hadn't mustered the courage to attempt a goodbye kiss when I left the next morning, but I was sure I'd get my chance sometime that summer.

It was an excellent summer for concerts...warm summer nights, exciting music. I attended several more with the same group of friends, including Heather. I had numerous long, wonderful conversations with this lovely young woman with whom I had become completely smitten.

As the summer wore on, my feelings grew stronger, even though my courage didn't. When I was with Heather, the conversations covered every possible topic—aside from our feelings for each other. But I just knew she felt the same way I did; I could see it every time I looked into those amazing eyes.

It took me until the end of August, but I finally summoned the courage to disclose the depth of my feelings. A Saturday picnic with Heather would provide an outstanding opportunity to express myself in the only way I knew how: music. The song I had written for her would proclaim my love in a way that would instantly connect us on an even deeper level.

As the final strains of the song crossed my confident lips, the stunning green eyes a few feet away began to well with tears. A faint smile brightened Heather's face. I smiled broadly in return, but my smile faded quickly as she spoke softly, "I've enjoyed spending time with you this summer, and I do consider you a good friend...I hope I didn't give you the wrong idea, but I just don't feel that way about you, kiddo."

Kiddo. For the first time, I felt our age difference, and the gap might as well have been twenty years at that point. "I hope this won't stop us from hanging out—I still think you're a pretty cool friend."

I never saw or heard from her again. Well, almost never...

July 2006. Almost fifteen years after that fateful August day, I encountered Heather-Rose. The still beautiful, though world-wearied green eyes told the story of a difficult life. We had traversed very different paths over the years. And as we talked, it became obvious that I hadn't known her as well as I had thought back then. As I pictured what my life could have been, and compared it to the life I've happily lived, another smile curved upon my lips...

Night Moves
by Sonia Suedfeld

YOU KNOW BOB SEGER'S "NIGHT MOVES"? Whenever I hear that song, no matter where I am, and no matter what I'm doing, I always think of Tim. We worked on those night moves all right, the two of us, stealing away every chance we could. And as the song says, he used me and I used him, and neither of us cared. We both knew we weren't in love, as Seger says in the song. Oh no, far from it. We were just young and restless and bored, waiting on the thunder.

Feeling the lighting.

I felt it when I first saw him, that hot, hazy July day. He was standing in the back of a rust-colored pickup truck, unloading bricks and bags of cement, his brown arms rippling with effort in the afternoon sun. My friend Sarah and I had only stopped at the construction site for a few minutes to drop some lunch off for her dad and his workers. It didn't take long to find out the guy unloading the bricks was Tim and he was working for Sarah's father over the summer, trying to save some money before returning to university in the fall.

He was tall, blond, and green-eyed. For me, the attraction was immediate. I was eighteen, had just graduated from high school and was looking forward to starting college in the fall. I wasn't looking for romance, but it came looking for me anyway. We introduced ourselves and exchanged phone numbers; it wasn't long before we were seeing each other every chance we could.

We made love on our second date, in the back seat of his car, after sharing a wonderful meal and a long walk on the beach. Soon we were seeing each other three, four times a week. And always we'd park down by our special spot at the beach, bats swooping in the night sky, and make love to the sounds of waves hitting the shore.

There was a lot of laughter between us. Tim was always cracking jokes, even when we were in the middle of it, him deep inside me and me wrapped around him. We loved, we laughed, and there was no sweeter sound than the sound of our crying out together in release on those hot, humid summer nights.

We felt the lightning.

But where there's lightning, there's thunder. We both knew it was coming; we could feel it getting stronger as the weeks went by. There were no expectations beyond the summer, and we both knew we would go our separate ways come the Labour Day weekend, he to start his last year of university in Ottawa, and me to start my first at a college in northern Ontario. I knew somewhere in my heart that once summer was over, we would never see each other again.

The weeks swiftly went by, and before we knew it, summer was over. We spent our last night together on the beach in each other's arms, gazing at the stars and the water all around us. We laughed and we loved and we heard the thunder. But we didn't cry and we didn't talk about the future. And we didn't say goodbye.

At dawn, he dropped me off at home and kissed me for the last time, just as the sun was cresting the horizon. I watched him drive away, and I knew he was gone for good. I would never see him again.

Twenty years have gone by, and I still think of Tim whenever I hear Bob Seger's "Night Moves." I still feel the lightning; I still hear the thunder.

His Heartbeat
by Mary Oak

TWENTY YEARS AGO. High summer in the low Sierras. Day by blazing day, we dug clay and fashioned it into form. By night, I learned another heat, a new geography: Brian's body. I had become fluent in the touch that flowed between us, but there was more to know. In a tiny A-frame cabin, darkness held us as we nestled together, my ear pressed against his chest. Beneath the arcing vault of his ribs, an ocean sounded, waves pounding unevenly.

"Do you hear it?" he asked me, dreamily

"Hmm?" I whispered

"My heart murmur."

"The shusshing?"

"Um-hum—there's a little hole between my heart chambers."

I thought of the Japanese climbing kiln that we were using to fire our pottery—the openings that allow a path of flame to ascend through the chambers.

Voice resonant in his chest, he continued as he held me close, "It's a heart defect. I was born that way. It causes my blood to flow through the hole and make that extra sssssssh at the end"

That night, I kept listening to his heart's improvisation: a steady beat doubling in echo and whoosh reverberating. Over that summer, close to him, I listened again and again, dreaming into that hidden generosity.

Decades later, I no longer have any of the pots I made during that pottery residency. I have lost touch with Brian. But when I am diagnosed with a rare cardiac condition, and I hear my own murmur, I remember that intimacy—Brian's rhythm that I knew by heart, an audible foreshadowing.

WORLDS APART

In the time right after Cupid has released an arrow, it is easy for couples to blithely ignore their different family, cultural or religious values. Love, if at first not totally blind, is at least willing to look the other way.

These stories are reminders of how complicated it can be to love someone when, for one reason or another, your two worlds will never become one.

No Small Change
by Savita Sachdev

*T*HIS STORY BEGAN five years ago. It was not an unusual day. There was the chaos of getting ready for work, with the usual scrambling around for parking meter money in the depths of my handbag amid the half a packet of chewing gum carefully re-wrapped in the original foil casing and the lipsticks without lids. As if that were not eough, there was the usual rush to buy more chewing gum in order to get change from a £10 note.

It was in an unremarkable shop that I met him.

It took twenty-four hours for me to fall in love. Later, it took even less for my world to fall.

The second worst thing a Hindu girl with several strict generations behind her could do is to remain unmarried. The worst thing she could do would be to marry a strict Catholic boy with pale blue eyes and the promise of passion.

So, we fell in love. We laughed a lot, we argued a lot, we traveled, we met each other's friends—all of whom would ask, "So when's the BIG day?".

Of course we laughed it off and acted coy, whilst my heart was breaking. You see, there is always a tradeoff with anything in life. In order for us to be happy, we would have to hurt so many people. Dramatic as that may sound, it's terrifying to defy decades of strong cultural fibres and religious beliefs, peppered with some politics.

We had talked about the future, our children's names, where we would buy our first house together. And we had talked about the impossibility of living without each other.

Still, after three years together, I kept thinking, wishing and praying that something would happen—a sudden change, a phone call out of the blue from my parents telling me that they wanted me to be happy no matter what. In my head I imagined scenes of walking down the aisle whilst our families applauded and cried with joy.

It was around this time that I was asked to be a bridesmaid for a friend. I agreed, but my spirit was crushed. I felt like an actress as one grueling scene played after another: dress fittings …tears over tablecloths not matching serviettes…overjoyed parents…watching someone be so unconditionally loved.

I wondered if some people went through life not realising they are truly blessed. I wondered if people realised that whilst tears were being shed over flower arrangements and menus, hearts were breaking.

During the ceremony, I was asked a thousand times about my "BIG day".

So, the BIG day finally came. Only, it wasn't to be mine. My current love slipped into the past as easily as he came. I let him go. There was nothing else to be done.

I hear his wedding day—with a beautiful French girl from Paris—was a happy one.

I imagined the rest: the wedding march, the walk down the aisle, the tears and applause, the cutting of the three-tiered cake, the father's moving speech telling of happy childhoods and how he had not so much lost a daughter but gained a son, the clinking of champagne glasses. I imagined it all.

In my way, I celebrated us; I celebrated the ties that bind, the childhoods and cultures that form who we are, the decisions one must make in love, noble and otherwise.

There are moments in your life where you feel you have already lived—and died.

The Peace of Knowing
by Lisa Kempke

THERE IS A TIME during college, when you are just discovering yourself, that you find a true love, someone to be with, laugh and enjoy activities with, and enjoy nothingness with, lying together. We had a beautiful relationship, and it truly taught me what real love is. He was my best friend and soul mate. More than that, he helped me uncover who I really was and what I really wanted.

We spent over five wonderful years together. We rarely argued, and almost always agreed on plans. We had fun and did adventurous things, like white-water rafting. As we were both semi-athletic, we ran and worked out together.

Unfortunately, I was from the local area and he was not. During the school year, as I did not dorm, he spent a lot of time at my home. I traveled to his home town, meeting his family. But at the end of college, we needed to decide where we planned to live and start our new careers.

I was very close to and lived with my parents. I could not imagine not living near them and being with them. He, likewise, wanted to go back home to his family and start his career. We talked this through and shared many tears about it. So it was a sad and bittersweet graduation.

We spent that summer together, but come fall, he had to leave. It broke my heart, because we were so perfect. But I did not want to marry and move away from my parents. He did not want to stay with me and try his luck in my hometown area. So, although it was very hard, we separated and went our own ways.

Initially, we spoke and emailed often, and cried and prayed for one of us to change their mind. But as time went on, we both became active with our new careers. Exciting things were happening to us. Contact became less and less frequent, but the feelings and love were still there. Eventually, we both began to date other people, and we each married.

It has been twenty-eight years since I have been with Mark, and I still think of him. I can remember our times together, and sometimes, as I run with my dog, I think of our runs together, especially if I do the same run now. I eat a certain dessert, and remember a time sharing it with Mark. I hear a certain expression or quote, and smile, hearing him saying it to me.

I think the biggest thing that came from our time together is that I feel comfortable with who I am. And we will always have memories of our time together. Although it is not always possible to remember the good, especially in challenging times, in this situation, I find that I can do that. We have not spoken in over twenty years, and that is okay, because nothing would change the past or the future.

My parents have passed on, my children are growing up. I love my husband and we have a good life. But I still think of my first real love, and wonder what would have happened if we had made different decisions. More than anything, I can remember and feel the peace of knowing that someone loves and cherishes me. That still brings a smile to my face.

Grease Revisited
by Maria B. Murad

"HEART AND SOUL." "How High the Moon." "Tenderly." Oh, how those songs bring back memories—of high school, of being young and my first love.

I was a sheltered, naive young girl when I met him. I had gone to a girls' school from the first through tenth grades. Then my mother suddenly decided I needed a change. She proposed a public high school for my junior and senior years. It was a change all right—from small classes with only females (wearing identical uniforms) to a large, noisy, coed institution full of strange new students and teachers. Somehow I made the transition, although there were lots of bumps along the way. But in the spring of my junior year, everything changed: I acquired a boyfriend.

I had liked this particular guy for several months. I palled around with his crowd, laughing at their antics and jokes, so different from anything I'd known. That spring, he approached me one day in the lunchroom, and asked me to the upcoming junior/senior prom. I was nonplused, because I didn't think he noticed me that much. But I was also thrilled and delighted. At fifteen, I had very little experience with boys, and I certainly had not dated at all. I accepted. From then on, through our senior year, we were a couple.

And what a couple. I was studious, an overachiever who did her homework as soon as it was assigned and chalked up a 4.0 average. He was—well, let me just say the writers of "Happy Days" could have based The Fonz on him: leather jacket, jeans, loafers, and a pack of Camels in his rolled-up sleeve. An indifferent student, he often sneaked out behind the school for a quick drag on a cigarette, and he frequently skipped classes.

The reaction of my parents, and even some teachers, was instantly negative. None of the adults could see the attraction between us, a decidedly odd couple. But what no one knew was that with me, he was sweet and tender and funny, never over-stepping the boundaries. He brought me into his large Irish family, who accepted me wholeheartedly and offered me a look at a normal, fun-loving home life, something I sadly lacked. I think it was his family as much as his charm that held me.

This was the Fifties. We danced the Lindy, did slow dancing, went to parties where the boys drank beer and smoked, while the girls, more conventional, merely gossiped and laughed at their clowning around. No harm came to any of us, which allayed, somewhat, my parents' fears.

Inevitably, though, we went in different directions. I was obsessed with ballet and spent most of my free time in classes. He was irresponsible, with little ambition. The awareness of this came to me slowly, but it culminated in one incident. A mutual friend of ours, who often made our twosome a threesome, died suddenly of spinal meningitis. One day he was there, blond and handsome, looking forward to graduation, and the next he was gone, with a closed coffin. My boyfriend promised to come for me to go to the funeral. I waited and waited, but he totally forgot about me. It was the first of many rifts that were to come.

I went to the University after graduation, and he drifted around, finally joining the army. We wrote brief letters, but when he asked me in one if I wanted to continue our relationship, I never responded. That was cruel and immature of me, but I had a lot to learn.

I never saw him again. I danced, got married, had children, and occasionally, if I went to high school reunions, tried to keep track of him. He never showed up on these occasions. At our last milestone celebration, someone said he had planned to come, but at the last minute was too ill with some undisclosed sickness. I got his address and wrote him a long letter, enclosing a photo. I didn't expect him to answer, and he didn't. But at least I could tell him how much he had meant to my growing up years and that I never, ever forgot him.

Invincible Inside our Love
by J. Victoria Sanders

JOHN WAS COFFEE-COLORED, with a false front tooth he sometimes clicked in and out of place. I adored him with the teenage innocence that allows us to truly give one hundred percent of our hearts. He would become my Panda bear, though at six feet tall and with a baby face, he looked more like a grizzly. He called me Bambi, because of my big brown eyes.

The winter I turned fourteen, John was sixteen. He worked as a locker room attendant at the Columbus Avenue Boys and Girls Club near his high school, Dewitt Clinton. I had started going to the Club with my high school classmate, Lanell, who introduced us.

In The Bronx, where we grew up, John and I were both so tall we seemed to rule every city block we wandered together. We dressed alike in matching Tazmanian Devil t-shirts or camouflage outfits.

My friends couldn't stop laughing when we showed up at a junior high school reunion dressed like GI Joe and Jane. But I didn't care. In The Bronx—a tough world of cracked sidewalks, drugs and violence—we were invincible inside our love, and nothing else mattered. We could be kids together, playing Streetfighter on his Nintendo, or, too grown for our own good, be engaged for a few months based on a pretty cubic zirconia ring and John's promise to love me as long as I loved him back.

All I loved more than John was books. All I had, really, was school. Ultimately, one of the biggest differences between us was that I had the opportunity to go to boarding school.

In four years of high school, John had attended maybe a hundred days of class. My mother, who is bipolar but does not take medication, was emotionally and sometimes physically absent from my life for long stretches of time. We had lived in the Bronx longer than we'd stayed anywhere when I was young. But before moving there, we'd lived in shelters all over New York City. School was my only way out, and when I got a chance to go to boarding school, I had to take it.

John, not one to show his emotions easily, cried. I went to the elite Emma Willard School on scholarship, trying to keep one foot on the manicured lawns there—and another on the crack-infested streets of the Bronx. I sent him drawings from school as if I were a budding artist in prison. And we talked on the pay phone a few paces from my room most nights of the week. But before I left Emma, our three-year relationship was over.

As big and comfortable as our love was, it taught me that not all love can withstand change. While John had protected me from the world, he had also kept me from dropping my defenses and growing beyond the survival tactics of anger and bravado that come with growing up in the 'hood.

After boarding school, I had several other loving relation-ships, but none of them equaled my love for John. We had accepted each others' lives without judgment. We had had so many firsts together and so many plans.

When I was a junior at Vassar, he found me again. He was engaged, working as a security guard in Manhattan. Life had changed me so much, but he hadn't changed very much at all. I still loved him—I always would. But not only did he belong to another woman, he also seemed angry that our paths had gone in such different directions.

Recently, he sent me a note on Myspace. It has been nearly a decade since we last spoke, fifteen years since we fell in love. We exchanged numbers the same day and talked for two hours. We laughed about how silly we had been, how much we adored one another, in spite of how and where we grew up. My Panda had taught me to walk in the world with swagger, but most important, he showed me that fully giving yourself over to the love of another person is an incredibly beautiful force of nature—and just as unpredictable.

Honesty
by Maryellen Wolfers

GLENN WAS A MAN when we met fifty years ago. He was twenty-six years old and had a career with the California State Fish and Game Department, living as a grown-up.

I was a college girl, twenty years old, studying to become a teacher. I lived in a dormitory on campus and had a curfew. In many ways, I was still a little girl.

I was at a college dance with girl friends from the dorm when Glenn approached me and asked me to dance. I liked him—he felt honest. He smiled with sincere interest and curiosity. Glenn liked what he saw in me and wanted to get to know me.

He was not a show-off kind of dancer, did not twirl me out and around the dance floor the way some men will, mostly to call attention to themselves. He was dancing with me because it was a means of getting to know me. That's what I mean by honesty.

Glenn and I went to his family cabin for a weekend. It was like being in another world, with just the two of us in a beautiful place, enjoying each other.

He was a man, ready to begin a married life. I was a naive girl, playing house, living a fantasy. Other girls start dreaming of white wedding gowns from a very early age. I did not. There were no bride's books, no sterling silver pattern, no vision of "happily ever after" in my experience. Glenn didn't know that, and neither did I.

I still didn't know what to look for in a man I would spend the rest of my life with. I knew Glenn was a good man, but he was too far ahead of me in stability. He was ready. I wasn't. When I told Glenn I was breaking up with him, he was sick, and broke out all over in big welts.

Then Ben—not a grown man—flew into my life. He was in the Air Force, but was still a kid. He was a smooth talker and a charmer who sold himself. I bought. He showed up, wearing a suit and tie, at the dormitory where I was working on the switchboard. I almost fell off my chair, he was so adorable. Adorable, but not honest—he did not know what honesty was. And I was a naive girl who vibrated with the excitement he exuded.

Ben asked me out on a date. He brought gifts. On our first date, he drove a big new black Oldsmobile convertible with whitewall tires. He asked me to marry him. On our second date, he drove a new white Volvo P 1800. He bought new cars like women would buy the proverbial new hat.

I divorced Ben after twenty-six years of marriage and four magnificent sons. When I had Ben served with divorce papers, he was bereft. He went to live with his mother and claims that the trauma of the divorce caused him to get Parkinson's disease. Now he lives in an assisted living facility, and I don't visit him. I never learned how to live with his dishonesty.

I am well, with no regrets. I learned from living with Ben that I am on my own, and I came to terms with that truth. I have built an internal strength. I am no longer the naive girl I was fifty years ago. I am a happy mother and grandmother, living alone, and I relish my freedom. This year I am celebrating my seventieth birthday.

Glenn lives in Alaska. He has a wife and children and is an outdoorsman. I assume he has taught his children about nature and about stability and honesty. He would be seventy-six years old now. I hear that he is well.

Incense Always Reminds Me of Yusef
by Sarah Bracey White

*D*URING A RECENT DAY-TRIP to a Long Island beach community, the cloying scent of incense drew me to a country store's display. I picked up a stick labeled "coconut," closed my eyes and inhaled. Coconut was Yusef's favorite. Its aroma saturated his sparsely furnished Baltimore apartment, where a blue light glowed above his front door. Unlike the pot-heads of the 1970s, Yusef didn't use incense to mask the smell of marijuana. He used it for atmosphere, the way he played John Coltrane albums.

By day, I worked in a law library; at night, my friends and I explored the wonders of the universe. Yusef's dark eyes had first mesmerized me at one of our house parties. "Be careful, girl," a friend said, "he's studied with a Yogi, and he reads minds." I laughed, and set out to seduce him.

Yusef was 5' 10," a gentle, soft-spoken man who could have been twice my twenty-five years, or anywhere in between. His soft, tobacco-colored skin seemed to have no pores, and he was totally hairless. His two front teeth were missing, but he smiled unabashedly, as if the gaping holes were a badge of honor. He told me they'd been knocked out during a teenage fight, and when his replacement bridge washed away during a swim off the California coast, he decided front teeth weren't necessary.

Yusef never read books, magazines or newspapers. Yet—without credentials—he worked as a therapist's assistant in group counseling sessions. I could just imagine him staring around a circle of reluctant soul-searchers and willing them, with his eyes, to speak. He certainly made me speak.

Some nights, we talked until dawn overpowered the edges of the black shades that hung at his windows. I shared things about my life that I'd never said before. "You're very powerful," he said. "You draw people to you, but keep them at bay. What are you afraid of?" When I didn't answer his insightful question, he stared into my eyes, then smiled and smothered me with kisses.

Yusef told me about his years in India and taught me to

meditate. "Life is an activity of the mind that utilizes the body for fulfillment," he whispered one night in a velvety voice.

"Then why don't you ever have an orgasm?" I asked.

"I practice Tantric sex," he answered. "The enlightened being's goal is not orgasm, but to become one with another." I gasped. He chuckled and added, "It's okay for you to have orgasms. You're not as evolved as I am."

We were so different. But time and again, I returned to his welcoming bed where our physical worlds collided, while a lava lamp undulated on his bedside table.

Some nights, I accompanied Yusef to a small jazz club where he played conga drums. He seemed to be in a trance while playing—eyes closed, thick body bent lovingly over his drum, bald head swaying in the spotlight.

"You two are soul mates," my girlfriend said. "You ought to get married this spring. Have the ceremony in my back yard." I was ashamed to tell her my interest in Yusef was purely physical. Though I was intrigued by mysticism and self-discovery, I liked things. Possessions meant nothing to Yusef. His only interest in money was for food and shelter. "The universe provides," was his mantra. "God helps those who help themselves" was mine.

After a mid-winter trip to Jamaica, financed as usual by friends, Yusef squeezed intricately carved silver bangles around my wrist. "I had these made especially for you," he said. I thanked him, but couldn't wait to get home and take them off. I felt like they were charms designed to trap me. Days later, I collected the few things I kept at his apartment, and never again knocked at the door with the blue light. However, if I thought hard about Yusef, he'd call, as if reading my thoughts from afar. After a while those calls stopped, and friends told me he had returned to California.

My relationship with Yusef was the equivalent of a grad course in human relations. I discovered that he wasn't a mind-reader, just a thoughtful listener who made it easy for me to share the contents of my heart. Whenever I smell coconut, I think of him, and of the power of listening. It is a power I try to exercise with compassion, as he did with me.

Reckless Eddies Around Us
by Judy Harwood

*H*AVING ESCAPED the antiquated social structure and poverty-perpetuating economic cycle of the land of my birth, I promised myself, "I'll go back when I have the time and the skills to make it a better place."

I never made it back to toil in the desperate field of need that is Eastern Kentucky, but I salved my conscience by concluding, "Those people don't want to change." Now, I know it was I, not they, who needed the area to change. Still, when I think of home, I remember the laurel and dogwood-covered hills in spring, the mountain twang of the hill folk, the early morning mists drifting through the hollows. They are part of me.

Similarly, I counted myself fortunate—and good riddance to my first love—when I departed for college, vowing I was through with love. I was the first daughter of a disgraced school teacher who ultimately abandoned me, my mother and six siblings, to start a new life in Ohio. I aspired to be valedictorian of my class just as my older brother had been. I ran the school newspaper and I was handling the small town gossip swirling around my family.

This first love was one of a loose-knit pack of boys from a nearby coal town, the scene of one of my father's indiscretions. I couldn't believe it when he started to throw paper wads at me, drop by my locker to chat, and choose a seat next to me in history class. He differed from me in important aspects. He placed no value on grades, although he scored higher than me on achievement tests. He articulated no vocational goals or plans for the future. He wore his disdain for others' opinion of him like a badge of honor. He felt dangerous to my future, but I loved the air of recklessness eddying around us when we were together.

His attention made me feel exceptional, but the notes he persisted in passing my way in geography class caused our teacher to lower my grade to a C, thereby killing my chance to be named valedictorian. I desperately wanted to announce we were a couple by attending the Senior Banquet together. His condition was that I go all the way with him after the banquet. So I went stag to the most important event of my life up to then. Afterward, he behaved as if nothing had happened.

Following graduation, we embarked on a summer of love as the time for my departure loomed over us. Then, inexplicably, he enlisted in the Marine Corps without as much as a word to me. He was gone before I was.

Despite the dozen who came afterward, when I meet a man with Robert Mitchum eyes, a Marlon Brando slouch and pouty lips, my heart flips in my chest. He is still a part of me.

We Were Dreamers
by Beth Carlson

*H*E WAS QUIET AND SCHOLARLY. I was young and anything but level-headed. We had no mutual friends, not even knowledge of the other's existence. It was not likely our paths would cross, only a fool's chance. But on that day we struck gold.

Looking back now, a year and a half later, I cannot remember quite everything. But certain images stand out in my mind, emotions caught in the current of reality and dreams deluded, but none the less beautiful.

I remember the initial rush and excitement of a first date. Not long after came the understanding that we really might have something beautiful and deep. You see, there was more to us than met the eye. We were dreamers, passionate and unafraid.

I recall snatches of memories. There is one of hot chocolate and a walk home in the snow, hand in hand. It was like a scene from a novel. The snow shimmered in the lamplight, flakes continuing to fall around us as he walked me to the front door and gave me a tender kiss goodnight.

Another time, dressed to impress, he took me to the high school prom…oh so cliché and innocent. And I still have a poem he wrote for me, one that would put Shakespeare to shame. It describes a blue-eyed beauty, with undeniable charm and a sweet, naive demeanor. I still cannot believe that the girl described lovingly in classic form is really me.

And then it was summer. Those sultry summer days stretched out endlessly, each more beautiful than the last. I can recall a night when we kissed in the rain, lightening flashing and not caring. That night there were no rules, no time, just youth, just us.

We were so different from the other couples. The bond was deeper, so beyond the frivolities of high school lust and whims.

We swore we were in love, that we would get married. I can remember the time we were by the creek, giggling and laughing as we made wedding rings out of blades of grass. At the age of seventeen, we named our future daughter Cadence.

I cried on the last day of summer. A gut feeling told me that when this day was done, things would never be the same. He reassured me, but I could see a glint of anxiety in his eyes. And I was right. The day that sweltering summer sun set, so did the heat of our love.

We tried to hold on, even as everything was breaking. We were engulfed in separate worlds, worlds that did not have a place for one another. When he said "I love you" it sounded like a plea. When I said "I love you" it sounded like a lie.

Sometimes things were as they were before. We could recreate those summer days, our unthinking passion and devotion. Those days were truly beautiful, but they grew fewer in number.

He wanted me to grow up, to accept our love, commit and to hell with the rest of it. I could not accept these terms. I could not give up my life for a chance at our future. I was young and still wild at heart. He knew this. His final gift to me was setting me free. But he still expected me to be his girl one day. And I just could not do it.

To this day, we maintain a strained sort of friendship. It is one continuously haunted by memories. We both remember what it was like back in the days when we believed love was easy, and we fell for the alluring delusion.

But our love was not in vain. I taught him that there is indeed beauty in this world and that he deserves to be loved. He taught me what it means to fall in love. He gave me integrity and strength, two gifts I will always hold close. The memories will forever flow through my veins. I would not be who I am today without him.

You can call it what you will: a high school romance, a first love, a lesson learned right, a love gone wrong. It is our story.

Spirit of Past Love
by Colin McClung

 SHE, A CAMBODIAN REFUGEE, and I, a suburban white boy, were transplants who had found our way to the left coast and were living out our California dream. As a child, she had escaped the bombing of her homeland and an assassination attempt on her family by the Khmer Rouge, while I played with plastic soldiers on the sprawling lawn of my back yard in Virginia with my older brother, who worshiped Richard Nixon.

Her teeth were the color of her skin, brown. I saw them when she laughed, her smile as easy and warm as those of the other downtown retailers who'd spent a fortune to make their Cheshire grins pearly white.

She worked in the bookstore. I loved to read the in-sleeve of books. We were inevitable. Her hair was so black and strong, we laughed the day I used it to floss my corn-colored teeth.

She drove a beat-up VW bug. I had no car. We both had little to no ambition, spending our paychecks on salty Mexican fast food and lying around on hot pavement, soaking up the sun while drinking Jarritos—time measured only by how long it took for our bloated bellies to subside.

That first autumn, we lived in a refurbished hay barn. We thought little of the future, other than in abstract terms, as we hunkered down under a sea of blankets, she knitting items we would don later that season while we sat watching old VHS tapes of Northern Exposure and dreaming of Alaska, our mutual love for the remote bringing us closer together.

During our first winter, the area of our already small cabin shrunk to a circumference governed only by the extent of the warm glow emanating from the wood stove. Our love was quite innocent, other than the biting. Besides sinking her teeth into me, she introduced me to yeast on buttered toast, chicory tea and (eventually) her family. I introduced her to the music of Hall and Oates, baby carrots as a nutritious mid-day snack, and ballroom dancing. We both put on weight that first winter together, me in the belly and her in the "back of her front," as my mother would delicately—if not so subtly—put it. We laughed at our transformation and thought it somehow confirmed we knew what it meant to grow old together.

At the height of our relationship, I was as sure of our love lasting a lifetime as I was sure of anything tangible in this world. But change is an intangible. She saw this, while I remained frozen in time. She bought the bookstore, having to spend her days among lawyers, bookkeepers and bankers, while I read in-sleeves about counterculture and pondered the life of Buddhist organic farmers. We felt the pull of opposite needs and the inevitable happened, again. She found someone with whom she could share her new vision.

She taught me about change. She taught me what the cliché "never say never" *felt* like. She taught me that I could look into the eyes of a lover and that a stranger could stare back at me, explaining love is not indebted to any past.

Motivated to complete myself, I moved to Alaska without her. This adventure eventually led me to my wife, my child and the wonderful life I now have in rural Vermont. Who I am, she helped make. I am not the man she knew. If we were to meet today, it would feel much like an introduction, two foreign bodies greeting each other in a world of passing objects heading toward separate and distant destinations.

Attempts to continue our friendship from three thousands miles away have proven to be nothing more than a sentimental dream. We haven't spoken in many years. As more time passes, she becomes more and more remote in my memory. I suspect she would find comfort in this. Memories are like graves: dig up the remains, assemble them in your midst and you will find the parts do not resemble the life that was once there. Even if the teeth, brown or yellow, still have their bite.

Worth the Wait
Anonymous

MAYBE IT WAS THE STARS in my eyes, blinding me to the inevitable. Maybe I turned a blind eye because I wanted so much to believe him when he said, "I love you." I know I was naive. I believed we would be married, that my life would fall into place as easily as saying "I do" and following my first love off into the sunset.

I was a junior in high school and he was a freshman at the community college. We instantly connected. Jon was good-hearted and sweet, always complimenting me and giving me inexpensive, thoughtful gifts. He began saying "I love you" within the first three weeks we were dating.

The chemistry between us smoldered. My parents thought he was wonderful and encouraged us. We went to movies, parties and had one memorable night of swimming in a nearby lake.

Then Jon took me to meet his family, who own and operate a goat farm in Montana. Believe me, it wasn't the "fresh country breezes" that caused me to wrinkle my nose.

Jon trotted off to help his dad, so I wandered into the big, homey kitchen. I offered to help Jon's three sisters with their chores. They suggested I change into "grubbies," so I pulled on the older pair of my jeans and a pretty pink top. I showed up at the main barn where the girls were already hard at work. They immediately dubbed me a "city girl." I didn't realize until later how disparaging the comment was meant to be.

The closest I'd ever been to a goat was seeing one outside a car window; now a teeming, nibbling, bleating herd surrounded me. To say I was a bit apprehensive would be to sugar coat the bald truth: I was terrified of the little creatures.

I gamely tried to milk Old Betsy, the "oldest and gentlest goat on the farm." It didn't go so well—she kicked me in the leg. I gritted my teeth and held in the tears. For a week after, I limped, which probably contributed to my fall into the picturesque little duck pond that afternoon. Jon's sisters could barely stop laughing long enough to help me out. I spent at least forty-five minutes in the shower, until Jon's father said through the door, "Ya'all gonna be much longer? This here's the only bathroom."

After that humiliation, I discovered supper consisted of goat's milk to drink and a lamb, liver and kidney bean stew. I choked down as much as I could, trying not to gag. I think now it was all a test, an elaborate, put-the-city-girl-through-the wringer test, that I failed miserably.

When we left, there was a conspicuous absence of the standard goodbye in that part of the country. No one told me to, "Come on back, ya' hear?"

Jon seemed more withdrawn after the trip, but I blissfully made plans to spend the summer having a blast with him and our friends. Jon told me all the time that he loved me and I reciprocated. My best friend was already planning her wedding and I was sure ours would be next.

Spring and graduation approached. I asked Jon to sign my new yearbook. He said he'd sign it later and get it back to me. Three days later, Jon's friend dropped off my yearbook at my house. I eagerly flipped through the pages until I found Jon's message.

"Dear Shaunna, This has been the greatest eighteen months of my life. I've had a blast! I'll never forget you. Love, Jon."

Stunned, I raced over to his apartment, but he'd already left. His roommate said Jon was taking a summer job in Medora, a town a few hours away. He left me a note: "Please don't contact me."

Utterly devastated, I went through depression, humiliation, despair, anger and finally, bitterness. I resisted all of my friends' attempts to cheer me up.

I saw Jon one more time, on a family trip to Medora that summer. He didn't see me. His arms were draped around two women.

That fall, I moved away to college and threw myself into school and part-time jobs. I dated, yet remained aloof from any hint of love. Then I met Wade. I resisted, but he patiently and lovingly broke down my walls. The difference is that this love is a mature love, growing and deepening with each passing year. We just celebrated our nineteenth anniversary. I have learned, the hard way, that broken hearts do mend and are capable of expanding to the limits of the stars.

When only memories live on

Whether the loss is very sudden or comes more slowly, the death of a heart mate leaves a particularly large rent in the fabric of your life. All your dreams of a shared future shatter, and you are left to find your way through a changed reality.

Each story here vividly portrays that poignant experience of love and loss, where, unlike what happens when a relationship ends some other way, not even the possibility of an ongoing friendship remains.

Inner Strength
by Dawn Carrington

ALMOST THIRTY YEARS have passed, but I have never forgotten my soul mate, the one boy who convinced me that dreams were possible, and that I could do anything no matter how the odds were stacked against me.

The late summer of my fifteenth birthday I'd just moved to a small town in Tennessee and wished I could be anywhere else… until I met Ren. He wasn't the boy in school that everyone loved, and he didn't stand out in a crowd. But I loved him instantly. Looking back, I think it might have been his country twang, or the way he could make me laugh when I felt like crying.

From the moment our gazes connected, we were inseparable. For one year my life was completely happy, fulfilled. Ren made me believe in the impossible. We talked about everything, even the stuff that didn't make sense to anyone but us, and we believed our futures were intertwined because we couldn't imagine living without one another.

My home life was a wreck, but Ren somehow made everything make sense. When I threatened to run away, he convinced me to hang in, to hold out for the final two years that would give me my freedom with a high school diploma. And the days I couldn't take the abuse, I snuck away to Ren's house where we sat and talked for as long as I safely could. Then he always walked me home.

Our first kiss didn't happen until two months into the relationship because he didn't want to rush me. He told me he wanted it to be as special as I was. Hearing someone tell me I was unique gave me a sense of hope for the future. And the moment Ren kissed me, I committed myself to him, knowing I was going to marry him.

I remember vividly the last day I saw Ren. It was the end of the first week of school. We always got off the bus a few blocks from our houses so we had a little more time together. Holding hands, we walked down the gravel road leading to his house. We didn't make plans to see each other that evening because he had company from out of town. I kissed him goodbye, promising to meet him at the bus stop early the next morning.

The next morning, I arrived at the stop before seven. At seven fifteen, I saw Ren's father's aging Ford lumbering down the gravel road, and I knew something was wrong. Ren's father worked the early morning shift at the local factory—he'd have no reason to be coming home so soon.

Forgetting all about school, I raced toward that truck. I'll never forget the broken words his father said to me: "Ren was killed last night."

My world collapsed around me, and I remember struggling to breathe. I'd never known such pain. My heart shredded, I fell to my knees on the damp ground. I didn't know what to do, how to think, to survive without Ren. He'd been my lifeline in this hellhole I lived, and I felt helpless.

The small funeral, held two days later, brought in most of the town. I sat outside on the back steps of the church because I had to say my goodbye to Ren alone. It was the last thing I could share with him.

That night, I expressed my words of love to Ren in the very first poem I ever wrote, and as the words poured out onto the paper, I felt his presence next to me. He'd always encouraged me in whatever I chose to do, so I wasn't surprised he was there. That poem spurred a lifelong writing career.

I have fulfilled a lot of my dreams, just as Ren said I would. Now, almost thirty years later, I still think about him. With every career achievement, I thank him. The love Ren showed me gave me hope, and though his death tore through my soul like a knife, I kept going because he would have wanted me to. His love gave me a strength I didn't know I had.

Beyond the Veil
by Xenia Schiller

YOU ARE BOTH TWENTY-SEVEN and in love. It's amazing, unbelievable. You'd suspect it all if it weren't happening to you.

He is movie-star handsome. And funny! No one makes you laugh like this. You just "get" each other. He's talking about marriage now, and it scares you, because he means it. Happily-ever-after is rolling into the station right on time.

You don't understand when he falls down the stairs, and into the bookshelves at work, or why the seizures are coming, why they won't stop. Right up to the diagnosis.

You're married now, and it's not at all how you imagined it. But still, bad times shared with him are better than the best you've ever had alone.

You're both thirty when he decides he's had enough of the less-than that medicine has to give. Not of you, never of you, but only of the cancer. But he asks you to let him go, and for his sake only, you say okay, knowing it will never be okay. This world has nothing to offer if he's not in it. And mostly, because you're in practice, you continue to hold on.

"Watch for the signs," someone says. And because you have nothing else, and also because you're desperate for any part of him, you do: the cell phone that spontaneously dials the old number still listed as "home" (because even though you've moved, that's what it is); the disembodied knock at the door when you forget to lock it; his very real presence when you first wake up. It's agonizing, but it's good; it's what you have, and you can't get enough.

The first anniversary, the first for your marriage, is the worst. A rogue calla lily blooms that day, and this happens every year, except one year when it doesn't. A close and empathic friend sends roses that year—except you get *two* bouquets, one that exactly matches the rare roses you held at your wedding, a gift made possible by Love, working behind the scenes. So you thank him, and the tears that come are different this time. There's joy mixed with sadness, where previously there was only despair.

More and more you are laughing—not the forced kind, but the knees-to-the-belly kind, complete abandonment. It doesn't hurt as much when you catch yourself thinking, "I can't wait to tell him this." Somehow you know he is there, laughing, yes, but mostly happy that you are healing.

One day you're watching a movie when the sound cuts out. The remote gives no satisfaction, so you consider his solution, mostly because it still amuses you. "Percussion calibration," he used to say. And thinking those words, you "dope slap" the side of the TV. Sound comes flooding back, and what you know right then is complete and utter joy at this inside joke that you will always share.

Now the plans you make are *your* plans, not *his*, not *ours*. And even though you're not yet in the practice, it's okay. It'll come. This new life is not perfect, but the happiness is exactly what he would have chosen for you, and that makes it okay for you to choose it for yourself.

Cherish the Memories
by Elaine Suelen

*I*T WAS A BEAUTIFUL DAY in the middle of May, and I was clearing a table in the local diner where I worked. You could hear patrons talking amongst themselves, the clanging of silverware and dishes, and the cook's bell when an order was ready. It was just another normal day.

I finished clearing the table and noticed a new customer sitting in my area. Walking over to the table with a menu and a glass of water, I offered him a good morning and asked if I could get him some coffee. He said yes, and ordered two eggs over easy, hash browns and a scone. During the course of his meal, he would stop me from time to time to make small talk. "I'm new in town, I'm here from California. Where are you from?" That sort of thing. When he finished his breakfast, he wished me a good day, gave me an unbelievable smile, and was gone. He came in the next three days at the same time, ordered the same breakfast. On the third day, he asked me out to dinner.

I, however, was not ready to date. I was a single mom of three small children and had only been divorced for eight months. I had made up my mind that I was going to raise my kids first, and then worry about finding love. I graciously said, "No, but thank you very much."

He took my rejection with a smile, saying, "Perhaps another time."

He continued to come in every day, and it wasn't long until half the town knew him by name. He was outgoing, generous, compassionate to a fault, and had a laugh that would fill the room.

Two months after his first visit to the diner, a group of us decided to go on a camping trip. He was among the friends that went. We spent two wonderful days taking walks, watching the kids play in the river, sitting around the campfire and sleeping under the stars. When we returned, he volunteered to drive my children and me home. He walked me to the door, and as I turned to go inside, he gently touched my arm and said, "You know, Elaine, you might as well give in. I'm in love with you, and generally, I get what I want."

I did finally give in, less than a week later, and we had our first date. So began one of best periods of my life. He was gentle at times, intensely passionate at times, hard-headed, patient and kind-hearted. He used to tell me I was the most stubborn woman he had ever met, and then he'd laugh and kiss me.

He taught me that a relationship takes compromise and communication, with more giving than taking. It takes forgiveness and patience. He also taught me that there should be joy when you're with someone. There were times we would laugh until we cried.

We also had our arguments. I remember once I refused to talk to him. He came to my house; I didn't answer the door. He called me on the phone; I didn't answer. It wasn't until the next morning, after I had spent the night crying, that the phone rang, and without thinking I answered it. He asked me if I was ready to talk. I said yes, and we did. I bring that up only because, as we were discussing the incident, he told me that when you refuse to talk to your partner, it makes them feel they have no control at all in the relationship. Everyone wants to feel as if they have some kind of control. I've never forgotten that.

We were engaged to be married the summer of 1996. The day never came. He was killed in a car accident on December 5, 1995. It took many years for me to recover from the loss, but I have come to a point where I can cherish the memories. And I do cherish them—very much.

Just Can't Find the Words
by Diana Lesire Brandmeyer

I AM AT THE MARKET, stuffing Granny Smiths into a bag when John Denver's "Annie's Song" pipes through the air. I gasp at the memories scratched with pain. My heart stutters and reverses. I am sixteen again. I practice linking my first name with your last. Scenes — of cool fall nights, sneaking into the park with a bottle of strawberry wine, and long walks in the moonlight — cascade over me.

You made me feel safe, wanted and loved.

The images make my world tilt. I can see the way your brown flannel shirt picked up the colors of coffee in your hair; the way you smelled of ivory soap, leather and horses; the way your hesitant fingers stroked my hair before you first kissed me. I knew then, at that moment, you were the one meant for me. The way you looked at me said you knew it too.

"For better or worse, in sickness and in health," we said in front of God and family. Later, I added, "No matter what," to those vows. I watched, confused , when instead of helping with our son's birthday party you preferred to watch cartoons. You quit going to work and talked in sentences filled with hate, then love, then insanity.

Still I said, "We're together, no matter what," even though I no longer felt loved, wanted or safe. Your debilitating headaches returned with the growth of the tumor. There were doctor's appointments and suggestions from them that I was the problem in our marriage. Still I said, "No matter what."

On our last night together, when you could still speak, I said I loved you.

Our sons' hands now represent your strong hands that once swallowed mine. When you laughed, your chin tilted in heaven's direction; now your sons' chins do the same. I laughed at your toes and said they looked like Frodo Baggin's. Both our sons have hobbit toes.

If I could speak to you now, I wouldn't be able find the words, not the best words that would tell you I understand now. You didn't choose to leave; it was your time and I know you always loved me, no matter what.

Not Enough Time
by Frances M. Rooks

I WAS FULL OF HESITATION when Bill asked me to move in with him. Each of us was widowed and retired, and we had been dating for six months.

After our first date, we were a twosome. We spent every day together, and realized how much we had in common. We played, laughed, and worked on flipping houses together. I was the one who did most of the interior work. Bill did the outside landscaping, and it worked great for the two of us.

My dilemma, when Bill asked me to move in, was that I was going to have to give up my apartment and all the furnishings, with no guarantee it was going to work. But I found myself hopelessly in love with him. And so I agreed to move in, and arrived with only my clothes and computer.

We had been living together for two years when he gave me an engagement ring for Christmas. I was thrilled and wore the ring proudly. We received congratulations constantly, and everyone we knew thought what a perfect couple we made.

We were both ecstatic and, as time wore on, found that almost everything was working for us. We continued to flip houses and enjoy each other's company.

Occasionally, the thought of no security passed through my mind. One night when we were having a beer, he told me never to worry, that his kids loved me as much as he did. He told me I could live in any one of the properties for as long as I wished, "Kind of like a life estate," he told me.

And of course, naive as I was, I believed him. Nothing was in writing—and what a mistake that was. But, you see, I had faith in him and believed him. Never, for one minute, did I think anything would happen to this paradise I had. We ate healthfully and were very careful how we lived. Then, lo and behold, one day he simply dropped dead.

Losing the love of my life destroyed me. I thought, though, that the kids would abide by his wishes, even though they weren't in writing. About a month after he died, they showed up and told me that I had to be gone by the next morning. I was in a state of shock, and couldn't believe it. I was totally unprepared for this happening. I had not even gotten over the sudden death of Bill and now, one month later, my world had collapsed. It was the cruelest thing that had ever happened to me.

I had no choice but to move out. I had no legal standing, even though Bill had already given me a ring and we were engaged. All of our friends had been so very happy for us, and I thought even his kids were. It had appeared that the family had accepted me totally. How wrong I was.

I packed up all my belongings, which consisted of clothes and a computer, and left in my car. I felt as if my heart had been ripped out. I asked myself over and over again, how could I go on? I prayed for an answer and realized that things happen for a reason.

Even now, though, a year later, I am still reeling from the turn of events. To this day I have no answer, but I persevere and have decided to pick myself up and move forward.

It's kind of like making lemonade out of lemons. I will never understand it, but I know now that what happened to me was my own fault. I should have asked for something in writing for protection, and I know Bill would have given it to me. I believe with all my heart that if he could come back, for even an hour, all hell would break loose with his kids.

Is it true that what goes around, comes around? I'll probably never know. But I know in my heart that I was one of the lucky ones, and had that once in a lifetime love. Even though our time together was short, I truly was blessed for having known Bill.

Jack Remembered
by Barbara Walker

*B*OTH OF US DISABLED from back injuries, we met at a pain clinic, flirting over the physical therapy equipment. He had an outgoing personality, bringing me out of a shell imposed by surgeries, pain and self-esteem issues.

After I met Jack, I began to see there were still positives in my life. We shared the same slightly sarcastic, irreverent humor. We would have these spontaneous "Burns and Allen" routines, never knowing in advance who was going to end up being Burns (the smart one) or Allen (the flaky one). Many times, we entertained friends and ourselves.

I loved that Jack was spontaneous in other ways. He would suggest taking off for a drive in the mountains or the desert on a beautiful day, grabbing food to make a picnic. It was always an adventure and I happily went along. One windy day, he came home from the store with kites for each of us. He put them together, bragging about how he was going to get his up the highest; then, off we drove to the beach to fly them. I filmed him, not too steadily, as I laughed so hard, watching him struggle to get that kite up in the air. That was another thing I loved about Jack: he could always laugh at himself.

He would make breakfast in bed for me when it was no special occasion. He took care of me when I was not feeling well, though he had chronic pain, too. Jack made me feel wanted, desirable and sexy. He loved to sit on the bed, watching me put on my make-up.

One day, he told me that he had a special night planned. He suggested I dress in my sexy black outfit. I went all out, make-up, dress, heels. He made me stay in the bedroom while he did his thing in the dining room and kitchen. When he came to get me, he blindfolded me, then walked me into the dining room. When he removed the blindfold, on the table was a lavish dinner he had prepared. The lights were off and beautiful candlelight warmed the room. He helped me to my chair, poured each of us a glass of wine. He put on some soft jazz, then hand-fed me strawberries dipped in chocolate. Dinner was medium rare steaks, baked potatoes with sour cream and artichokes. It was the best dinner I'd ever had, and was such a beautiful night.

My children, all young adults, loved Jack. He joked with them, listened when they had a problem, offered suggestions, but never lectured. We took my first granddaughter on outings, frequently. Jack treated her as if she were his own, playing with her, showing her new things, explaining things to her. He read to her before bed when she spent the night.

I lost Jack in 1994, just months before we were to marry. I didn't see how I could go on without him. But Jack was right. I am stronger than I give myself credit for being. I still hear his voice encouraging me and making me laugh.

Jack gave me the gift of being less fearful of life and the way it can blindside you at times. He showed me that you have to see the humor in life and not take yourself too seriously. Jack showed me that you can carry on when you are feeling you are not capable of doing so.

I became a better version of myself being with Jack, and I became a better human being for having known him.

He will, always, have a place in my heart.

Sinikka
by Gary Winters

WHAT DO YOU SAY to a blind girl
in an after-hours wine bar?
that was the problem facing me
I decided just get going
like a nail drawn to a magnet

I plopped two fingers on her leg
and started rambling on about
nothing really, but she listened
so I said, do you mind my touch?
my hand on her leg after all

how else would I know you're still there?
she said in a low tone. I was sunk
her shape was fit for a statue
back in Finland where she came from
with Notan her black Lab guide dog

she asked me if I wanted to
go home with her and I said yes
nothing more nothing less, just yes
inside her building she said watch
as she took off Notan's harness

the floor was waxed linoleum
Notan took off at a dead run
halfway down the corridor now
he toppled over and then slid
to the end with a silly grin

then he raced back did it again
Sinikka gleeful, me amazed
coming from a late-night venue
to a realm where life's magic
makes bald fun of adversity

in the morning she cooked breakfast—
bacon and eggs over easy
when I casually mentioned this
later on, my old pals were stunned:
how'd she know when the eggs were done?

from that night we were an item
she was my girl and that was that
she took five minutes in the shower
no more, shook out her short loose curls
sparkling electric flaxen hair

and she was ready to go out
at a famous jazz club, she said
they've got a pool table in here
no, I said, then looked back, oh yes
she smiled, said I heard the balls click

Sinikka saw things I didn't
like this is a nice restaurant
she'd say, then smile at my silence
and gently guide my fingers to
the fine embroidered tablecloth

one time she walked up behind me
at an outdoor café table
and put her hand on my shoulder
Sinikka! how did you know it...?
she sniggered with delight—the dog

Sinikka taught me Finnish words:
minä rakastan sinua
it means I love you in Finnish
a spell cast down from vast glaciers
reflected in rivers of ice

time for Sinikka to go back
close out that chapter of her life
Ernest Hemingway said one time
all true stories end in death
and this one is no exception

we talked on the phone every day
I said we'd meet in Italy
a woman would come from Sweden
and bring her to me in Venice.
from there we'd travel on to Greece

then her sister called from Finland:
bad medical report, Big C
Sinikka's dead—she hanged herself
with the dog lead, she said through tears
in a flash it all became clear

in olden times aged Inuit
didn't want to burden the clan
pull the sled over here, nephew
this snowbank's a good place to die
Yrag stops, nods, he understands

minä rakastan sinua
my Scandinavian princess
minä rakastan sinua
Sinikka daughter of Odin
minä rakastan sinua

BRIEF ENCOUNTERS

A brief encounter, especially with someone whose vibrations resonate with your own, can continue to sound an echo in your heart. That fleeting connection, with its sense of inevitability and strong emotional impact, may have changed your life. Its memory, now a permanent part of your story, radiates an almost tangible warmth.

Far From Forgotten
by Diem Kaye

I'VE HEARD SOME PEOPLE SAY that they fell in love at first sight, but dear God, you annoyed the hell out of me at first.

We were at a party, just another bunch of high school kids pretending they were adults, fueling the fantasy with alcohol and smoke. I'd left the noise inside, wandering out to the balcony where I could be left with my own cigarettes and thoughts. I'd been feeling glum, alone in the crowd, and the weather outside was oddly fitting.

The rain was pouring down so hard I didn't even hear your footsteps as you sidled up beside me, plucking the cigarette from my lips. "These things will kill you, cowboy..." Your lips twisted into that crooked grin I'll never forget. You took a single drag, then held it out, "...unless you share."

I grunted and snatched it back, determined not to let a pretty redhead ruin my foul mood. I could still taste your cherry lip balm as I inhaled, blowing the smoke out in the rain and doing my best to avoid looking into your eyes, bright as a cat's and twice as mischievous. In fact, I was doing such a good job of not looking at you I failed to notice you had managed to snatch my cigarette from me again.

"Do you mind?" I asked, wishing I could kill with a glare. Or at least wishing I could come up with something witty enough to make you go away.

Instead, you laughed, that crooked smile on your face the whole time. "Course I don't mind." You puffed away on the cigarette, the ember on the end nowhere near as dazzling as your hair. "Why do you?" You held out the cigarette for me, as if it was yours and you were doing me the favor.

I grabbed it back, knowing I still had half a pack in the pocket of my jeans, but they didn't have the taste of your lips on them. "Because," I said, leaning forward and looking out into the rain, "life sucks and then you die." I didn't want to talk about the things bothering me: work, school, and a bipolar mother I had to practically force-feed her own medication so she wouldn't spend our grocery money on some zany scheme.

Before I knew it, I was holding the cigarette out for you. You took it as if this were to be expected, and shrugged. "That's why you got to find the good times when you can." Your eyes sparkled. "Like now." You grabbed me by the hand, pulling me along. "Let's dance."

I tried to think of a dozen things to say, to explain I couldn't dance, didn't even want to dance. But the best I could murmur was something about not wanting to go inside.

"What makes you think we're going inside?" You put the cigarette back in my lips with a wink. "Get ready."

"Wait, wha?" Before I could say anything more, you had dragged me out into the rain, your laughter as pure as the water cascading down around us.

I can't remember much of the rest of that night. Just the cold fingers of the rain crawling down my back, the softness of your hand and the warmth of your body as we twirled like children in the rain. The thump of my heart rivaling the bass in the house for noise. Your sparkling green eyes. That crooked smile. Those cherry-flavored lips.

But I'll never forget what you taught me that night: that life does suck, and then you die. Despite this, though, or perhaps because of it, you have to grab onto the good moments all the more. You have to fight for them, make them yours, no matter if the sun is shining or the rain is pouring. I'll always remember this.

To this day, whenever I see a redhead with a crooked smile, I feel my heart leap into my throat and hope block out all common sense. Sadly though, it's never you. And whenever this happens, I wish for only one thing: I wish I had asked your name.

A Gift of Love
by B. Gael McCool

THE FIRST TIME I SAW PATRICK I was riding the number 20 bus from downtown to Commercial Drive. There was something in his aura that set him apart from the other passengers. Not that I could actually see his aura, but if I could have, I imagine it would have danced with the blue-white flames of a welding torch. I couldn't help but stare at his astonishing face.

His features were chiseled, his skin warm and lustrous, and his eyes were a penetrating icy blue. A deep scar carved a path from the corner of his left eye down to his jawbone. I was completely overwhelmed by his beauty.

When he got off the bus, I followed him into a neighborhood café and watched him stride toward a table at the back where he joined a group of friends. Completely mesmerized, I could not look away. One of our neighborhood know-it-alls approached me, and I asked him about the man with the amazing face. Moments later I was introduced to Patrick.

I flushed and blurted an apology for staring at him. Patrick looked at me in a kind way and said it was all right. But the next words that escaped my lips were as surprising to me as they were to him. I literally sputtered, "It's just that I've never seen anything so beautiful...may I touch your face?"

His eyes widened in confusion, but then he smiled. I took this as silent assent, then ran my fingertips gently from the edge of his eye down the length of his scar. I felt an inexplicable chemistry between us that was neither romantic nor sexual. Words seemed irrelevant.

There was something ineffable and magical about Patrick. I was humbled by his equanimity. I learned a bit of his history, how he had earned his scar as a junkie inmate, and how he ultimately repaid his karmic debt by counseling drug addicts in prison. He was the most compassionate person I have ever known. To many people, he was a hero, but this wasn't what fascinated me. Patrick had what I can only describe as an illumined presence, and although I only knew him for a short time, that presence altered the course of my life.

A few months after we met, I unexpectedly ran into him downtown. It was 11:45 on a Wednesday morning when he came bounding across the street toward me. He seemed even more oddly beautiful than usual; he was pale and luminous, highly charged, and almost breathless. Although our chance meeting surprised me, Patrick acted as though he had been waiting for me to arrive.

He said, "Thank God you're here," and swept me up in an unusually intimate embrace. Then, standing back for a moment, held me at arm's length and looked deeply into my eyes. His gaze penetrated my soul, and I felt truly loved. Without another word, he dashed across the plaza and disappeared.

The following day I learned that Patrick had died in his apartment shortly after our brief encounter. The official cause of death was *heart failure*. But no one who truly knew Patrick would ever put those two words together in reference to him—that heart never failed him or anyone else.

It took me a while to fully appreciate the gift Patrick had given me in his final greeting, but today it is clear. With wordless equanimity, Patrick saw into me. He acknowledged and accepted my depression, he tipped his hat to my death wish and then, with perfect presence, showed me what it truly meant to be ready for death. With grace, ease and beauty, Patrick simply exited his life—complete with it. He had loved his life, and he left it with an act of love.

His departure left me with my own unexamined life in my hands. I knew then that it would be a waste to leave this world without achieving such luminosity myself.

For the priceless gift of love and life he awakened in me, I will always be grateful. Bless you Patrick, wherever you are.

Palladium Nights
by Beda Kantarjian

*I*N THE SHIFTING VOID between the dancing couples, I saw his searing eyes. Figures on the floor blurred as the face on the far side of the ballroom came into focus. The set ended, and the man began to saunter across the room with the easy grace of a dancer. His eyes never left me.

I looked down at my skirt, buoyant with crinolines, and twisted a tissue between my fingers. "I'm a fool to think he is coming to me," I thought. Then two neatly polished black shoes appeared in front of mine. My gaze lifted to pressed slacks, stylish striped shirt with a tuft of chest hair at the neck. I stared at his chest a moment, then blinked and slowly looked into his face. He was smiling, those liquid eyes crimping at the corners. I must have smiled back.

Without a word, he slipped his arm around my waist. We glided onto the dance floor. Tall and thin, Luis moved like a willow as we joined the crush of dancers at the Palladium on 25-Cent Social Wednesday. The loneliness I felt for my home and family in Puerto Rico was briefly forgotten that night in New York—and on others to follow.

The Arthur Murray Dance Studio gave lessons on Social Wednesdays for those who needed them, but Luis and I did not. With the lightest touch, Luis masterfully guided the two of us as one. I had always loved dancing, but had never danced quite like this. It was as if his prowess had transferred to me. My long legs matched his, step for step. There were times people stood back and gave us the floor. When my coal black hair raked his hand on my waist, it seemed to give him a chill. And if his eyes were demanding, mine were submissive.

My girlfriends and I, all about twenty, sat at the same table each week. Luis began to stand nearby, though he never joined us. We danced only with each other. Each night near closing, he would whisper to the DJ to play "Because of You." His breath ruffled my hair as he sang the words. It was the closest we came to conversation.

More than fifty years later, I can tell you his first name and that he loved to dance—but that is all. I had a theory: he was married and simply loved to dance. He was near thirty, and in the fifties, most men were married by that age.

My best friend had a wilder theory: Luis was a spirit. She would fall into her rapid-fire Spanish, while offering her proof. "We never see him come, or go. He simply appears and disappears. Luis is a spirit. *He's not of this world*," she would say. I could not deny that I had never seen him walk into the ballroom, nor walk out the door, but that was crazy talk.

Then, one night, a fall chill fell on Fifth Avenue. I felt dread in the pit of my stomach as we entered the ballroom. Almost a year of rhythmic connection that needed no words felt suddenly out of reach. Did it ever exist? Of course it did. I would open the doors to the burgeoning sound and Luis would materialize. But he did not.

I continued to go to the Palladium every Wednesday, my eyes darting between the dancers, searching for those intense brown eyes, that ready smile. I never saw them again.

Perhaps my friend is right; perhaps Luis is a spirit, because the man I remember is not one who grows frail and crooked and slow of speech. He's always young, lithe, and melodic and sees the beauty in me, allowing me to glimpse it, too, even now.

Scarlet Begonias
by Beatrice M. Hogg

*H*OW COULD I EVER FORGET a man who wrote a poem about my smile? Even though I have no idea what I did with the poem David wrote almost twenty years ago, I still remember him with fondness. And I will never forget the weekend we spent together in October 1990. That weekend, for the only time in my life, I felt beautiful.

David was a handsome Deadhead who entered my life back in 1984. After discovering the music of the Grateful Dead, I had placed an ad for Deadhead pen pals in "Relix," a magazine devoted mostly to the Dead. Soon, I started to get letters and pictures from Deadheads around the country. But one letter caught my attention.

David was different. Not only did he write about the music, he talked about his life. He told me about his plans and goals for the future. He talked about growing up in a large family outside of Boston.

I started to look forward to his letters. They made my boring life as a welfare caseworker in western Pennsylvania a little less dull. He enclosed a picture with one letter. As I gazed at the photo, I felt as though I knew this mysterious young man with bright blue eyes and a wide smile. I found myself responding in kind, telling him about my life and the things that were important to me. I hoped that one day we would be able to meet in person.

When we started corresponding, David was living in Washington State. In 1986, he decided to return to his hometown. On his way home, he stopped by to visit me. He stayed with me for three days, sleeping on my sofa bed. Even though he was seven years younger than me, we had a lot in common. We spent hours talking, laughing and listening to music. It felt as if we had been friends forever.

Over the years, we kept in touch sporadically, exchanging birthday cards each January and occasional calls and cards throughout the year. After I moved to northern California in 1988, we didn't keep in touch as often. But on March 31, 1990, David called me. For the next few months, we talked frequently and I promised to visit. One day, he called me with a beautiful poem he had written for me. Once I heard the poem about my smile, I knew I would be going to Boston soon. I decided to visit him over the Columbus Day weekend.

The fall foliage was in full color when I arrived in Boston. David met me at the airport, warming my heart with a smile as brilliant as the leaves outside. From the moment I arrived, he lavished me with attention and affection. He made me feel I was special, like a rare and beautiful creature. On our first evening, we sat by a lake on the outskirts of Boston, drinking champagne and watching as the sun set behind the trees. Once again, we talked about our lives, sharing our hopes and dreams.

I never saw David again after that wonderful weekend. Our lives were too different, and we lived too far apart. The last time we talked on the phone was August 9, 1995, the day of Jerry Garcia's death. We were both devastated. But he sounded distant. Somehow, I knew I would never hear from him again.

Recently, I searched my apartment for that poem David wrote, but couldn't find it. I did find a letter from him dated a month after my visit. It reminded me of the joy we found in each other for a brief time. Twenty years later, I still think of that weekend as one of the best of my life.

I hope the last two decades have been kind to him. Wherever he is, I hope he is happy. I know I can never repay him for the happiness he brought into my life. Whenever I think of David, I think of "Scarlet Begonias," one of our favorite Dead songs. "Once in a while, you get shown the light in the strangest of places, if you look at it right…"

City Corners
by Anahi Arana

*F*OUR DAYS were all I had. My sister Anna and I were in the city filming a documentary. A steak dinner with wine started our night, and we then got drinks at Plaza Serrano, where everyone spends their evenings drinking, playing, and finding love.

There he stood with his friend on the brightly lit, bustling corner, passing out flyers for their small theater production. They quickly caught sight of us, two lonely girls zigzagging our way through the streets, happy and laughing and waiting for the next thing to happen. We talked about something, I am not sure what, but we spent more than an hour on that corner talking. He had a pretty, David-like face, and dreamed of being an actor. He knew little about politics, film, or sociology. But he smiled anyway, and had a confidence in everything he said.

I remember he made a stupid word play on my name, so that I somehow became the pretty one, even though I preferred to be just plain. He made me feel more than myself, more than my jeans-and-sweatshirt self, than my straight, unmade-hair and book-in-hand self. With flyers in hand and a plan for the following night, my sister and I sleepily crawled into a taxi that took us home.

I don't quite remember the play, only that it was a comedy and that he was smart, sharp and funny. Afterward, he and Javier were schmoozing with their friends until they finally came to us and said, "So, you came? What do you want to do now?" And it was set. We smiled and kissed on the cheek, then left for the supermarket, where we bought some snacks and a Malbec wine, Argentina's finest.

At his apartment we ordered a pizza and they played us songs. He looked at me while he sang and strummed his guitar lightly and softly, already touching me. His dirty blond curls gave him boyish charm while his tall, lean body gave him the allure of a man. I felt wooed and yet not wooed. I felt that I could leave then, being his friend forever, or stay, maybe never to see him again.

It came time to play: a tickling contest. All I saw was his face. I turned down his first kiss. He swept me away to the kitchen, where he propped me up on the counter. We talked about everything. He told me I had honest eyes. His confidence made me feel his strength. And yet he was innocent like me, even if I was his prey and he the vulture, loving my naive openness.

My sister and Javier left, and I stayed with him. He held me in his lap and kissed me for hours. On the sofa, he took off my clothes and I took off his and we did nothing but kiss and touch. I took a taxi home at daylight.

Between that night and the next, I thought about him and nothing else. When I ate, I felt his hands and I couldn't swallow. When I walked, I felt his warm body and wanted to sink down into the ground. Asleep, I smelled him and heard him, and his voice was like an echo that never died.

Our second date was sweet—we held hands the entire night. It was as if we had known each other since childhood and didn't have to say much to understand.

For our last meeting he came to see me where I was staying with my sister. We listened to music and looked at each other in silence. We kissed at the front door for an hour until he finally left.

In the bedroom, I cried, while my sister eyed me and smiled. Our next stop, visiting our family, filled me with the usual joy, but I was slow in forgetting his face and touch. And, to this day, I still know him to be my first, in so many ways.

Exotic Petal
by Rochelle Potkar

*H*E WAS MUCH YOUNGER—and I was much married. Yet when we first met through an internet social networking site, we did not discuss age or marital status. We just hit it off as friends dabbling in a forum of poetry, introduced as participants.

We started exchanging free verse, poetry of all forms and kinds, subjects and contexts, till finally veering to our favorite topic: love. How precarious are the lines drawn when two people are attempting to write poetry on and about love—and share it with one another?

How thin is this veil?

How do you know if the strapping guy in the profile picture is sharing love poems for your evaluation and critique only—requesting you to be truly objective—or that the substance and hope of love in his poems are not, in some way, meant for you? Or that you, by writing poetry, are not doing so for him in the capacity of receiver and muse?

It got complicated. We didn't know for whom we were writing these love poems. Did the frequency of writing these poems increase because of the sudden surge with which we met each other every day on the net, or was it one of those heavy moments of sheer inspiration that was to befall us in any case?

This boiling and roiling and steaming and simmering had to reach a peak at some point. And it did. We met at a conference for poets, located between each other's towns. The travel distance, and taking away time from our work and families, did not seem to get in the way. But I needed to ask myself what I wanted from such a meeting, such an arrangement. Would I walk the fine line into infidelity? How distant and far, or how warm and cordial would I keep this relationship, now that we were going to meet in person?

I thought I would wait for a time to decide, that I would cross the bridge when it came. But we arrived at the venue of the conference with all those nights of yearning poetry between us, and we flew into a warm hug. I inhaled the smiling scent of his after-shave mist, his body scent and maleness, and told myself that no matter what, I would not allow myself to cross the line, however difficult it got.

You see, the line was so delicate. This was the hardest friction my feet had felt in years, to stick to my ground on the pixel of earth, longitude and latitude intertwining the determined position I took in this equation, while my heart flew around recklessly. It twirled and somersaulted and went through gleeful strides and trapeze rides.

We attended the conference hand in hand, and we kissed in the dark at the end of it. That much I permitted myself before tearing myself from him.

And I am glad. It was a slippery slope—this love. A sense of maddening multitudes. Psychedelic. Dizzy. Whole. Those days after the conference were some of the worst. I could not sleep, eat or concentrate. I stared into open space. I had to read a paragraph five times till it made any sense.

He was a breath of mint fresh air, a feeling of youth and possibility. And I think every human being should be rewarded by falling in love every so often. It keeps one alive. You pay closer attention to yourself. You care for yourself once again, and more.

I allowed us to drift away. It was better that way. But I carry with me the fragrance of this love like neatly drawn-out petals from an exotic plant that I can bring to my face and inhale every once in a while.

Love is the only thing that can truly turn the tide, turn the tables on you, fox you, fool you and your vision and wisdom, and have the last laugh. Love is what can blind you or shake your balance. It is truly a drug, well almost. It made me feel new, ten years younger, for sure.

SOUL MATES

Many people think of a soul mate as the one person they are supposed to be with, a sort of foreordained pairing. And those who have actually found a soul mate often describe a sense of mutual recognition, a familiarity, a kind of intimacy that cannot be accounted for in any other way.

Most of these stories do not use the words "soul mate," but they do share a quality of unaccountable and immediate connection, something that seems to exist the moment the two meet.

A soul mate, however, is not necessarily a life partner. Having met and loved, soul mates, after they part, remain psychically "with" each other in the ether as a sort of support, a lifelong touchstone. A soul mate can provide a way to recognize—in future relationships—the elements truly necessary to nourish and sustain body and soul.

Voices
by Liz Mugavero

I RAN OUT OF GAS in my driveway and he filled my tank.

A love story not born of any particular romantic event other than this: my car, towed. He, a gas station attendant, diagnosed the problem.

My first semester of college, late for class, I still made time to flirt, because I liked his smile. Even though I was a college student cultivating dreams of faraway cities and writing awards, and leaving my mark on the world, and he was a gas station attendant, clearly older than me, I flirted.

I liked his smile.

He asked me to go for coffee. I met him that afternoon. He told me I had nice eyes. I knew he was a bad idea. I still fell.

For the next year, we traveled together through miles of uncharted territory. He had never been with someone so stable, he said. I had never been with someone so adrift, I said. He drank. Did drugs, when he thought I didn't know. He pined for his ex. I loved him. He loved me. We loved each other in the best way we knew how at that moment in our lives. He wanted to be a marine biologist, or a chef. He was unemployed most of the time. He cooked like a fiend. When he finally found a job at a classy restaurant, it closed.

He suffered from epilepsy and didn't take his meds until the seizures came. A family member took pity on him and bought it. He lied a lot—to me, to everyone. He spent time with bad people. I cried a lot. His sisters befriended me. I went to class every day and met people who were more like me, who were academic and educated and going places. But I wanted him.

He drove a ratty station wagon we took to the state forest late at night. I let him drive my car, even though he didn't take his meds. We listened to Air Supply and saw Meatloaf and The Steve Miller Band in concert. He drank.

He took me to a lake in Maine where his family had a cabin. There, I learned to nap during the day. I loved those weekends.

Then he left me. In that moment, I learned more about heartbreak than I would again for a very long time. I really did love him, this baby faced, ne'er-do-well man who couldn't hold a job or move out of his mother's home. I started to get over him. He courted me. Drew pictures of me. Tattooed my name on his arm. Called me "bella." I took him back.

It ended again. For good. I threw myself into graduating. Found someone new.

He had a seizure, this time while driving. Landed in Mass General Hospital. I visited him. We cried together.

He went home. We never spoke again.

One summer day, at another lake, I couldn't stop thinking about him, his lake in Maine, the trips we had taken there. The memories, after blocking them for so long, were so vivid, and I had no idea why.

I went home that night and listened to my answering machine.

"Richard died," his sister's voice told me. "He had a seizure in a boat, on the lake in Maine. He drowned. I'm so sorry."

I went to his wake. He looked the same. My name was tattooed on his arm, still. I heard he dated someone briefly before he died. I wondered what she thought of that tattoo.

Childishly, I pictured him in a grave, his skin somehow preserved, that tattoo still linking us long after he had left.

His mother cremated him and put the urn in her living room.

But he visits me sometimes, as he did that day he showed me the lake in Maine—when he told me what happened to him.

Had he lived, I would never have gone back to him. But he's with me now, in the background: a friend, a co-pilot, a guardian angel. He doesn't visit every day. But when he does, I know.

He tells me.

No Sad Goodbyes
by Lynn Radford

*T*HE MOST MEMORABLE LOVE of my life came at a time when I was struggling to define myself as something other than a wife and mother. My creativity had been abandoned in favor of caring for my family. I'd resigned myself to my new reality, never suspecting that another person could show me the way back to myself.

In my twenties, I became fascinated by a man more than twice my age. He was a wounded romantic, a lover of nature, a composer of music and a writer of songs. He was a Vietnam War veteran who saw terrors too numerous to recount. They haunted him endlessly. Sleep was no respite from the torture he suffered.

As tragic a man as he was in those days, I was drawn to his presence. His quiet confidence drew me in and the example of his own creative journey anchored me to his side. I desperately longed to absorb whatever it was that motivated and inspired him. Countless hours I spent at his knee while he wrote song lyrics, played guitar, told stories, cried, and taught me Life Appreciation 101. It was there that I also fell in love with him.

My senses had never been so acute. I'd never felt so alive! I felt free, once again, to expose myself to the naked page. My creativity levels were soaring and I was producing some of my best writing. He taught me to embrace my dreams, honor my voice and give flight to it. It was a valuable lesson.

Our relationship was platonic, but not without the passion of lovers beneath the sheets. Stolen moments were all we had, but they served us well. His cottage in the woods became our refuge as we explored the world and one another. We wanted no more and no less than what the universe spread before us.

Our hikes were filled with a shared appreciation for nature's canvas as it unfolded before us. We drank in flora and fauna, their colors and textures becoming part of us. We delighted in glimpses of rare species and listened as our avian companions serenaded us from on high. Quiet evenings in front of a fire found us sharing a book or writing companionably.

We knew, even as we grew ever closer, that we had no future. We would never marry. As a couple, there would be no happily ever after for us. We didn't talk about it, it was simply an understanding. And so, we enjoyed each other for the moment, living and breathing, sharing and creating.

All good things eventually come to an end, and our season was no exception. Our ending was free from teary goodbyes and broken hearts. He simply returned to his home state of Virginia and I remained a wife and mother. Only...a change had taken place. I was a better version of myself for having experienced him.

For long months, I desperately missed his presence. But gradually, I learned to live without it. As the years passed, I have clung to the memory of our time together. It was a gift of blessing and great spiritual growth. To this day, I am thankful for the deep connection we formed in that brief time when our lives and souls touched.

Recently, I came across my poetry from that period. The last line of "You Alone," says it best; "You, alone, have shown me that to which I was blind; I am ALIVE!"

Something About That Boy
by Nanci Block

WHEN I TELL PEOPLE that I dated the same guy from eighth grade through my freshman year in college, the first question I always get is, "God, why?"

The answer that I consistently give is, "I don't know." And it's the truth. I don't know what made me stay with Scott so long, and I have no idea what made him stay with me. I only know that there was just something about that boy.

On a basic level, even at thirteen, I was ridiculously attracted to Scott. From the very beginning he made my toes tingle and my fingers go numb. All the blood in my body would rush toward my core in his presence; my heart would pound and, for a girl who could chatter away with the best of them, I would lose my words. That initial amazement never went away. It may have paled as time went on, but every time I looked at him, the butterflies took flight. Each time he glanced my way, my body would warm from the center out.

Together, Scott and I had easy conversations and uncomplicated fun. Despite the fact that we had very few common interests, we held each other's fascination. We could talk for hours, and we loved to play together as if we were nothing more than two little kids. I can remember roller-blading and sidewalk chalk, Marco Polo and one-on-one basketball games in his driveway.

During the precarious age when everything you do is open to criticism from your elders and peers, Scott and I never judged one another. When he was outcast for being different, I supported his long hair, his affinity for art and comic books, and his devout following of grunge rock and Kurt Cobain. When I took a whole lot of crap for joining the cheerleading squad, Scott was front and center at every game, cheering me on. For everyone else, Scott and I both had to be someone else: the best friend, the perfect daughter, the responsible teenager, the learned student. With each other, we just were. The world fell away when we were together, and the pressure of being a teenager—yes, being a teenager has its own special set of pressures—lifted.

All of this worked when it was just me and Scott. It was when the rest of the world interfered that we started to fall apart. We had knock-down drag-out fights about how much I loathed Jen Robinson—his best friend who happened to be female. There was his thinning patience that I wouldn't accept her as his friend. And we argued about my friends, and how he seemed to think I became a different, a shallower person around them. We both became suspicious of what the other was doing when we weren't together. We would make a case for independence and time apart, then complain that we weren't making enough time for one another.

On several occasions, Scott and I made the declaration to go our separate ways, dated other people, and attempted to move on. It never worked. On my end, no other guy ever fit right. Conversation was stilted. Kissing was awkward. The element of unadulterated fun was missing. No one else got me. No other guy could make me feel the way Scott did—like slowly melting chocolate. And it was the same for Scott, or so he would always tell me when we reconnected, which we always did. He would smile, and I would forget. I would kiss him, and he would forgive. If we lay in each other's arms long enough, and blocked out the white noise of reality, we could get through anything—except for that one time we didn't.

Even now I smile when I think about him. I shudder to think what would happen if I ever saw him again. Even though I am blissfully married to the man of my dreams, I would be willing to bet that, however involuntarily, I would light up from the inside, begin to tremble and start to melt just a little.

Because there's just something about that boy.

The Australian
by Michelle McAlister

KNOWING THAT THE GIFTS OF TRAVEL are often unplanned and unscripted, I had chosen my destination only the night before. I had resigned myself to fate, having realized that fundamentally this is what I had been wanting all along.

I arrived in Pelekas, a Grecian hilltop town on the island of Corfu, where homes wore stains of passion fruit pink, saffron yellow, and stucco white. Like citizens-on-guard, the homes stood wedged together, backed by an army of dense emerald vegetation.

Out strolling, I spied a fair-haired man lounging in the doorway of a dusty pub. He had a deliberate, languid lean that told me he had nowhere to be. I set out to cross paths with him.

He was Australian, with nothing subtle about him. His voice boomed and twanged with sarcasm and unabashed observations. He was without couth and was opposed to modifying himself to his surroundings—perpetually unapologetic at all times, in all places. Hailing from Adelaide, on the southern lip of his country, he arrived in Greece, tall, lanky and with sandy, unkempt hair. Penniless, the Australian had somehow landed in Greece, now possessing nothing of value except the drink in his hand that he conned from the bartender.

I had discounted him, but then quickly realized that he was grounded and ungrounded at the same time. I watched him stoke the locals, instigating a bar-wide laughing fit. When he finished with the crowd that gathered around him—that's when I, all of a sudden, could no longer recall the life I had lived before him. A glimmer in his eye sparked powerfully familiar; an invisible lure drew us toward each other.

Having banded together with mutual fiery appetites, we linked arms with lemon popsicles in one hand, ice cream cones in the other. Smelling of sticky lemons, we rented a moped and rambled recklessly to red sand beaches. The Australian ran into the sea fully clothed and hurled himself atop a giant wave, losing the moped key on the ocean floor. We waded around in the clear water holding hands, laughing, drawing the Grecian sand between our toes, searching for the golden key, fruitlessly. Finally, we pushed the wet, salty, slippery-handled moped up the beach cliffs back to where we paid our fine for our carefree abandon.

At night, a massive, low-slung orange moon watched over us, while donkeys, goats, horses, dogs and roosters swooned and sung tunes. We, too, swooned, sitting under the eerie orange glow on the balcony of my hotel, drinking wine from the bottle.

"I had a dream last night," the Australian said. "I was locked in a room, afraid. The devil was coming to get me."

Normally upbeat and fearless, the Australian seemed vulnerable for the first time. "Were you trapped?" I asked, taken aback by his serious turn.

"No, I wasn't trapped. I was just waiting. I knew he was coming, and I was scared."

"Then what happened?" I pushed.

"You came through the door. You saved me," he confessed.

The Australian's revelation took me to another place, even forced me there. I had taken him lightly, had chalked up our days to nothing more than a summer of Grecian romance. The Australian left me speechless; I rearranged everything I'd held true.

That night, as the Australian slept far from the home he had fled, I thought back to the moment when I arrived in Pelekas. I was transported to an unknown place, trusting in fate. I thought of the Australian, seeking an escape from his life, trusting in travel to deliver it to him. Before the sun had risen and while the orange moon still hung outside the window, I sat on the edge of the bed, bewitched by the gifts of travel.

I thought of the promises we made, wondering if he'd be able to charm his way across the Atlantic, back to me. Yes. Yes, I thought. I kissed the Australian on the cheek and whispered, "I'll see you in America."

As it turned out, fate continued to have its say. The Australian passed away before he could get to me, but his spirit still caresses the fibers of my memory, bringing him back to life.

A Relatively Innocent Love
by Marcia S. Gaye

OUR MOTHERS WERE BEST FRIENDS. Born only months apart, we were tucked into the same bassinet while they visited over coffee. We even had the same initials. Indeed, since our fathers were related, we had the same last name. I could have become his wife and still been totally me.

Our families were close in heart, but not in distance. As we grew up, we saw each other only occasionally. Yet his blue eyes and dark curly hair caused me to tumble each and every time. When he teased, it was with a smile so guileless that I never felt defensive, never felt the sting like I did from other boys.

He had an insight, an attentive spirit. When he looked at me I knew he saw me, even if only in a glance—and that he understood more about me than I did myself. He spoke slowly, as they do in West Virginia, and with the consideration of a poet, choosing words of significance. His humble manner encouraged my aspirations to know myself and to be aware of my own influence.

During our pre-teen years our families once vacationed together. He watched, bemused, from the deep end of the pool while I tried in vain to learn to swim. Other kids pulled me underwater as a prank. When I emerged, sputtering and spitting, he was gliding through the water, cutting a smooth boundary between them and me, breaking up their line of bedevilment. He did this without looking in my direction for acknowledgment.

Our relationship was like that, an undercurrent from which we would surface to breathe, to gain our bearings and to keep perspective.

We played putt-putt golf and counted my missed strokes as the number of children we would have. I bought long strands of angora yarn to wrap around a charm he hung from my neck, secured discreetly under my blouse.

When we older kids played "seven minutes in heaven," I prayed fervently that he and only he would be my partner. While the other boys practically slobbered with anticipation, he stood aside, aloof. When the two of us entered the closet booth behind the dark curtain, his eyes sparkled with naughtiness, but his smile was shy. We sat quietly until he finally touched my hand, holding it through the long minutes of privacy.

As we became teens, our visits were less frequent, coming as interruptions in the lives we led apart. We would steal moments to rendezvous, taking short walks or claiming a corner of the far yard to look at the night sky. I had only to look into his eyes to feel the mysteries of the world, to know the benevolence of God, to feel gravity spin upside down, and to know the complete warmth of utter safety.

Music vibrated through him. He sang from his heart, voicing hymns and prayers. His praise had no hesitation; his pure love for the Lord glowed openly on his face. I bore a similar glow, but I was not so singularly minded. I concentrated on disguising emotion that would have required a response which could not be declared.

When I went away to high school, he wrote letters warning me of the drug culture I would encounter, expressing concern, hoping that I would resist that influence and the other temptations that would present themselves. When I began to date, my boyfriends were always West Virginia boys with thick dark hair. Sometimes their eyes were blue, sometimes brown, but never with the sparkle that undid me. I married one of those boys, a brown-eyed one, and changed my name, temporarily becoming someone else until that boy returned me where he'd found me.

Now I see my first love every few years, he with his wife, and me with my true forever husband (who is not a West Virginia boy). We exchange photos of our grown children. He brings a guitar and sings the old songs and some new ones. His smile is confident, and if his blue eyes catch mine unexpectedly, there is a flash of familiar sparkle

Facing the Fall
by Autumn Conley

I CAN STILL REMEMBER his eyes in the dark—like tiny sapphires dancing in the moonlight. It's strange the things you remember about your first love. His strong, gentle touch...his blonde hair wafting across his forehead...the scent of Eternity cologne.

My first love started off as my best friend. He was younger than me, but we had everything in common, as if we were meant to complete each other, and we had fun together. I was naïve to think that it would remain platonic. It didn't.

One evening, over fast food pasta, he simply said, "If I were older..." I was completely thrown. I'd never had a boyfriend before, there was an age gap, and I knew it would not be accepted by our families. But I gave in, and the months that followed were the most heartwarming and heartbreaking of my entire life.

We remained "just friends" in the eyes of everyone around us. But we spent every waking moment together, stealing private ones when we could, daring to flirt and cast wanton glances at each other. We were so close, and had so much in common, that it seemed I had found a piece of myself that I didn't even know had been missing. He woke me up from the shy, dull girl I had been, and I lived. He became my solace, my project, my reason to laugh or cry or feel anything at all.

I am not much of a romantic, and had never really understood why people refer to it as "fallling" in love. But I fell, and I fell hard. We laughed all the time. We knew what the other was thinking, and we did sweet things for each other when no one was looking. We were, as far as I understood it, in secret love. I felt so happy, young, full of life and invincible. I never wanted that feeling to end.

The problem was, it did end—inevitably, painfully, bluntly, and with few answers. It was like being robbed of all your dearest possessions and never finding the thieves. I spent two days sitting in my closet, snuggling the stuffed Dalmatian he won for me, playing "our" songs, staring at his picture, and crying my eyes out. I remember physical pain in the pit of my stomach, as if someone had ripped my insides out. I didn't know what to do the next day—I had forgotten how to live without him.

When I think about it now, I realize we never could have lasted. But he taught me how to love better...how to feel more ...how to live instead of just existing...how to deal with pain...how not to be afraid of falling in love. My past love, for all of its ups and downs, is what gave me the courage to face the fall again and love someone else. I remember it with smiles and tears, which is what love is all about

Something Remembered
by Ariel Hafeman

WILL I EVER COMMIT? I take his hands from around my waist and wrap them into my fingers. In these moments, I am somewhere else. Because there is something that will always be with me, like the imprint of a fossil in stone, something remembered.

I was not a different person then, but I was younger. By the sea he held me, and we fell into a wave where the ocean hit us. He had searched through a cardboard box, tearing through folds of clothing to pull out a dark blue sweater for me. It was wool, thick, with interspersing lines of dark and light blue across. He held it out and gave it to me, never letting me go.

We sat on a boat dock, our legs hanging over the water. It shimmered. It was late, midnight of a young summer so full of life it was seeping like sap from a tree. We were separate from the rest of the party, had stolen away when he took my hand and led me off. Within the light from the house thrown out through the windows, I could see the others as they scattered across the lawn ahead. Their laughter and noise varied, feral and distant. He was the most real thing there.

The dock where we sat rocked gently when we stepped onto it. Light climbed down from the moon onto the surface of the water in white shock that spread like fingers. I gazed into the water as he murmured about his father. He was just a little boy when his father left. He doesn't know the rules anymore, how to be a man. Later, I will find myself in relationships with men who are bad, and I will remember all the goodness of him, how he could not see it. I will see the difference in people; I will remember the sameness in us.

We collected ourselves against each other's lips. We fought against our miseries. We were too young then to know what we had. The summer was too distracted with life to see us beyond itself. Insects filled the air, crickets, frogs, the hush of wind in the trees and the grass. We were hidden as I touched my head to his, leaning into him so that I would never have to leave. We stayed like that until we were broken apart by the night.

How did it take me so many months to touch his hand? Sometimes I think it is harder for us to be near what we really want. Maybe I had to learn what precious means.

Now, years have passed, and I know I am lucky just to have known him, my synonym. In that single second we first met eyes, I knew. After that day, when falseness made me doubt myself, when I questioned who I was, then I had a reason not to let go of me—because I knew, because I remembered.

Sometimes I feel it in new places: midnight, autumn leaves, the curl of vines across a doorway. I look for it, trying to unveil it in paper, drawing it out across the surface with kohl-colored pencils, chalk, etching from the dark corners some sort of paint in shades I have experienced before. He is like water washed down a river that comes back again as rain. What he gave me is not gone or given in rations or parts, but only swells continuously. It is an impression, a perpetual compass to remind me of who I am.

There was a strength in him, a seriousness in his voice that does not allow me to doubt, but only be grateful that it existed, even for just that summer. It was always something bigger than us but still as simple as listening, waiting, like a lion in the shadows and the long grass above swaying, but with everywhere else to explore while it dreams.

That Piece of My Heart
by Lee Ann Sontheimer Murphy

*I*N HIGH SCHOOL, he wore a blue jeans jacket frayed and faded to white. His hair was long enough to flirt with his shirt collar, risque in a small town. The socially acceptable stuck-ups would call him "hippie," but never to his face. They knew better—Ike (named for President Eisenhower) moved with the careless grace of a big cat, and could be just as deadly.

We were both outlanders, strangers from outside the provincial realms of Newton County. That was our common bond, the tie that brought us together and made us friends. Rebels at heart, we were different from the common herd, and from one another. But enough strands of common thread existed to pull us into the eye of the needle together.

My first real kiss, the one where I realized that I was female and he was male, came from Ike. I was thirteen, so young that I had no idea what I was doing. We were buddies until the day in math class when a single strand of my hair fell into my face and he lifted his hand to brush it aside.

Our world narrowed in that moment to a small sphere. Something like electricity jumped from his hand to my face and traveled through me as his fingers caressed the curve of my cheek. Without thought, by some ancient instinct, I reached out to him and touched him. Like iron filings drawn to a magnet, we moved together, heads touching, and he put his lips over mine.

I was lost and I was found. The classroom around me faded into fantasy as I let him kiss me. Like Sleeping Beauty, I felt awakened (although Ike was no prince, just a ragged, rough teenager with too many dreams and not enough money to find them).

I surfaced to find the class united in laughter at Ike and me. I blushed and he got mad. His angry response earned him a trip to the principal's office, where he was well known. My shame and embarrassment were my penance, but the cost was greater.

Ike avoided me for weeks but, after the fuss died down, after our peers forgot, our friendship was restored. Over the next four years we smoked many a forbidden cigarette together, passing the smoke back and forth with camaraderie. We never had a formal date, not the kind where he came to the house and picked me up before my parents' eyes. There were football games, however, where we huddled together against the crisp November cold, or field trips where we shared a single bus seat. A few dances in dim rooms draped with colored streamers, where we hugged and swayed to the music, were the most intimate moments we shared after that kiss.

He met the girl he would marry during our senior year, but our paths had already diverged. I went away to college and he joined Life. And, in time, I married, too.

Three children later, my husband came home to tell me about his new co-worker. It was Ike. He was straight and he had a new lady in his life, this time perhaps the right one. The other guys at the plant couldn't believe they were friends, my man and my old friend, especially after they joked that they had kissed the same woman. Me.

We used to listen to Janis Joplin scream her rage, her pain, her heart: " Take it," she sang, "take another little piece of my heart now, baby..."

They all take a little piece of your heart, the ones you let within your sacred circle, into that inner sanctum. Those little pieces make up a cosmic soul, all parts of the whole, and all part of me. Mine are scattered out across the world, some in the keeping of people I'd rather not think about.

Ike has a piece of my heart and he carries it. "I've always loved her," he told my husband last year. And he does. I read it in his eyes when he looked at me. But he loves his wife more, and he should.

You and Me, Always
by Gergana Chinovska, a. k. a. G. Goldwyn

*T*HE NIGHT BEFORE DEAN LEFT, he kissed me in a different way. It was the most gentle touch on my lips, just for the smallest second, and then he whispered, "Please take care of that heart for me."

I've been over this story about a hundred times in the last week–staring at the empty screen, with nothing coming. It's funny, running out of words, since I have spent the last two years elaborating on this story, trying to figure out all the ways in which loving Dean had changed me. Replaying all of the memories we've had together, trying to find something that would ultimately lead me to some sort of a sophisticated and wise solution that would bring him back into my life.

Now, with me drunk and dizzy, should be the worst moment for writing that story. And yet somehow it's probably the only one possible.

The first word that came to my mind when I met him was NO. He was working with me, and I came to know him quite well over the next few weeks. But that day we met, I knew he liked me—and frankly, I didn't care. My life had no place for him.

Dean was a peculiar guy. He had blondish hair in messy spikes around his face, and watery eyes that looked deep blue in certain light or almost yellow at other times. He had the habit of staring right at you as if that would give him some secret knowledge to help him see inside you.

The first real conversation we had was when he said, "Sometimes you're smiling but you look as if you're going to cry." I stared at him, startled and irritated that all my trying to hide my feelings was not working very well.

When he found a girlfriend, I was happy for him. In fact, I was so happy I teased him until he admitted they were together. I was so happy I kept repeating it until I wasn't happy anymore.

When I started talking to him every hour, going for dinners and walks, and finding him for a hug every time I needed one, I should have realized that we had become more than friends. When he kissed me for the first time, I was so happy I could accept the fact that he was with someone else. I assumed he was going to break up with her. When I understood he wasn't, I was already in far too deep.

He was nothing I wanted, and everything I needed. I loved every moment we were together. He knew how to make me laugh when I wanted to cry. When I was with him, he looked at me as if I were the most beautiful woman in the world, at least the most beautiful for him. He taught me how to live when I wanted to give up.

We sneaked small moments at work to be together. Every moment was different, special, unexpected. Every moment was like a last one. When we were together, there were no rules, no expectations, no problems, nothing but me and him. He made me who I am and yet somehow, here I am, two years later—I look better than I did then, and I am still an artist. Here I am, still the same, without him.

I knew if Dean ever needed me for anything, I would do it, regardless. I knew if he would give me one chance to be with him, I would give up all I was, everyone I knew and all I had worked for—just for that one chance.

Loving Dean was the first time in my life I had put someone else's happiness before my own. If now that happiness has excluded me, loving Dean was still worth it, even for the small time it lasted.

We met like fireworks in the sky and the world exploded, blooming and changing. The fact that we ended up scattered to different places in the world, leading completely different lives, didn't change the truth. I had loved.

And now I have finally owned up to my promise, letting myself be happy without him—and be happy for him.

I had loved, and that would never change.

Annabel Lee
by Danielle Abbatiello

When **I met Bobby**, who I affectionately referred to as My Bobby—ironically taking possession of something that I would never actually own—he was a teenager. I was his slightly older boss, working summers at a concession stand at the beach. Upon meeting him, I instantly found this young man charming, silly and funny, and very intelligent. He made me laugh. But mostly, he made me feel special. My Bobby had this way of making everyone he met and interacted with feel special.

I knew from the beginning that I wasn't the only one. All right—I wasn't the only female that he made feel special. But as I sit here and write this, I am sure that the connection we shared was unlike any other relationship that either of us had shared with anyone else in the world. In fact, some of his friends, who also worked for me and didn't particularly like me, gave My Bobby a lot of grief over his relationship with me, and over the affection that he obviously had for me.

Still, My Bobby never kowtowed to his friends. Instead, he agreed to attend the wedding of one of my best friends with me. This wedding would become our one and only "date," the attendance of which was highly discussed by those we worked with, who speculated what was going to happen.

Truth is, and at the time both of us were evasive about what had happened, we shared a singular and spectacular kiss. Ours was the type of kiss where time stopped in order for us to capture every second. Even as I close my eyes now, I can see his hand reaching out, touching my chin, pulling me closer. I can see him leaning in and, in what I can only describe as the purest moment of bliss that I'd ever experienced, I felt his soft, red lips touching mine. I can't say that our shared kiss was a romantic kiss. But what I can say is that our souls touched and that, for the rest of my life, I will forever feel connected to My Bobby, and know that someone, somewhere, sometime, truly loved me.

Though I've kissed other men since then, and though I've been in love and thought I've been loved by others since then, I have never felt that soul connection with anyone other than My Bobby. I often wonder if that means I haven't really loved these other men, or maybe they never really loved me. But why else would I feel this soul connection?

Then I think that maybe the connection My Bobby and I shared was strengthened by our lack of romantic fulfillment. Perhaps My Bobby is so dear to me because the memories of him intertwine with a time in my life that seems so long ago and idealized, like a pleasant dream of people and places and un-adulterated happiness. Whatever it is, Bobby holds a special place in my heart that I fear no one will ever match or live up to. Thus far, he remains my dearest and deepest love.

I no longer speak with My Bobby. We lost touch several years ago. I often think about him, hoping that he is well and happy and making some woman feel as special as he once made me feel. I'm sure he is. I'm confident that he has a wonderfully successful life, with a beautiful wife and lovely children. I smile when I think about him.

As for me, I teach English. Every semester I have my students read Edgar Allan Poe's poem "Annabel Lee." I read it for the first time when I was in my junior year of high school, and I was always attracted to the imagery of the poem. It takes place "in a kingdom by the sea" and speaks of "a love that was more than love." Every time I read the poem, I am transported back to the period of my life where My Bobby was to me what Annabel Lee was to the poet in the poem, and I know that nothing "can ever dissever my soul from the soul of the beautiful Annabel Lee."

The Summer of '62
by Jim Landis

MOST DAYS ARE RATHER UNREMARKABLE, nothing special, nothing to get excited about. But occasionally something special *does* occur, and that day is etched in your memory forever. Your life is changed forever. I experienced one of those life-changing days in the summer of '62.

I was on assignment at an Air Force Base in Lincoln, Nebraska, a systems engineer sent out to Atlas Missile bases to assist with base activation programs. When in Lincoln, I always stayed at the Holiday Inn; I found it clean, comfortable, well staffed, with a very good restaurant and a large pool. It was at that pool that my life changed forever.

I was walking along pool-side, wearing swim trunks, with a towel around my neck and a cup of soda in my hand. I noticed a gorgeous blonde woman reclining in a chaise lounge. She was wearing a straw hat with a very large brim. As I approached, she gave me a slight smile. I kept walking, but couldn't take my eyes off her. As I passed her, I turned my head, looked back, and walked right off the edge and into the pool. When I bobbed to the surface (clutching my cup of now chlorinated soda) she was laughing.

She leaned toward me and said, in her very British accent, "Are you part of the entertainment here at the hotel?"

I replied, "Act One, Scene One!"

"I'm Peggy." She offered her towel.

"I'm Jim." I dried off, and we started to talk.

We talked, and talked—and talked. Peggy told me that she was from Oldham, Lancashire, England. I told her I was from the Bronx. She laughed, thought that was funny, then asked, "Is the Bronx a real place?"

I answered, "Yes. The Bronx is a real place—and it is also 'unreal.'"

We kept talking. I called the missile site and told them I would not be on the complex that day, and they should call me only in an emergency. We talked for more than five hours. I knew, by then, that I wanted this woman *in* my life—for the *rest* of my life.

After dinner that evening, we returned to the hotel and to my room. We held each other for the first time, and in that moment I was overwhelmed by feelings of love, peace, joy, and contentment, the likes of which I had never experienced before—nor since.

We told each other everything about our lives: the good, the bad, the happy, the sad, the joys, the miseries, the sweet dreams, the nightmares, our failed marriages, marriages that never should have been. It was an intense catharsis; we laughed and we cried, and we fell asleep holding each other. It was the beginning, the first day of a life together that lasted twenty-six years.

Beating in Time
by Laurie Weed

*H*E'D HAD A FEW DRINKS, and it was too late for the train. When I returned with the bedding, he stood between me and the sofa with his arms folded across his chest. Clowning, he straddled on long legs and sank down like a tripod to look directly into my face. "I want to kiss you," he said, "but sadly, I'm no longer allowed." His playful tone was tinged with longing.

"Your loss." I replied lightly, stepping around him. I floated a sheet over the sofa cushions, then offered him a pillow and a daffodil-colored blanket.

"Thanks," he said, taking the bedding from my hands.

In one circular motion, he tossed it carelessly behind him, grabbed me by the hips and rolled backward onto the sofa, tucking me into his chest like a football. He was so much bigger; he easily contained me in one arm and draped the yellow blanket around us with the other. We hadn't been physically close in years, but he folded himself around me, fitting to me as if we'd been cast together in bronze, or entwined in the womb. His cheek nestled against my ear and, swaddled to his solid body, I relaxed like a cat. He would talk until we both fell asleep, hypnotized by his voice.

Fully clothed and half-dreaming, I drifted, imagining the salted-honey elixir of his skin on my tongue. I felt his hair—that great animal mane he had long since chopped off—falling around me in waves of toasted barley. As always, when we stepped into our shared orbit, a new universe opened, and the Earth dropped away, frozen in time until our return. There was no one else here with us; there never could be.

STAR-CROSSED
LOVERS

Like Romeo and Juliet, some lovers—or potential sweethearts—just seem to have the stars against them. But even if no one dies, circumstances, sometimes dramatic, sometimes not, can create an insurmountable obstacle. Having found the possibility of true love, these pairs then find that their dreams of a future together have been swept away.

No matter how deeply these lovers care for each other, outside forces have conspired to orchestrate an end to all they have worked and hoped for. They are left with an unsettling sense of "if only things had been different."

One Unusually Warm Winter
by Daniel Mullen

W**HEN I THINK OF CHRISTIE,** my mind grabs a hot cup of coffee, settles into an overstuffed chair and stares out the window at slowly falling snow. Christie wasn't my first love; she wasn't my last love, either. She is, however, the one about whom I still write poetry, stories, and songs that no voice will ever sing.

Her memory I keep locked away; she's mine. Like holding a favorite blanket in my child-like hand, I long feared that if I shared her with the world, she would vanish from my mind and heart forever.

I had known her years before. Though she was young, she already stood a head above the other girls. She had brown hair that tumbled like a waterfall down to her shoulders, and a smile that could wake a man from a coma. She had yet to grow into the woman I would meet again a decade later.

Our interactions then were innocent, confined to Bible studies after school and late-night chats with friends at the twenty-four hour diner downtown. She always left a tip, though the waitresses would simply leave a pot of coffee at the table. I wondered what it would be like to be alone with her, without our friends guiding the conversation. If my heart hadn't been devoted to following God, I might have pursued a deeper understanding of "Christie."

As we both stepped through the heavy wooden door of adult-hood at the end of the hallowed halls of secondary education, she traveled to the Far East in search of peace. I traveled to the Middle East with the Army to enforce peace. Both missions failed, but would provide a foundation for conversation ten years later.

By then, divorce had jaded me; children had matured me. This time, I was unfettered emotionally, free to engage her in a relationship. I quickly affirmed my attendance to her birthday party one November. Any chance to catch up with this old friend would kick all other plans to the curb. I found out Christie had a guy waiting for her in China, but that didn't deter me.

I remember us cooking in her mother's kitchen. Every night was a different flavor: fajitas, salmon, curried chicken, hamburgers. We were both so lost in the joy of cooking together that we doubled a recipe once and ended up with enough masala for a large Indian family to flavor their meals for a week. Her mom watched in amazement as we wove around each other, grabbing pans, chopping vegetables, seemingly as one body.

Over Christmas, I went so far as to introduce her to my children and parents. They all thought she was wonderful, funny and gorgeous. I did too. We frosted dozens of cookies and accidentally frosted her backside. My daughter howled as Christie stood up and displayed the new yellow and blue accents on her black, skin-tight jeans. She took it in stride, though, laughing along with the rest of us. That was the moment I knew I loved her.

With the New Year came new experiences. I would pick her up from yoga and listen to her complain about the instructor's incompetence, while trying not to get caught stealing glances at her slightly sweating face and hair.

But my heart sank when a letter came from a school in China. Her teaching position would be available that May. She was ecstatic—until she saw the sadness in my eyes.

We promised to make the most of the couple of months we had left together. I cautiously agreed to the plan, but knew I was hurtling headlong into heartache. On Valentine's Day we threw dietary caution to the wind and ate pizza with wine while watching a movie.

The big day arrived, and I almost stayed away. Our good-bye lasted all day, save for momentary interruptions for insignificant activities like eating and talking. At 11:30 that night, I held her in my arms for the last time. She cried into my chest and I cried into her hair. She smelled like a winter's worth of memories—and flowers.

How One Wrong Number Changed My Life
by Adna Jahic

I REMEMBER HIS SKY-BLUE EYES and his curly brown hair. It was a warm summer's day, the day I had to leave town because my dad found a better job in the UK. I gave Andrej our future phone number and he promised to call.

"Don't forget me," I said.

"I'll remember," he said, and gave me a memorable kiss on my lips.

We were twelve.

After two years, I was still wondering why he never called. *Maybe he did forget you,* I thought. But I got my answer ten years later, when I went back to visit my grandmother.

There was a place where Andrej and I used to hang out when we were kids, a cliff by the sea. We used to play UNO cards there, talk about what we were going to do the next day, or just sit there and enjoy the silence. We often spoke with no words.

During that visit I was on the same cliff, for the first time alone. I was just sitting there, thinking of my childhood — thinking of Andrej and how he might look now. Then a guy came and sat down next to me.

"I didn't know this place is so attractive to others too. Do you mind if I sit here?"

Then he smiled. At that moment I realised who this guy was. I would never forget his smile. People change, but their smile is always the same. His beauty mark under his right eye just confirmed it. *It is him,* I thought. He didn't know who I was.

"Do you come here a lot?" he asked. " I mean, I never saw you here before, and I'm up here every day. You look so familiar."

"It's my first time after ten years," I said with a broken voice.

He looked at me for a few seconds with a question on his face.

"What is your name?" he asked with a broken voice too.

I couldn't hold my tears anymore. Even after so many years I felt that I loved him. And even after ten years he could still understand my silence.

I felt his fingers moving my hair from my face to place it behind my ear. That is where I have my mole. He stood up, so I got up too. Then he hugged me.

After a couple of minutes of silence, with me in his arms, feeling his chest rising as he breathed in and out, I asked him why he never called. He said that the number I gave him did not exist. I thought he was lying. But he pulled out an old piece of paper and I recognized my handwriting. It was the number I gave him. One number was wrong. *So it was all my fault.* Today I think that it was meant to be like that.

Six months later we were still truly, madly, deeply in love. We still played UNO cards, went to our cliff every Friday to drink wine. We visited his parents every Monday and Thursday when we got our own apartment. We never fought and I felt like the luckiest woman alive. We just loved spending every single minute together.

Sounds perfect, ha? So, how did he become my past love? In the worst way. One afternoon he went to buy some wine for dinner. He never came back. An hour after he left, his mother called me to tell the terrible news: "He was driving too fast and lost control over his car. They say he died immediately." On that day, a part of me died with him.

His mother gave me all the things he had with him that day. There was an engagement ring with our names on it. It was the toughest year of my life.

Today, I think of him with love and pain, with laughter and tears. These events taught me some things. The most important thing: you never know what tomorrow will bring or take away from you. We enjoyed every day as if it were our last.

To love someone that much...again...I think I will wait for a long time for this to happen. Maybe I have a lot of days still in front of me. Without him, yes, but with the most beautiful and painful memory of him.

I Hope She Found Her Way
by Brian Greene

*M*Y MOST SIGNIFICANT past love was Susan, who I fell for when she and I were both in the ninth grade. Susan was tall, blond, and pretty, and she was an honor roll student and a cheerleader. But unlike most of the cheerleaders she was no snob. Susan was humble, self-effacing, awkward, and incredibly kind and gentle.

I first asked Susan to "go" with me shortly after the beginning of the school year. We quickly became nearly inseparable, and got closer and closer as the year went on. She was named runner-up in the Homecoming Queen contest at our junior high school. After the Homecoming football game and the halftime pageant, the Queen, the other runner-up, and their two boyfriends—all of them vacuous, elitist types—were going out to an expensive steak and seafood restaurant. I figured we had to go, but Susan surprised me by telling them we had other plans; and she and I, along with her mother, went to Pizza Hut and had the most wonderful time. Susan and I held hands under the table the whole time. If I didn't already love her before that day, I fell hard for her then.

Susan's mother, who was a sweet and generous person, died suddenly. Susan was initially brave and optimistic in handling her mother's death. She was almost *too* together about it. I kept wanting her to break down so I could be there for her, and so that she and I could share the pain. But Susan kept smiling and doing well at school, kept wanting us to just sit on her family's couch and hold hands and kiss.

The first sign Susan showed that her mother's death was finally getting to her was when she went to a slumber party with several other girls one Friday night. One of the girls called me at about ten o'clock and told me I needed to come and talk to Susan, that she was a mess. When I got to the house I found Susan in a room by herself, sobbing and saying that her mom's death was her fault. When I got her to calm down a little, she told me something shocking which she had been withholding from me up to this point: on her death bed, her mother told Susan that her dad was not her real father.

Now I was really going to be strong for Susan, and hold her up during this impossible time. But she didn't let me. She changed, and after that I couldn't connect with her anymore. She met a wild girl who was adopted, and started drinking and doing drugs with her. Susan told me once, "She can understand me in a way you can't, because she doesn't have any real parents, either." I told Susan that didn't matter, that I would always understand her, because I loved her. But she was moving away from me.

At one point I told her she had to choose between her new friend and me. When she said she couldn't make that choice, I told her she just did.

After our break-up, I saw Susan just one more time, the night before she, her dad, and his new wife (he remarried just months after Susan's mom died, and his new wife was a horrible woman, mean-spirited and domineering) moved to South Carolina. Susan called me that night and asked me if I wanted to come over and say goodbye to her.

We sat on their front porch and lightly held hands. Her wild friend had run away with a boyfriend by then, and Susan seemed to have calmed down and gotten back to being herself. At one point I cried and told her, "If you don't want to go to South Carolina you don't have to. You can stay with me, I'll take care of you." Susan squeezed my hand and said, "I have to go. I have to go there and find a way to be happy."

I hope she did.

Where the Streets Have No Name
by Libby Cudmore

*N*ICHOLAS WAS A KNIGHT in slightly dented armor. At first glance, he seemed impervious to damage; he laughed easily and always seemed to have a good time. Look a little higher than the smile, deep into the forests of his eyes, and there was a pain there, a frustration no one ever questioned. It was wanting to ask that question that drew me to him.

One night, after rehearsals for *A Midsummer Night's Dream*, I invited him out to my favorite after-hours spot, a playground. We talked about the play. We talked about ice cream. We talked about movies we loved when we were kids.

As I unraveled his layers, I realized he was unveiling mine. I told him about the boyfriend who had recently dumped me in favor of spending more time playing video games. He told me about his girlfriend, Sarah, who never let him have any fun — they couldn't go dancing because she felt fat; she wouldn't see action movies because the violence made her squeamish. He joked that she'd kill him if she found out he was out with another woman, but admitted that the pleasure far outweighed the threat. We sat on the swings until midnight, then drove home with U2's "Where the Streets Have No Name" on the radio. I felt as though I were flying, the stars swirling past us, the rhythm of the song pounding out the rhythm of the road.

The playground time became our nightly ritual, and it seemed as though whenever we got in the car, that same song came on the radio. Nicholas went home on weekends to visit Sarah, and I found myself counting the hours until he came back. Every Sunday he returned to me with no life in his eyes. But after some ice cream and a long chat about nothing in particular, he hugged me goodnight and left with a grin.

One night it rained, so I invited him back to my dorm to watch a movie. We fell asleep on my bed, and when I awoke I realized we'd stretched out on our sides, his arms enfolding me. We were close enough to kiss and his lips looked so inviting. For the first time since I'd met him, I found myself envying Sarah. Watching him sleep, I couldn't understand how she could treat him with anything less than adoration. He was so sweet, so wonderful, so kind and thoughtful, he deserved someone who appreciated all he gave. Lying there beside him, I confronted the feeling that, girlfriend or not, I was in love with him.

"I love you," he murmured.

His eyes were still closed. Was he dreaming, and if so, of whom? He drifted awake and we examined each other for a moment, wondering if the words hovering between us could be spoken again.

"I love you," he repeated.

I felt as though a gate had opened. Finally, I could say the words in my heart! "I love you too."

He leaned in and pressed his warm lips to mine. Our first kiss seemed almost unreal, so I went in for a second, just to be sure I wasn't dreaming. We kissed for the rest of the morning, for the rest of the week. When he left on Friday, he said he would come back without the chain around his heart. I counted the seconds until he came back to me.

He told Sarah they were through. She cried and begged him back, exploiting his gentle nature, insisting she'd die if he left her. He believed her. When I went to kiss him, he put his fingers to my lips and told me the bad news. "I love you," he said. "But I have to be with her. I'm sorry." We finished the play and the rest of the semester in an awkward silence, and parted ways for the summer.

It took me a long time to realize we weren't meant to be together. I married a man I met in college. Nicholas married Sarah. Even now, when I hear our song, I think of him, the soaring feeling of pavement beneath the wheels of his car, the wind across my outstretched hand, the sensation that, for one moment, we tore down the walls around our hearts and built something beautiful in their place.

The Affair
by Marian Lane

Was the affair a part of the insanity surrounding me, or the sanity that saved me? My marriage was slowly being ripped apart by alcohol and drugs.

When love burst upon my consciousness, I was not prepared for its impact. Words are limiting, but there seemed no limit to our expressions of love. How does one describe the moment, so auspicious, that will change a lifetime?

I was managing a Christian thrift store and enjoying the kaleidoscope of people passing through our doors. He stood there, in deep thought, inspecting a couch. He turned and looked at me—the intensity of his eyes piercing mine. It was like an electrical surge, warming my body, leaving me trembling, knees wobbly and weak, my hand so sweaty it stuck to the ticket I was writing for his purchase of the couch. His smile was inviting as he asked me to have lunch with him. The emotions and sensations his presence caused were a relief from the chaos I'd been experiencing, and I began to relax.

I felt excited and comfortable in this new relationship. It never occurred to me that our openly seeing each other would be viewed as something to be hidden. But the store committee, hearing rumors, felt compelled to ask for my resignation. "Why couldn't you have been more discreet, Marian?" Would being discreet have made our relationship right? We were both married. Maybe it was wrong. But I was drawn to Jack, felt loved and accepted. Our intimacy was beautiful and liberating, an ultimate act of release I had never before experienced.

Jack opened a new world for me. He taught me to fish. On my first try, I whipped the line out into Nylan Lake. I felt the hook catch on something solid. "It's a whopper!" he said. It was a ten pound, thirty-inch brown trout. Fisherman marveled at its size, congratulating me.

Another first was skiing. After I had practiced on the "dope slope," he said, "You're ready for the 'OH MY GOD.'" We got off the lift at the top of the mountain. I looked down, stunned and frightened, my stomach in knots, and shouted, "Oh...my...God!" Falling many times, I finally plowed into a snowbank at the bottom. Skiing was not for me, but through the fright, what exhilaration!

We had a honeymoon type of weekend at Fairmont Hot Springs Resort. It was winter and snowing. We changed into swimsuits and played like children, throwing snowballs at each other and diving in and out of the heated pool to keep warm. That evening, we dressed for a candlelight dinner, he in a suit, I in a long skirt with a red, off-the-shoulder blouse, but barefoot. "You delight me, Nice Lady."

Sunday morning, Jack went out to warm up the car and found all four tires were slashed. "What will I tell my husband, Jack?"

Driving home, we created scenarios to try to explain the tire incident, scenarios so preposterous we began laughing at my predicament. I needn't have worried about Bill's reaction. He said nothing. I believed then that he wanted out of our marriage.

The day of my appointment with the divorce attorney, Jack laid a bouquet of apple blossoms in my arms, saying, "Go for it, Nice Lady."

Returning home from a weekend visit with my parents, and leafing through the "Tribune," I saw a picture of Jack in the obituaries. He had died of a heart attack. Shocked, I rushed to the mortuary. I had to see him. His wife had prepared Jack for burial in the brown leisure suit I had made for him.

I attended his funeral service and stood among the crowd at the cemetery. Alone, I watched as they lowered his coffin into the ground, covering it with dirt and new-fallen snow.

I never remarried. The impact of this love of only two years continues to evoke emotions of love and laughter, excitement and happiness. I have yet to shed a tear over his death.

This love affair happened in 1979. I am now eighty-three. The memory of that magical love, so long ago, has endured.

The Love I'll Never Forget
by Kathryn Radeff

I FIRST SAW ANDY on a cool and rainy November night. I had just finished Thanksgiving dinner with my family when my girlfriend called and asked me to meet her in a restaurant. I was tired and not really interested in going out, but she talked me into it. We were carrying on a conversation when I spotted him sitting at a table. He was dark, mysterious and absolutely gorgeous; I couldn't take my eyes off him. He smiled as our eyes met, and I found myself feeling heat in my face and stammering a hello when he walked over to our table,.

As we talked he said, "I just moved back to the area to help my brother fix up a restaurant on the lake. We plan on opening before summer."

"I work in a restaurant," I laughed. "If you need help, I'm a good waitress."

At first self-conscious and tongue-tied, I was soon talking with him in a way I had never known. Before long, we were seeing each other often. We'd meet at the movies, and on spring days stroll along the lake's boardwalk, or in the summer lie on a blanket at the beach.

I was a summer person. I loved sunsets. We'd always stop to watch the sun go down, changing the color of the lake from blue to purple to black. Every summer seemed better than the last one. The sunsets became more spectacular and my time with him more precious.

Some nights, the beautiful moonlight lay across the water, connecting the shore to the horizon. He asked, "Where would it take us if we could walk on it?"

"Wherever we want to go."

"Where would you want to go?"

"I don't know, but I'd want to go with you."

Other days, we sat in my apartment listening to songs of the early 1970's that seemed to speak directly to us. I can still remember our conversations, and how his mere presence excited me.

I had known other guys, even had a high school sweetheart. But what I felt for them couldn't compare. He was my first and only true love. I was consumed with him, a sensation I had never felt before. My heart still jumps whenever I think of him.

A few years later, a tragedy struck his family and he needed time to accept his loss. After that, he was never the same, and we drifted apart.

Twenty years later, we ran into each other. He was married and had two children.

I gazed at his handsome face. He still touched my heart. "You were the only girl that really got to me," he said. "I loved you so much. I was young and foolish to let you go."

I couldn't talk. Not through the tears.

"Why didn't you ever tell me that?" I asked.

"I was never good with words. You know that."

"Yes, I remember, a man of few words. But the little things you did made me happy!"

Sometimes I think about how time sweeps us along and puts us in a place where we're faced with different roads, knowing we have to take one or another. We make choices, choosing one life, leaving behind other lives we could have lived, full of perhaps different passions and joys.

After he left, and I was alone, I thought that if his heart had been ready, or the timing had been different, we could have had a beautiful life together. After all, he was my only true love.

A True Test of Love
by Lori A. Nason

FROM THE MOMENT WE FIRST MET, I knew we were meant to be together. He was everything I had ever wanted in a man; he was kind, caring, compassionate, and we shared many similar interests. For the first couple of months we dated, we were almost inseparable. And, when we were not together, we spent endless hours talking on the phone, not because we had anything to say, but just to hear the sound of each other's voice. He made me feel so safe and secure, as though nothing bad could ever happen to me as long as he was by my side. But that all came to an end, shortly after my life was struck by tragedy.

I had finally found true happiness, and in a matter of seconds it was taken away. It was going to be our first night apart, and I decided to go out with a friend. I never made it home that night. I was struck, and nearly killed, by a drunk driver. Weeks later, I woke up and found myself in a hospital bed, covered in cuts, bruises and bandages. I had tubes coming from every part of my body. I was scared and in pain, but when I looked across the room, there he was.

The nurses told me he had been there every day, talking to me and caressing me, hoping to get a response. But I just laid there, lifeless. He looked at me and told me I was beautiful, but I knew I wasn't looking too good. He told me he loved me, and that we would somehow get through this together. We had a long and difficult road ahead of us, but I could survive almost anything as long as I had his love and support.

I remained in the hospital until I was eventually transferred to a rehabilitation facility, where I'd learn to walk again. He visited me every day, and assured me that I was going to be all right. It was there, in the rehab facility, that he asked me to marry him. Even with the unbearable pain I was in, it was still the happiest moment of my life.

Once the feeding tube was removed, and I was able to eat solid food again, he never showed up for a visit empty handed. He would bring me all of my favorite foods, and he always knew exactly how I liked them prepared. He remembered that I don't like pickles on my burgers, and that I like lots of garlic on my pizza. He knew my favorite drink was a Starbuck's Vinte Café Vanilla Frappaccino.

One day, he showed up for a visit, hiding something behind his back that he didn't want me to see. He asked me to close my eyes, and then slipped a large plastic bracelet over my hand. Written in beads it said, "Aaron loves Lori." To me that was the most special gift I have ever received. It was ugly and gaudy, but it meant the world to me, because he took the time to make it especially for me. All of my life, I thought I knew what love was, but until I met him, those three little words (I love you) were just empty words, void of any meaning.

When I finally returned home, our relationship started to change. Besides working and going to school, he now had the added responsibility of taking care of me. He would help me shower, clean my wounds, take me to doctor appointments, and do all of my cooking, cleaning and errands. I felt guilty for relying on him so much. I knew it was hard on him, and I could see he was under a lot of stress. I wondered how much longer he'd be able to take it. And, unfortunately, it wasn't much longer, only three months. I was heartbroken when he left me, but I can also understand why he did, and I am still grateful for everything that he did for me.

Gleam and Glow
by Janine Harrison

SOMEHOW PAUL AND I MANAGED to spend the night we met alone in a dorm at a Lutheran youth convention at Kenosha's Carthage College. The next day friends nicknamed him "Gleam" and me "Glow." We were inseparable until the trip ended.

It wasn't that we were basking in sexual afterglow; it was that we had sat together, holding hands, exchanging our lifetimes, our spirits equal. Clear blue eyes tangoing warmth and intelligence. Arm-in-arm we watched dawn break through a sable sky over the lake, and then savored our first kiss. He was, and I was almost, sixteen. We said our good-byes on the beach, hugging, caressing, promising.

Paul called the next day.

We lived fifty miles apart—he, in wholesome Wheaton, and I, in rundown Riverdale, Illinois. We exchanged a lot of love letters. Even today, in a cedar cupboard, resides my "Paul Box." Although I never open it, it contains every sweet word he wrote.

We met next for a luncheon cruise along Lake Michigan's shoreline. Sun shone in the sky and in our hearts, which his father captured in a photograph.

Just after Paul's first visit to Riverdale two months' later, my father went into the hospital. He died three days later. Paul stood by my side through the funeral. What he couldn't know was that my father was an alcoholic and that we had never come to any resolution. At first after he died, I was elated. With him gone, all discipline, all fear died. My grades shot upward. I felt truly pretty; danced for my high school dance group, the T-Ettes; took mom grocery shopping; cooked dinners; dotted I's, crossed T's, aimed for perfection.

Almost everything about Paul's life seemed a storybook. His spacious, white-sided home on a tree-lined street, picturesque; the mural of a waterfall amid a forest covering his bedroom wall, quaint. His sister Brenda, spiritual, giving, seemed faultless; his mom was gracious and kind. I didn't want him to know how ashamed I felt of my life, so I tried to be twenty-four-seven wonderful and never spoke honestly. He was, after all, a prince. What if I turned into a frog? What I didn't realize was that because I couldn't confide in him, neither could he in me—and his life wasn't as unproblematic as it appeared.

For homecoming, he watched as, in 1920's style ivory fringe body suits and ballet slippers, we T-Ettes performed "All that Jazz." Afterward, Paul, in his suit, and I, in my mini-dress and stilettos, danced—him occasionally swinging me under each arm.

In December, I popped out of his coat closet, yelling, "Happy birthday!"

He gave me a gold heart necklace with a diamond for Christmas.

At one point, Gleam even pinned me to my bedroom floor, asking, "Will you marry me?"

"Yes," answered Glow.

We knew, however, that it would be years away. Still, I would practice signing "Mrs. Paul Allen Schewe, Janine Schewe."

Late winter, I plummeted. All I wanted was to lie in bed. It would take years of overcoming "don't think, don't talk, don't feel," to comprehend the turmoil I felt then. Paul tried, but I remained mute. Worse yet, I needed to feel bad about myself as I had when my father was alive, so I cheated with Lohnny, five miles away, who wore muscle shirts and parachute pants, jumped full beer cans thrown into fires, and took me on my first trip to third base.

Paul found out.

"What we had wasn't even real, Janine!" he argued as we broke up. I couldn't understand.

We dated others for three years, drinking, drifting apart. But when I last saw him, entering junior year, we were beginning to mature.

"I'm going to break up with Kelly," he confided.

I was hopeful.

However, before the semester closed, she was pregnant with what would be their first child. They would marry and have two more.

Looking back at our brilliant blue-eyed innocence, I wouldn't have chosen another first love, or a first kiss, with more ambiance than daybreak. Although I became who I was meant to be, if a parallel universe actually existed, Gleam and Glow would be strolling lakeside arm-in-arm until their sun set.

THE SPACE
MY HEART CIRCLES

Because the focus of Heartscapes is remembrance of loves now past, each of its stories involves some degree of loss. But a few seem to highlight the loss itself, one by offering a loving portrait of what the couple had shared, others by describing a particular experience of the absence of a beloved person.

This void exerts its gravitational attraction, just as the person did. Like a planet that has lost its sun, each heart circles an empty space, finding only the warmth that comes with remembering.

Road Picnic
by MJ Henry

*H*ARVEY WAS THE ONLY MAN I EVER LOVED. As the years went by, our love was tossed and beaten like one of his old trucks. In the midst of all our trials and turmoil, the one thing that was always able to bring us back together was our road picnics.

We always took an old car. When I say old, I mean rust, dents, torn seats...

"Wait! What's that smell?" This was always me talking. A search would ensue until the offending item was found. "Oh Harvey! It's a package of shrimp shoved under the seat. How long has that been there?"

"Don't throw that out. I'm saving that for fishing."

It was all okay though. We always started early, allowing time to either fumigate or choose another vehicle, and there were always plenty of old vehicles to choose from. Harvey was a nut about old cars and trucks. For him, these represented all that was good about his youth. For me, they represented a time for us to be together without fighting or competing.

We dressed comfortably and tossed some blankets and pillows into the car. We took only a few dishes; the fare wouldn't require much. We would pick up food at some little mom and pop store. There the cheeses were fresh, the meat came off a slab, and we could usually find some homemade jerky, baked goods, and let's not forget the homemade root beer.

The picnic usually took place in the car. We would eat as we drove, or if we found a good spot we would sit on a blanket in front of the car or in the bed of the truck. It was nothing to lie down and take a nap in each other's arms, letting the day glide past.

Times were not always happy for Harvey and me. We went through a bitter split and lived apart for a number of years, but we never divorced. Then the day came that he was diagnosed with cancer. In the early days of his diagnosis, nothing changed between us. As time went on and his illness worsened, we drew a little closer.

Each day it became more evident that he was losing his battle with cancer. He began asking me to take him places. Church was difficult. I drove him to church one Sunday evening. It had been a few months and I knew that he had changed. The once vibrant man with thick brown hair was now a feeble soul whose hair, lost from chemo, was coming back white. I heard the whispers as people asked who he was. Someone said, "Is that Harvey?" All I could do was turn my face away from him so he wouldn't see me cry.

One spring day Harvey drove his old truck down the road that led to my house. The bluebonnets were especially lush and beautiful. "MaryJane," he said, "I sure want to go see the bluebonnets. Let's take a road picnic."

I don't think we had been on a road picnic in ten, maybe fifteen years. I wasn't going to refuse him now. We loaded up in his old truck and went looking for one of the mom and pop stores we used to visit. Most were closed, but we found one. We got our meat and cheese and homemade bread and sweets. They didn't have homemade root beer, so we bought A & W. We also got a couple of pounds of homemade jerky. What a feast.

We drove for miles until Harvey saw a spot with a roadside park. The bluebonnets in the field close by were perfect. The air was scented with their fine bouquet. We spread our blanket on top of the table and lay down together. There we spent the day enjoying the flowers and our royal fare of salami and hard cheese with homemade bread.

Harvey died in July of that year. With the exception of the incident at the church, I never cried. It's been thirteen years. And today, with the writing of this piece, I am unable to control my tears. I still love you, Harvey.

My Girl
by Jill Cordover

*T*HE TELEPHONE BILL was the only thing in the mailbox this morning. As I walked back to the house with that old familiar hollow feeling, it distressed me. I thought I was past expecting.

My approach to the mailbox has been increasingly straight-forward and direct as the months have passed since *the* letter. I can casually wait at least an hour past delivery time now. I flip the box open with unconcern and take a thorough look inside, not lingering. When there is nothing there, or when it holds only bills, my mind quickly absorbs itself with the next activity on the morning agenda as I stride back to the house without giving it more than a second thought.

It didn't use to be that way. It used to be that I would ease the box open just a crack to glimpse out of the corner of my eye. If there was a flash of white, I looked away as I gentled the envelope out between two fingers. I would run my fingertips around it, still not looking, as I made my way hesitatingly back to the house, having lost my stride.

Most of the time, a plasticine window or metered stamp dashed my hopes and soured my disposition. But once in a while, my fingers told me they held a letter. I made a mental inventory of those who write letters to me, and those to whom I owed letters, to narrow the possibilities.

Mostly they were from my mother, wonderful letters that I barely read because they weren't from him. I would scan them for the key ideas, making sure that nothing was required of me. Then, disappointed and empty, I'd toss them on the desk.

I was happy to be getting over the morning reflex of pain that colored the course of the day. I was tired from having my life determined by whether or not my former husband, who is now married to someone else, would write me another letter.

He wrote once when I wasn't expecting it, and that's what started all this. Before that, the mailbox meant nothing. Some days I didn't even check it.

His letter was on top. The dear familiar handwriting leapt out at me, reminding me of all the ways it had addressed me in all the years when we were everything to each other, reminding me of all the notes propped on the kitchen table between the salt and the pepper, notes starting with "Dearest Girl," or "Darling Girl," or "My Girl." And I remembered what it was like to be Dearest Girl and Darling Girl and his girl. I held the letter in my hand for a long time.

The Fijian stamp was beautiful, a brightly colored bird in flight against a blue sky and a bluer sea dotted with atolls. The return address was a hotel in Nadi, embossed in the upper left hand corner. I don't remember the name. On the envelope he titled me, "Mrs. Jill Cordover." I read the message in the "Mrs." and a warm flood of pleasure surged through me.

Sitting on the back step with my finger under the flap of the envelope, I opened the letter gently, trying not to tear it. The paper crackled as I smoothed out the folds in my lap. There were four pages of hand-written onionskin.

I don't remember a single one of the written words. If I read them another hundred times I still wouldn't remember them — because he touched me from between the lines, cried in the spaces, and spoke through things unsaid, "Dearest Girl, Darling Girl, My Girl."

He didn't write again, and that's mostly all right. There is a connection between us that transcends the betrayal, is as eternal as love, and as clear as the "Mrs." And I don't have to do anything about it, except maybe start to savor my mother's letters. It's just that sometimes, when I hear the mailman, I forget.

The X-factor
by Shari' Wright

SOME THINGS ARE EASY TO FORGET. Some must be forced...

I push the small burgundy box farther back in my drawer, making room for the gold cuff I've taken off. The box is now in the back right hand corner, hidden behind all my jewelry— behind my hoop earrings, my bracelets and all my necklaces. But, somehow, the gold ribbon that had been gathered to make a gorgeous bow, and was wrapped around the heart of it, lingers in the middle of the drawer—in plain view, begging to be remembered.

Xavier gave it to me as a birthday gift—for my twenty-first. It would've been mistaken for a ring box, but it wasn't black velvet, and this wasn't a fairy tale. It was Xavier. Reality. In the midst of all the gifts sitting on the table, it was the box that stood out, the small box sitting in the shadow of a pink Victoria's Secret bag, on top of cards from family and friends that all knew how I adored the celebration of my birthday. The box sat, between sentiments, declaring its own.

A tiny card with my name written on it was taped to the box. "Nicole." No alias. No nickname. "Nicole." Reality.

In the belly of the box was a silver chain holding a circle of diamonds. It was easy to wonder, "Why the circle?" " Why not a birth stone or a heart?" My family and friends never knew the dynamics of our relationship, or how those, too, were held in this box. Only Xavier and I were privy to all that was inside.

After nothing but torn wrapping paper and cake crumbs were left of my birthday, I received a text from Xavier explaining his gift. It meant "forever." Even if we couldn't be together physically, we would remain vital factors in each other's being.

For years following that college love affair, my first love in fact, I've had moments and memories that I want to force away. But I can't seem to make it permanent with Xavier.

So, as I sit here doing my best not to cry, I acknowledge how I keep everything in its place. I reorganize my space in order to reevaluate ideas and feelings. I do this when my mind twists and jumbles thoughts.

Cold-weather jackets, skirts and dresses: color coded; jean jackets—from darkest to lightest; dress shirts—also arranged from darkest to lightest. His dress shirt, matching nothing, unable to fit into a category, is in the back of the closet. I've worn and washed it four or five times, so not much of him is left on it. The collar is limp, the color is faint, and now, where his cologne used to be, the scent is all mine. Still, faint or bold, Xavier lives all over my space; he's in and around so many intricacies of my life. The circle.

It's almost absurd, what we were, what he was to me. It has become clear that he made part of me—the part that is all woman and all emotion, that needed the satisfaction of love, comfort, and companionship—he made that come alive. I feel my pulse. Rhythmic and true.

He knew what to say, his words always right. Always grounding. Always revealing. He made things plain. He made things better. When all I needed was a touch to take away the loneliness, he would hug. When all I needed was the chance to close my eyes and find safety in sharing his breath, he would kiss. He would offer a simple gaze when everything could be saved by just looking across the room with eyes that I believed knew what it took to really see me.

Now, unable to keep from crying, I realize that I do not have to see the circle for it to exist. Xavier does not have to be around to leave an impact. Even when I want to forget.

I Am So Over Her
by Bryan Braun

*H*ELLO, LADIES. I SUPPOSE YOU'VE HEARD ALREADY. Yup, I have been released from the burden of being a perfect boyfriend. That's right…I am single. Boy, am I over Danielle…and ready to hit the market again!

I love girls. The way their hair gives that misty smell when you walk behind them; shoot, the way they walk is like a musical number all its own. I love the way they look at me, too, and I feel wonderful inside. And the way they hug you…after a hard day. The way her eyes squint when she smiles. Um, I mean…their eyes. I am so over her.

I suppose I should start at the beginning. I was a junior in high school and there was this girl, Danielle, in drama with me, who I had a crush on.

"Ask her out," my friend Gustav said, "she likes you. She told me."

Cha-ching! Instant happiness overcame me. I did my happy dance and went off to greet Danielle. She was just about to get changed out of her costume. Thinking fast, I tore a button off a nearby girl's shirt. By the way, the show we were doing was *Bye Bye Birdie*, where Hugo and Kim get pinned. (Did they really get pinned?)

"Hey, that's mine!" I ignored her and ran down the hall.

"Danielle! Danielle!"

"What?" Danielle turned and everything froze.

Now was my chance to ask her out. So me, being the suave devil that I am, pulled out the stolen button. "Danielle Hopson, can I pin you?"

"Awe, of course." I was in heaven! Man, there is nothing quite like asking a girl out, and her saying yes.

So this was the start of a beautiful relationship. I really liked her, even thought, after a while, I loved her. And I made the *huge* mistake of telling her of my feelings.

Yup, shortly after telling her that I had fallen in love, she dumped me, dumped me good, got all emotional, started crying. How do girls do that? Cry on cue?

The dumping went down as so: "I don't think we are working out," she said, confidently and strong-willed. She didn't think it was working; I did. So we had reached a controversy. That's when she turned on the faucets. She started crying and talking (horrible combination, hard to understand.) I just sat there, straight faced, not showing any pain. Shoot, like I was going to let her breaking up with me get me upset.

I said goodbye to our relationship and drove off. Exactly three minutes after leaving her house, "Danielle!" Yeah, that's right, I cried. See, women have this power over men. Girls can make men cry…like…like girls. Anyway, to make matters worse, she called me.

"I'm sorry, don't hate me. I want to stay friends."

"Danielle, I don't hate you. I still want to be your boyfriend too.

"What?"

"I still want to be your friend too."

The next day eventually rolled around. That means school… that means facing her…that means the test I didn't study for because I was sobbing like a wounded dog.

So when lunch rolled around, I sat down at my table and began talking to my buddy Nick about whatever. Danielle then walked up to the table, and our eyes met. Boy, you would have thought that was awkward. Well it was. But, from that moment, I had the biggest crush on her.

It's hard; she doesn't rest her head on my shoulder anymore.

Well, anyway, summer began. But really, I was waiting for the next year of school, the moment where I would find out if my efforts to get over Danielle were put to good use.

The first day of school, I walked into that building saying "Danielle who? Ha!" I was extremely confident that not only did I not want Danielle, but I didn't want a girlfriend. They just complicated things.

Then, I saw her. It was like...slow motion. Her hair swaying from side to side, beau...I mean, no, I am over her. She walked by and said,"Hi." And I melted. I love her. No! I mean, no, I don't love her. I am so over her!

IN THE SHADOW
OF WWII

All wars have a profound impact—on both those sent to fight them and those left at home. But in the 1940's, during WWII, at least one factor was dramatically different: communication with those overseas. There was no email or texting, no satellite phones or skype. The only viable way to stay in touch was with pen and paper letters that traveled to and from overseas war zones by ship.

A serviceman would climb the gang-way of a ship, then travel across an ocean. Weeks or months later, if the ship had not been torpedoed by a U-boat, the girl he left behind might receive a censored letter or V-mail.

Couples were separated for years—so it was not unusual for a romance to fizzle out. When letters stopped, a person was left to wonder what had happened—perhaps for the rest of her or his life.

These stories, like the popular songs of that time, evoke the mood of the whole era.

In the Mood
by Florence Haney

"Hey, Betty. I found out our dance tonight is formal. Okay?" So like Blake. He's picking me up at my dorm before the hour. Everything's last minute with him. That's what makes him fun. I hung up the hall phone and shot upstairs to my room.

"What are you doing?" Ann, my roommate, asked, as I flung the sweater and swing skirt I'd chosen earlier on my bunk.

"Formal dance!" I pulled my long gold gown over my head, adjusting lace on sweetheart neck and puffed sleeves. Bless Mother's artistic sewing fingers.

"He did it again!" Ann fluffed out my side bang, ran her fingers through curls over my ears. "I'd dump him!"

I shucked out of saddle shoes and anklets, slipped on high heels, then tossed compact, lipstick, hanky into my beaded bag. "He's the best." Best dancer, best writer, best looker. I was envied by everyone in our tiny oil town high school.

"You enjoy so many of the same things," everyone said. "Like you were made for each other." I agreed.

Glenn Miller's "In the Mood" pulled us through ballroom doors. Driving rhythms called us to join other brightly dressed girls and their dates. Many young men were in ASTP or Navy V-12 uniforms. Blake would be Navy-bound soon. A submarine somewhere. Pearl Harbor had changed all our lives.

"This might be our last dance." I kicked off my shoes. "Can't jitterbug in these."

Mellow sounds from trombones slid down my spine to my toes. Blake's hand took mine, twirling me onto the dance floor. Saxophones sang their way into every nerve. We knew just what the other would do. Our bodies moved faster as other dancers moved into a circle—gave us the whole dance floor. Deep-throated growl of slide trombones urged us into swifter steps. He swung me out as far as he could. Our shoulders moved at the insistence of Miller's music. We met back in the center, falling into each other's arms as the last beat throbbed.

Panting, leaning on each other, we accepted spontaneous applause. Blake. Betty. We belonged together, always "in the mood" when we hit the dance floor. Benny Goodman, Harry James, all great bands. But Glenn Miller brought out our best.

The day he left for duty, we kissed good-bye.

"We'll keep 'in the mood.'"

"Till you come home."

V-Mail didn't give much room to share thoughts, so now and then I sent a story. "Dear Blake, here's my latest writing effort, called "Blue Vase," about Mother during the Depression. Hope you like it. Waiting for your article. In the mood, Betty." He sent back a critique.

We wrote about high school days and our freshman year at OU, remembering the fun when we danced, when we worked in the Press Building wrapping and mailing out books worldwide. Mostly, we looked forward to writing a book together.

The war grew more intense. My family moved to California where we worked at Mare Island Naval Shipyard. Somehow our addresses were no longer correct. Blake and I lost track. I met other young servicemen, even danced with some. It wasn't the same. Glenn Miller disappeared while flying to Paris, big bands faded away. The world was so different when the war ended. I wondered, *where are you, Blake? Are you still writing? Dancing? Are you still alive? Where are you, my lost love?*

I entered a new way of life at the University of California, majoring in Liberal Arts. Returning service men, sporting the "ruptured duck" on their lapels, registered under the GI bill. One turned out to be "love of my life." Fred, good musician, terrible dancer. He always played his alto sax when other students danced. Glenn Miller was his favorite band through our years of courtship and marriage. We played those melodies over and over, cuddling in his parents' car.

Fred never knew why I felt so loving when Miller music played. Yes, even after these many years with the most wonderful man in the world, "In the Mood" still makes me wonder, *Where is my lost love? Is he still "in the mood?"*

Though I Have No Regrets...
by Jeanne Pafford Glasgow

CONSIDERING THE BREVITY of my World War II romance with Barney, I wonder why my thoughts of him have never ceased over these many years. After he left to enter Annapolis Naval Academy, I married Jimmy, a handsome young serviceman. I loved him deeply over the sixty-four years we were married. So why did lingering memories of Barney surface occasionally, when I easily forgot other boyfriends of yesteryear?

I remember my neighbor, Kay, calling to me, hurrying across the street waving a letter. "Jeanne, my brother Barney has a furlough and is at home in Phoenix. And he'll be coming to Tucson to visit Aunt Dode and me this weekend."

Breathlessly, she told me, "We can take him to the servicemen's dances. Won't that be fun?"

"Wonderful." I answered. I knew he was her favorite brother.

The week crept by slowly as I attended classes at the University of Arizona. Young men were in short supply on campus during World War II, but Tucson was inundated with servicemen at its three air fields, and I didn't lack for dates.

Friday evening the doorbell rang and I opened the door to greet Kay and her date, Lee. Behind her was a tall, attractive blonde fellow in a navy uniform.

After introducing us, Kay smiled as they came in to greet my parents. I could see that Barney was looking me over as he said, "Hi." Later he told me it was love at first sight.

The dance at the Y.W.C.A. was filled with couples jitterbugging to the "Jersey Bounce," and we joined them. Barney was a good dancer, and a great date. When we heard "Goodnight, Sweetheart" playing on the phonograph, we knew it was the last dance. And at my front door we ended the evening with a passionate kiss that thrilled me to the tips of my toes.

Saturday afternoon Barney and I saw a movie at the Fox Theatre, and in the evening the four of us went to a Young Women's Defense League dance. Kay drove her aunt's car, with Lee in front and Barney and me in the rumble seat. After the dance, we drove up to "the mountain" to look at the shimmering lights of the city while we talked...and kissed.

Sunday, Barney rode the bus back to Phoenix. But that wasn't the end. Monday night my sister answered the phone.

"Jeanne," she called, "Barney's on the phone."

He called every night that week and took the bus back to Tucson on Saturday. Once again we went dancing, ending the evenings with root beer at a drive-in and a ride to the foothills for another panoramic view of the city lights. Barney returned to Phoenix on Monday. His furlough was nearing an end, but he had time for one more trip to Tucson.

"Let's go to Sabino Canyon, alone, and have a picnic," he suggested.

"Good idea," I answered. "I'll pack a lunch."

He borrowed Aunt Dode's car and we drove to the canyon. We hiked, climbed on the rocks, and waded in the mountain streams. We ate our picnic lunch sitting on a big white boulder surrounded by cool rippling water. Barney took pictures and we talked, learning more about each other. He treated me like a princess, putting me on a pedestal. I felt regal. Was I in love?

That evening we joined Kay and Lee to go dancing at the Pioneer Hotel. Before the evening was over, Barney asked me to marry him. I was swept off my feet, finding myself an eighteen year old college sophomore who said, "Yes." Surprising myself, I promised to wait for him till he graduated from Annapolis.

"You can date," he said, "Four years is a long time to sit around and wait."

We wrote letters; he sent me a dozen red roses on Valentine's Day, and our song was "Give Me One Dozen Roses."

Then I met Jimmy, and even though I sadly wrote Barney a "Dear John" letter, he was always there in a corner of my heart. Though I have no regrets, I find myself wondering what my life would have been like, had I waited for him.

Falling in Love with Love
by Sara Wolkow

*J*ULY 4, 1943. I had just turned fifteen in June. Harriet, my dearest friend since the sixth grade, would be fourteen in August. We were two very young, impressionable girls.

"What shall we do today?" I ventured.

Harriet responded, "It's the Fourth, why not go into town and see the goings-on at the Commons? There probably will be speakers for the holiday."

"That should be fun," I mused. Anyone could get up on a soap box and air their views, much like Hyde Park in London.

Harriet's older sister had recently given me a powder blue summer dress. "I'll wear the dress your sister gave me, and my new three-inch high heels." They were the white leather, slingback, open-toed shoes I finally had permission to buy.

"I'll wear my favorite dress," Harriet said, "the one with the large red cabbage-like flowers on the white background, and my white heels, too. Lana Turner, step aside, here we come!"

Riding into town on the orange-colored street car with the hard slat seats, the hot breeze blowing in through the open windows, we began to feel the excitement of the day. It was war time; Boston, a port city, was awash in sailors in blue, interspersed with soldiers in khaki. This was not lost on two high school teenagers.

We got off at Park Street station, and walked to where a speaker was spouting forth. Flags waved in the warm breeze, martial music played celebrating the Fourth. While standing there listening to the speaker, to our amazement, two soldiers jumped down beside us, like birds flying out of the nearby oak tree.

"Hi girls. We noticed you and wanted to say hello."

"Well, hello," we replied. "So what are you doing in Boston?"

"We're training here. I'm in reconnaissance, and my buddy is in engineering. He'll be off to the China/Burma/India theater, and I'll be off to the European Theater. In the meantime, we'd like to get to know you. My name is Johnny Swartz."

"And I'm Johnny Seamen," the other soldier volunteered.

And so it began; my first brush with love. Things worked fast during war time, an exhilarating and frightening era. Johnny Swartz was a tall, handsome fellow with blue eyes and light brown hair. Square of jaw, thin-lipped, nineteen years old. I was immediately smitten. They asked for our addresses and eventually walked us back to the Park Street station, each putting a dime in the slot to cover our carfare home. A few days later I was elated to receive a letter from him asking for a date. Harriet, too, got a letter to double date.

The day arrived. It was exciting to walk down the street on his arm, sit beside him as we saw the film, "Rommel." And then it was over.

So smitten was I with puppy love that I kept the stub of his cigarette, putting it to my own lips. I read that one letter over and over, and as the weeks went by, I almost gave up hope of ever seeing him again.

It was now September. As I emptied the mail from the box, I saw it, a letter from him! I was euphoric. He asked to see me and, once again, I proudly walked beside him, he in his heavy army coat, I in my beige wool coat with Lynx fur decorating the front, and a matching Lynx hat. Once again, I felt the thrill of sitting beside him as we watched the film, "It Happened One Night."

The evening over, he kissed me goodbye and said he was leaving for Camp Pickett in Virginia for training before heading overseas. Again, I pined away, hoping for another letter. It never came.

In desperation I wrote to the Adjutant General in Washington, D.C,. to try to find him, to no avail.

I saw this soldier only three times, and still wonder, on occasion, if he made it safely through the war.

A New Traveler in the Adventure of Love
by Albert J. Rothman

SHE WAS BEAUTIFUL, not conventionally "pretty." But when she walked into a room, all turned to her: her self-assured energy, her spark, her passion.

When I met June in 1944, I was in my final semester of Columbia University, and soon to be called for service in the war. She was attending Juilliard School of Music, studying voice with a special interest in operatic singing.

Soon after being introduced to June, I was wholeheartedly in love with her. She was two years older and seemed a woman of the world compared to this naive guy who bucked against his virginity. I had had only puppy loves—one couldn't call them affairs. For one thing, I was too uncertain and self-conscious to pursue the girls in grade school. Only later did I learn that many of the girls had wanted me to pursue them.

June's mother, who was a friend of my mother, told June, "Be careful. Albert is so deeply involved that you could hurt him."

June had responded, "But mother, I really like him." (June's mother related this conversation to my mother, who related it to me.)

Between classes I spent time with June. It was winter and we played in the snow, throwing snowballs at one another as we laughed. Our mutual love deepened.

Even though June was a music major, I had never liked opera. Every Saturday afternoon, my mother listened to the Metropolitan Opera's broadcast, and the singing left me cringing, especially the soprano voices, which I labeled as screeching. But June wanted me to experience an operatic performance, aware that I had never seen one. She purchased tickets and we attended. To me it was more screeching.

June saw that I was bored. On the way home, she said that she had made a mistake taking me to that opera. But our affair sizzled on.

I remember an occasion when June prepared a special dinner for us, accompanied by wine. Wine? A current aficionado would consider vermouth a wine, but only for aperitif or mixed with gin for a martini. I was unschooled in wine. Occasionally I had a glass of sweet Manischewitz wine at home and had learned to drink beer in college. I was enraptured by the dinner, by the wine, but mostly by the attention of my love.

During dinner, Franck's D Minor Symphony was playing on the record player. While June served dessert, she told me that she would be gone for a few days to visit her former lover, a dentist upstate. I was heartbroken, fearful that she would resume her attachment to that previous lover, but June tried to reassure me. She acknowledged that he was part of her past, but now she was only concerned that he might be suicidal over losing her. She wanted to try to comfort him.

I began to weep. June thought that the music had moved me, and said she was impressed that I was so sensitive to music. At the time, I thought my tears were for fear of losing her. Years later, I realized that she had been right. I love and am easily moved by classical music.

Our affair ended, as is so common, because of misunderstandings, and probably because I was too new a traveler in the adventure of love.

Shortly afterward, I graduated and reported for the Big War, World War Two. I learned years later that June subsequently married another singer and gave birth to a little girl.

But even now, after sixty years, Franck's D minor Symphony brings me back, with a tear, to my first real love, my incomplete —and incompleted—romance with June.

I have never again felt any love like hers. She spoiled my heart forever.

RESOLUTION
AT LAST

Uncertainty about why a relationship ended can haunt you, even years later. If you
were left wondering just what happened and
questioning how the other person really felt
about you, that uncertainty may wander
out of the shadows from time to time, like a
ghost, disturbing your equilibrium.

Then, one day, you and the other person
have a chance to revisit that earlier time. You
learn about factors that were not evident
when you were together, and gain a larger
perspective. Seeing there was nothing you
could have done, you are finally free of what
had haunted you, free to truly move on.

How Little I Knew
by Amy L. Thomas

WE WERE HIGH SCHOOL FRESHMAN, and he was my best friend's neighbor. I would see Danny every time I visited Kate's house, and thought he was the most handsome boy I had ever seen. He was funny and seemed to completely understand me. We talked for hours on the phone, and decided we were officially "going out." But after that year, I moved on to like other boys.

Flash forward to Senior Year. Danny asked me to the Senior Prom, and we shopped together for a tuxedo and flowers. He took great care with his appearance, and had won Best Dressed for our class. I got such a thrill when he picked me up in his yellow Firebird.

I could tell him anything. He always told me about his family and his job, how he wanted to move away when he graduated and find a new life. I would listen and imagine what it would be like to be with him, what our life together would be like. He was completely different from the other boys I had dated, and I felt safe with him.

Danny and I would see each other when I came home from college on breaks. But he had changed. He seemed angry and often very quiet and depressed. After a few years, we completely lost touch. My best friend had not heard from him either, and he did not come to any of the high school reunions our class had scheduled. I heard he had moved across the country. By this time I was married and had my two children, so I was settled into my own life and routines. But I would wonder where Danny was and hope that he was happy.

After our class's twentieth reunion, I asked if Danny had responded to any of the invitations, or given any of his current information. The woman who organized the event gave me the last known address she had for him, and I decided to write. I was thrilled when I received a long letter in the mail a few weeks later. After I read it through a few times, I called the number he gave me. He picked up the phone, and his low, smooth voice brought back a flood of memories. We were crying and laughing at the same time.

Danny began to tell me what his life had been like in high school—things I had never known about. Danny is gay, had known since he was ten years old. Coming from a very religious family, he would pray every night that he could change, that these feelings would go away and he would be normal.

Danny felt persecuted. He told me some of the horror stories of how he was teased and heckled, things I never knew about. He had decided that the best thing he could do was try to like girls. He believed this would "cure" him. It did not.

After high school, he finally felt he was able to date men, and had been with his late partner, Samuel, for ten years. They had had a good life, or so Danny thought. But Samuel's family had shunned him for his life choices, and the pressure eventually caused him to commit suicide.

Danny could not live in a community that would not accept him and who he was, so he had moved to a location that was more tolerant. He has been with his partner Evan for over eight years. They are very happy and travel extensively, an "old married couple," as he put it.

I was sobbing, and thought back to how little I knew of this man who I claimed to have loved and cared for. I felt guilty for not understanding and for sometimes criticizing a lifestyle that is different from the one that society considers "normal."

Danny made me realize what being true to oneself is about; I only hope that my children can take something from his example and live in a world without prejudice.

A Heart's Renaissance
by Stephanie R. Pearmain

*H*E WAS THE FIRST MAN I ever loved completely, and perhaps the only one to ever know and love me completely. I was nineteen the first time I saw him. It was a moment out of the movies: a tall, incredibly handsome man, with a smile more beautiful than sunshine, walked into the room. I told the woman next to me, "I'm going to marry that man." And I did.

We were both young and naive enough to love freely, without the shackles of hearts that had been torn apart and moved through the world in fear. We were open to the madness and raw beauty of a love that enraptures the soul. And so we lived and loved on a crash course that could not sustain itself. We grew into different people as we navigated our twenties. We hurt each other as much as we loved each other.

After five years, he left. And though the weight of the world lifted when he said he was leaving, the connection remained. For years we dropped in and out of contact. He was always the one I knew would be there to love me from afar when everything else might be going wrong. I could feel when he was thinking of me, and he would call when I really needed him to. I would know instinctively when the flashing light on the answering machine was signaling a message from him.

The last time I saw him was September 1, 2001, right before the world seemed to fall apart. I was almost thirty and in the process of moving out of a relationship and into my own apartment. He was an eight hour drive away.

We met in Phoenix, intending to explore some of our old haunts. We wanted a night of fun, to remember the partying of our youth. The point was not to recapture the feelings and emotions of the past, but rather the freedom we knew at that time in our lives. We tried a few local bars and clubs, hoping to dance. It had been so long since I had danced. But no place felt right. So we drove out of the city and into the desert. We parked on a hill overlooking the city lights and talked until dawn.

It was a night of closure for both of us, after many years of circling each other, bound by an invisible connection we could not completely understand. We sat back beneath the black sky, far enough from the city that the stars were countless. The air was still and almost silent. We asked questions we had never dared to ask about the past. We answered honestly in a way that can only be done after years apart. By sunrise we emerged, reborn as lighter beings free to go their separate ways and begin anew.

I will never love with the reckless abandon that I did at nineteen. There is joy and sadness in that. I will forever send love to those two young souls we were once upon a time. My life would be unimaginably different had I never met him. With him I experienced immense love and happiness as well as great sorrow and emptiness. With time, those extreme feelings have been quelled, leaving me at peace with the knowledge that he is a piece of my soul for always, and I am thankful for that.

Love and Hope
by Laura Lee Carter

I FELL DEEPLY IN LOVE with a world class mountain climber back in 1977, in Colorado. Together we moved to Seattle in the summer of 1978, and soon after, he left for a first ascent in Alaska.

When he returned a month later, he was a different person, aloof and unfriendly. He seemed so isolated, I decided to introduce him to a new friend of mine. Slowly and painfully, I realized my lover was more interested in my friend. I was devastated. At age twenty-four, love no longer made sense.

In March 2003, nearing age forty-eight and two years past a difficult divorce, I spent three days completely alone as a gigantic blizzard raged outside. During the storm, I decided to read my old journals and reminisce about my lost love from so long ago. I wanted to understand love, why it lasts, and why it doesn't.

By spring of the next year, I became convinced that I must make contact with "the one who got away." I needed to know for certain what had happened so many years before. After sending him a couple of letters and receiving no response, I finally gave him a call one bright July morning.

His voice still sounded warm and familiar, and I was stunned to find him so pleased to hear from me. As we spoke, the years fell away, and we were both twenty-four again. After a few long talks, my love for him re-ignited. Was there a chance we were falling in love again?

But this was not the reason for our renewed bond. For decades, I had blamed myself for the failure of our relationship. He now explained how depression had ruled his life and ruined his relationships. He apologized for the trauma he had caused in mine.

Through our discussions, I finally found some closure over this heartbreak from decades past. There was now no doubt in my mind that I had not ruined the best love relationship of my entire life. Bless him for having the patience and courage to share his truth with me, and listen to my accumulated anguish. Our talks unearthed years of excruciating pain, which then flowed out in one gigantic cathartic wave of relief.

This healing experience gave me courage to join Match.com. Online dating had seemed hopeless at times, and I was just about to give up when I received a wink from Mike. He seemed sweet, was wonderfully responsive by e-mail, nice on the phone, and only ten miles away. We decided to meet three days after our first e-mail exchange.

As he walked up to my door, I spied on him from behind my curtain. He seemed to be trying to decide whether to hide his big bouquet of flowers behind his back. I was touched. With a great smile, he introduced himself and presented me with the lovely bouquet. He was lanky and lean in a very sexy way. I fell into his greenish gray eyes immediately, thinking I would never get out.

We discovered we had much in common. We both had spent years in Asia, he in the Navy, me as a China specialist. It was so easy and comfortable being around him, like a meeting with an old friend. Before we knew it, ten hours had passed.

Mike and I married eight months to the day after we met, finally convinced that soul mates do exist. Now, six years later, our love has blossomed. Our dearest wish is that this easy synchronicity of mind, body and spirit we share will never end.

Shattered Spirit
by Ann Blanton

I WAS AN INNOCENT GIRL of nineteen when we met. He was older, more experienced, a Navy Seal. He was home on leave visiting his family after carrying out a special assignment. I thought it was so exciting that he had such an important job.

Immediately, I was captivated by his charm, sense of humor and how handsome he looked wearing his Navy uniform. His bronzed skin and big brown puppy-dog eyes had my attention at first glance. He was tall, well-built, and his dark hair was in a crew cut. The first time I saw him, I knew I wanted him to be my first serious boyfriend.

That summer we spent all our time together. We revealed our deepest secrets and laughed, too. We fell head over heels in love.

Everyone thought us foolish for spending so much time together, but we didn't care. We spent every possible moment wrapped in each other's arms, our naked bodies clinging together, making love under the magnolias near the water as the waves crashed against the rocks.

The indicator symbol in the tiny window of the pregnancy test immediately confirmed my suspicions. It was proof positive I was pregnant. And the love of my life was leaving on an assignment in five days.

At the end of the week, we said our goodbyes at the bus station. I was alone and pregnant, but I knew his mission was dangerous and secretive. There was no guarantee we'd see each other again.

At first, he called as often as his mission allowed. By Thanksgiving, the calls began to taper off. When Christmas came, the calls stopped altogether.

By this time, my belly had expanded; I could hardly see my feet. The new life growing inside me never stopped kicking, not for a single moment. I couldn't sleep. Worries and uncertainties filled my brain, making the nights seem endless.

I forced myself to eat, but nothing would stay down, and my weight began to plummet. My doctor ordered bed rest. I frowned at the thought but, for the baby's sake, did as he said.

Nevertheless, I went into labor in my seventh month. Paramedics were called, and they rushed me to the hospital, where I was prepped for delivery.

I knew something was wrong when I saw the doctor's face. My baby girl had been born with the cord tangled around her neck. The doctor fought to save her life, but it was too late. Her tiny, frail life had passed away before it began.

I was alone again, with a broken heart and a shattered spirit. I didn't know if I had the courage or the strength to go on without my beautiful little girl.

Years later, when I had managed to get my life back together, my first lover came back into my life without warning. I thought my eyes were deceiving me—or maybe I was dreaming. I had loved him once so completely, and that had never changed.

The years had been kind to him; he was more handsome than before. He had a mustache, and his hair had grown longer, with a touch of silver emerging from his sideburns. My heart fluttered, my palms were sweaty, and thousands of tiny butterflies filled my stomach.

He walked with a limp and was clutching a cane.

Then I noticed he had lost one of his legs. My heart nearly burst from the pain of seeing him like that. I raced into his arms and gazed into his eyes. We held one another and cried as I told him about our daughter.

He was grief-stricken. He whispered, "I still love you. Please forgive me for not being there for you."

"I have forgiven you a long time ago, and I love you, too." I was crying. "That will never change. But we can no longer be together."

I had to tell my first love that I loved another now, and could never break his heart the way mine was broken.

Missing the Tingle
by John Anderson

I HAD BEEN LIVING AS THOUGH a good job, career, and house just happened to people automatically after a certain age, as if tubes of toothpaste just showed up magically in their bathroom cabinets. I found out that I had a long way to go.

The love of my life was gone. Not without a fight, mind you, but gone. She loved me, but wanted a taste of freedom, and took it. Her decision never allowed our love to grow and bloom, and prove its worthiness. Growing up can be a wild ride, with a lot of temptations. Sometimes temporary situations can, if you're not careful, turn permanent.

Her perfect body, her shock of brunette hair, her funny ways of telling me when I had crossed a line were things that I loved, and they made my heart tingle. It was the tingle that directs and makes people's lives worthwhile. I knew what I'd had, and wanted it back.

In the meantime, I was trying to purge myself of her memory at local bars. Unfortunately, I had too many good memories and they wouldn't leave. At my age then, I didn't realize that instead of getting poisons out of my system, I was actually putting more in.

After another difficult night of trying to forget, I went to her house. I knew that at three in the morning it would be difficult to get her attention, but my broken heart's logic was talking louder than my mind's. It had to tell her that I missed that tingle, and couldn't imagine living without it.

After stopping for a rose at a local 7-11, I was off to her house to let her know she was not only a big part of me, but about the only part I still liked. Ringing the doorbell was out of the question; I wanted her and no one else.

By the soft light of the distant street lamps, I climbed the snowy back porch, rose in my mouth, to access the roof. I crawled up toward the steep peak, proud of my newfound romantic side —and so badly wanting another chance.

Three taps on her tiny bedroom window finally roused her. And as the window scraped open, there were no tears, no "How have you been?" just, "John, it's over, get out."

"I need to talk to you," I begged. The rose dropped onto the roof as her window slammed shut in front of me. From that moment on my life would be irrevocably changed.

I lost my footing on the snowy roof as I awkwardly struggled to get off my knees. It was the price of wearing cowboy boots for the mission; they looked a lot better than they gripped. After sliding down the slope of the roof, I ripped off part of the gutter and fell to the ground ten feet below.

Oddly enough, I felt contentment as I lay in the snow, outside a place that I wasn't welcome, with a broken gutter hanging above me. Her actions told me the truth, and I finally realized that the foundation that had supported our love—faith, hope and trust—had taken a serious blow. We did not have the maturity to repair it, and later, when we did have it, wouldn't be able to go back.

A couple of years after that night on the roof, we talked, still hoping for a chance to regain the miracle we had shared, the miracle of someone making your heart tingle with a phrase, a look, a smile. But the temporary situation that had turned permanent was her relationship, then pregnancy, with her next boyfriend after our breakup. I realized then that we had thrown that miracle away, to be felt again only in my dreams.

Some twenty-six years after that night, investigating more myself than anyone else, I found her picture online, posing with a group of her patrons at the counter of the bar that she and her husband own. My heart tingled again as I saw her smiling and so at ease with her friends—strangers to me—the woman who taught me the best of what love is and, unfortunately, the worst.

Editors' note: John later wrote to us with this reflection:

"After writing about losing my first true love, the effects on me were so dramatic that I tracked her down to figure out some long-standing questions and to let her read it. Something that had rooted itself within me, living dormant but still with a lot to say, needed to come out and be fully explored. She's since told me that her two grown daughters have read it and cried with her, happy that their mom had been in fact in love and treated well, fought for, and missed."

REKINDLED LOVE

What ever happened to...?

It is not surprising that wonderings about an old flame occasionally slip into a person's thoughts. And, in this electronic age, it is more possible than ever to find an earlier sweetheart, making it is easier to act on curiosity, maybe just say "hello."

Those renewed connections offer myriad possibilities. One may find that the other person is still married—or married again, now happily. Or maybe she or he simply isn't interested in renewing any connection, romantic or otherwise.

But if both are now free to explore the possibility of an encore romance, they may decide to meet— to see what, if anything, is there. And sometimes they find a spark that rekindles a love that began long ago.

You Just Never Know...
by Leslie Mastrianni

*I*T WAS **1967.** The world was changing in so many ways—music, fashion, social values and politics. University was an exciting place to be, and I was going into my second year. I was nineteen and naive, ready for life and love. There were many parties, and I remember the fun of flirting and dancing. One night, at a fraternity party, I was surrounded by young men and was enjoying myself thoroughly. I chanced to look across the room and met the eyes of a tall fellow with black hair and twinkling eyes. He walked towards me, and I knew that this was the man for me. It was love at first sight.

Michael and I dated on and off through our university years. I loved him so much. But each time we got too close to the flame, he would pull away and I wouldn't see him for a while. I dated others, but he was the one against whom they would be measured, and somehow they never measured up.

Finally, at the end of university, we drifted apart. In an old diary, I read that he wrote letters to me. I don't remember writing back. I do remember my heart aching for him, wishing that perhaps I'd been less cool. But it was the time of love with no strings attached, and I was so afraid of being an unwelcome string. I was twenty-two and the love of my life was gone forever.

Through a mutual friend, I would hear news of Michael from time to time. Then I would wallow in memories for weeks, all the while telling myself to get over it and just leave him behind once and for all.

New opportunities and new chances came. I married a good man whose life offered me travel, education and, of course, children. But always, in a little corner of my heart, was the memory of Michael, and all the "what if's."

As is the way of things, my children were suddenly grown up. My husband and I had grown too far apart for our relationship to heal. I was looking at retirement and ready to sell the house that had become too big for one woman. It was time for a reckoning —time to clear the decks and start life anew. As it happened, the daughter of Michael's and my mutual friend was getting married, and I was invited to the wedding. After much thought, I resolved to write and ask him to lunch. I wanted to see Michael one more time, and then put memories of him away forever. He called, wanted to have lunch.

It had been thirty-six years since we had last seen each other. He looked at me and smiled that old smile. The twinkle was still there (although the black hair was not). We talked about everything, trying to squeeze thirty-six years into a lunch time. I told him that my husband and I were divorcing. He said that his marriage also was ending. My heart skipped a beat, but, as always, I maintained a veneer of coolness and calm. We went for a drive in the country and stopped at a little place for coffee. There was a lull in the conversation and, for once in my life, I didn't try to fill in the blanks—I just sat quietly.

After what seemed an eternity, he looked up and said, "I want this to continue." So did I.

That was almost two years ago. Now I am married to the love of my life. Neither of us regrets the years we missed. Our children were meant to be. Past loves and lives were meant to be.

At our wedding, Michael said that he had thought about me every day for forty years. There had hardly been a day when I had not thought of him.

In these, our later years, we have been given a second chance at love—not the love of youth, but a deep and mature love where being cool has no place. This time, there are many strings and a strongly burning flame.

The Love That Heals All Wounds
by Jim Womack*

*M*Y FIRST TASTE OF LOVE was just as exciting as the romantic writers portrayed it to be. Flowers smelled sweeter, and the sun shone more brightly. I met Harriet Burnette during the summer of 1967, when we worked as summer employees at Fort Belvor, Virginia. She made me laugh and helped me overcome a serious case of shyness. For some reason, known only to Harriet, she found my naivete´ and country attitude refreshing; she enjoyed my company, and I made her laugh. Before long, we fell in love.

We made many memories that summer. We cried during the sad part of "Born Free." We shared love songs at a Righteous Brothers concert in Washington, D.C. We had long conversations about our future together. We made plans. Before we knew it, the summer had ended, and we returned to college.

Unfortunately for me, our love did not stand the test of a long-distance relationship. Harriet met someone else and moved on with her life. Whether I liked it or not, I moved on as well. Eventually, my only remaining memories of Harriet consisted of a Righteous Brothers LP and a Polaroid picture taken on our last date. Occasionally, I ran across the photograph and wondered what had happened to my first love. And when I played that record, I fondly recalled a truly special time in my life.

Over the next thirty-eight years, I married, raised a family, and had a career in education. I committed myself to being a good husband, father, and teacher, but depression and alcohol abuse took a great toll on my family. Even though I put away the bottle in 1991, the damage was done. In 2003, I ended the unhappy marriage and retired from an unrewarding career in education.

For a time, I lived quietly and enjoyed a simple life. I traveled, ran ultra marathons, and worked at a variety of jobs. But, despite the fullness of my life, a steady and compelling feeling began to rise within my soul. That old Polaroid picture of Harriet spoke to me. The Righteous Brothers sang to me about love and inspiration. A truly wonderful idea came over me: I would search for Harriet.

In 2005, I returned to Stafford, Virginia, and made some inquiries about Harriet. In a series of serendipitous events, I made contact with her sister. And one day, Harriet Burnette re-entered my life with a simple cell phone call. Her name was different now, and her voice had changed due to some vocal chord surgery. But she was the Harriet of my youth. I discovered that she, too, had experienced a difficult life. Widowed at thirty-one, divorced by forty, she was currently in an unsatisfying relationship.

We reunited that summer and rekindled our love after all those years. Time stood still for us. We were young and giddy again. We enjoyed the intoxicating nature of our love, and married in December.

Two months after we married, Harriet found a tiny bump in my neck, which turned out to be thyroid cancer. Although the necessary surgery and radiation put me out of action for a while, the doctors told me that Harriet's timely discovery had saved my life. My second chance at love became a saving grace. Harriet's commitment and support during my cancer treatments taught me the real meaning of love. She raised me up, challenged me to be active, inspired my creative talents, and helped to heal many of the wounds from my past.

Since our wedding, I have had an opportunity to help Harriet as well. She has had several surgeries, and suffered the loss of some special relatives. She tells me that I supported and loved her more than anyone else in her life. She says that I have helped heal her wounds as well.

By following the voices of our hearts, we were able to have a second chance at love. That opportunity has been life-changing. Our love has, indeed, healed our wounds and made us whole again. Are the events of our love and reunion just chance? We think not.

*Editor's Note: Jim Womack died in October, 2010. Story used with permission of his wife, Harriet B. Powell Womack.

Lost and Found
by Glanda Widger

*I*T WAS A LONG TIME AGO. I was all of fifteen and totally smitten. He was on the football team, but not the first string, of course. He was far too gentle for such a rough sport—I could see that the minute I looked into those hazel eyes. Tall and dark, not really handsome, but sweet and soft spoken. Hair that was neither brown nor black, and cut short.

I was the exact opposite. Short, plain, and wild as a March hare, I was game for anything that was fun. I chattered a mile a minute, and rode my dad's eagle motorcycle around the subdivision like a crazy thing. I was a nerd, but covered up that fact with totally outrageous behavior.

I was the oldest of seven. He was confused by my boisterous family, and a little intimidated. Still, I was determined to have him. I went to all the football games, even though I detested sports. I lurked in hallways where I should not have been, and employed every female trick I had ever read about: batted my eyes, dropped my books, stepped in front of him so he would have to trip over me. You name it, I tried it. In the end, he had no choice but to notice, and finally asked to carry my books. From there things just progressed naturally. We dated steadily for two years. I went to his senior prom with him.

I attempted to seduce him on numerous occasions, but he refused to fall prey to my charms. I wanted to get married and raise kids. Sensible boy that he was, he decided that he needed a good job before taking such a step. He agreed to buy me a ring and become engaged, but wanted me to wait until he enlisted in the Army and finished a couple of years to gain some rank and good pay. I had a fit. He didn't listen and off he went. I ran away with a local mechanic six months after the love of my life joined the Army. I felt devastated, betrayed and angry. I was going to pay him back for his rejection.

In the end, I only harmed myself. I married several times and raised three wonderful children. I thought of my past love often during those years. I still carried the snapshot from our prom in my wallet. I spoke of him and told stories to my children about the things we did: walks on the beach and trips in his dad's old Buick. I wondered about him, where he was and what I would do if I ever met him on the street. That was unlikely, but the dreams were nice.

Then, a miraculous thing happened: the Internet, or more precisely, a reunion site. I would wander through the names of my old classmates and search for news of him.

One day, four years ago, an email came for me. I was stunned. It was him. I answered back. He was divorced, as I was. He had been looking for me for five years.

He wanted a photo. I was never pretty, and photos did not help the situation. I was also old and overweight. What was I supposed to do? He sent his picture to me. He was totally bald now and a little overweight, but he still had those same, soft hazel eyes and gentle smile that had made my heart skip a beat so long ago. I braved the camera and sent a picture to him. When he invited me to come to Florida for the weekend, I was thrilled.

The rest is history. I flew to Florida three times that year. And the next spring, I packed my little station wagon and drove down for good. When I took him to meet my children, my son grinned, shook his hand and stated, "It's about time. I already feel like I know you."

We moved to the Carolinas when he retired, and settled into a small house in the hills. Oh yes, we got married a few months ago, and are going to live happily ever after.

KEEPING THE JOY
OF FRIENDSHIP

When a romance doesn't work out, it is possible for the former lovers to remain friends. They do, afer all, have a common history. They know a great deal about each other and may even still care deeply for one another.

But post-romance friendship is not exactly easy. There are so many painful reminders of how it once was—and now is not. You may fear that you will have to relive your loss again and again. Then, to further complicate things, you have to take into account each other's new loves.

Making the effort, however, can be worthwhile, creating for past loves the chance to keep some of the best of what they had and find great comfort in mutual support. life-long friendship may be the most valuable gift former sweethearts can give each other.

When He Looked Like James Dean
by Terri Elders

WHEN I WALKED INTO THE FOYER of the Little Brown Church for Bob's memorial service, I broke into a grin. Our son, Steve, had posted a blown-up photograph of his dad. There was Bob, at nineteen, shrugged into a leather flight jacket, eyes squinted against smoke from his corona, looking jauntily suave, the perfect embodiment of early 1950's cool.

We had been divorced for nearly twenty-five years. In fact, when Steve called me with the news, while he related the details, I was doing the math. If we hadn't been divorced back in 1980, if we had remained in our genial but increasingly disunited marriage, and if Bob hadn't succumbed to lung cancer, we soon would have celebrated our golden anniversary.

Though I'd not seen my ex since I had remarried five years earlier, I had continued to send birthday and Christmas cards. I knew of Bob's hospitalizations and painful decline, that over the past few years he had lost nearly seventy pounds, that he walked hesitatingly with a cane, and looked closer to eighty-five than his actual age of seventy-three.

A career police officer, Bob had remained quite active with the Southern California Juvenile Officers Association and with a Twelve-Step program he had lead for decades, even after retirement. I found it tough to picture how deteriorating health had laid siege to his robust appearance.

Now, staring at the photo of the Bob of my youth, I remembered how we met. In 1954 I had been editor of the Compton College Tartar Shield, and Bob, a Korean War vet attending on the GI Bill, had been taking a photography course. Since the photo lab was housed in the journalism building, Bob used to joke about trying to lure me into the darkroom.

I took my seat in the chapel, and listened as my son welcomed the crowds of people who had come to celebrate his father's life. Steve spoke of finding the photo of his dad, how astonished he was to discover how cool his dad appeared, and how he had looked like James Dean even before Dean became a star. The audience chuckled.

Then he mentioned how his father had been smart enough to marry not one, but two, smart women. The audience laughed again, and I heard somebody in the back whisper, "I wonder if Terri is here."

Others came forward to relate appreciative memories. As they talked, I reflected on how our divorce had opened doors for both of us. Bob had found a more compatible woman, one who shared his interests, which involved recovery programs right in the town where he had been born.

Our divorce had released me geographically so that I could work with the Peace Corps. I have heard gray wolves howl on the spring equinox in Mongolia, stared down a baby octopus while snorkeling in the warm Indian Ocean waters of Seychelles, dined on armadillo at Macy's Café in Belize City. I've seen the Toledo, the castle in Spain I had dreamed of since childhood. Whenever I returned to Southern California, Bob would take me to lunch, and smile at my adventures.

Steve asked if anybody else wanted to speak. I rose, approached the dais, and heard somebody say, "Why, it's Terri."

"With the exception of his niece, I have known Bob longer than anybody here today," I began. Then I told of our first encounter. As I exited from a rigorous Western Civilization test in late 1954, Bob gave me a wolf whistle. I walked over and said, "That's cheered me up." I stood on tiptoe and pecked his cheek. Bob grinned and said, "If I get that for a whistle, I'm going home and get my bugle." The audience roared.

I recounted some of Bob's earlier achievements, how he had been the quintessential optimist, and vouched that he had indeed been cool. "I'm happy to say," I concluded, gesturing towards the photo, "that I knew Bob Elders when he looked like James Dean."

A few days later I found an abelia shrub called Golden Anniversary. Bob and I had been married for only twenty five years, but had remained friends for an additional twenty-five. That chilly afternoon I planted the Golden Anniversary.

Gifts that Endure
Emily Joyce

*N*ERVOUSLY I WAITED for the knock on the door that would herald the arrival of a man I hadn't seen for over forty years, the man who was my first love. He had been my beloved "F" and I his "E." Bound in our teens by matching friendship rings, we had pledged to love each other forever. Forever, in this case, proved to be only about four years, but they were years of growing and learning and loving.

In high school, he was active and I was shy. Following in his wake, I discovered the joys of the debate team and the theater. He was the Dramateers' director and a performer. I was the backstage prompter, never having the nerve to act, but loving the closeness to the stage and its magic, and, of course, to him.

No ordinary dates, ours. Together we walked many a mile, always discussing our dreams and philosophies, movies—whatever happened to run through our heads. We spent hours sitting on the wall outside my house, still talking or just being together. When his arm was around me, I felt the world was right and I was secure.

We spent many happy hours sitting on the floor in his den reading through plays. I did all the female parts and he the male. He had been writing his own plays since early in grade school, so this role-playing was as natural as breathing for him—and it gave me joy.

My parents had instilled in me a love of classical music, but with him it became even stronger. We would sit and listen for hours to the classics. Rachmaninoff's "Second Piano Concerto" still brings a smile and fond memories, especially the rhythmical and powerful end of the first movement, which we both loved.

As the two years of high school stretched to two years of college, we gradually grew apart—inevitable, I suppose, since we were at two different schools. He grew up faster than I did, and when he said we should date other people it broke my heart. I said some hateful things that I like to think were very much out of character. For years thereafter I was greatly ashamed and wished I could unsay them.

The things I got from him—a sense of self, a love of music and the theater, and confidence in dealing with others—stayed with me. We both married and had successful lives. Then my marriage fell apart after twenty-four years, and occasionally I wondered where my old friend was, and what had happened to him.

Shortly after I retired, I had a chance to find out. His marriage had dissolved, and he asked a mutual friend for my address. After asking me if it was okay, she gave it to him, and he wrote. In my return letter, I apologized immediately for what I had said all those years ago—only to find that he didn't seem to remember what it was—and of course I was forgiven.

Now we were meeting for the first time. Would he still find me worthy of friendship, or for that matter, would I still find him interesting? We had been writing for several months, but writing was not in-person contact.

I suppose he was as nervous as I was. He hadn't changed much in appearance—grayer, but still slender and attractive. I was heavier, but still recognizable. After an awkward dance of conversation, we found that we could indeed maintain an active friendship. What a delight to rediscover a friend from long ago!

In the subsequent months and years, we have gone from letters a couple of times a month to e-mails almost every day. Modern technology is wonderful. We see each other occasionally, even though we live several hundred miles apart. Neither of us is interested in romance at this point in our lives, but oh, the joy of rekindled friendship. Once again, he is my "F" and I his "E," and our emails are signed "Love," even though at this point it is the love of friends and not romantic love. At this time in our lives it is enough.

Smile Your Smile
by Julie Hooker

*I*T STARTED UNDER A CHUPPA in Birmingham, Michigan in 1994; I married Dwight Hooker. He was sixty-five. I was twenty-three.

Six months earlier, he had given me a 1.7 carat diamond set high in a gold swirl. There were four small diamonds leading up to mine. "One for each of my wives—Margaret, Carol, Sharon, Penny, Julie!" he joked.

Dwight didn't ask me to marry him. Asking wasn't his style. Instead, he called his friend Lois, whom he'd known since the eighth grade, and asked, "What if Julie and I get married when we come back to Michigan?"

I could hear Lois smile as she replied, "You'll get married in our backyard, under the oak tree. Richard will give Julie away and we'll have a rabbi."

Neither Dwight nor I was Jewish. But his friends were, and he hadn't had a Jewish wedding. Dwight was my friend, my lover, the man who cheered for me. All six of Dwight's children, along with his five grandchildren, came to our wedding.

The day after we returned to Utah, I went to the Social Security office and filed for a new card as Julie Ann Hooker. Next stop, driver's license division, where I lied. Because Dwight liked the photo on my license so much, I told them I had lost my license.(Dwight, a former photographer at *Playboy*, taught me early to drop my chin, look up and smile. From behind the lens, he'd say, "smile your smile.") Whenever I feel a camera focus on me, I hear him say, "smile your smile," and I do.

Months later, armed with *Bon Appetit* and a recipe for sweet potatoes straight from the south, I made my first turkey dinner. Lois called to say "Happy Thanksgiving," and I heard Dwight say, "I'm so proud of her."

For a decade, friends and family sat in our Sundance home, eating, drinking, celebrating and relaxing. For a decade, flames crackled behind the glass of the octagonal fireplace and, after dinner, the Trivial Pursuit board came out. For a decade, I cooked. And my husband was proud of me.

Together, we adopted a Samoyed, a Golden Retriever and a Himalayan kitten. Dwight named them all. Since he was a Russian dog, Dwight called our Samoyed Gorbachev, because he didn't like Yeltsin's politics. I found a Golden puppy for sale on a street corner. I called Dwight, thinking he'd say, "No way." Instead he replied, "We need a touch of gold around the house. Bring Midas home."

Dwight wanted a kitten. One day, in town, I found a kitten in a pet shop. Smaller than a can of Coke, it looked Himalayan. Years before, he had given a Playmate a Himalayan. Dwight called him The Cat, Mandu.

A decade filled with holidays, weddings, births and deaths passed. We lived through the death of Dwight's youngest son, depression, heart attacks and strokes. I grew up. I was loved. The difference in our ages grew. "I have to let you go," Dwight told me one day. "I'm too old. You need to get on with your life."

Together we sat holding hands in the attorney's office. Our lawyer smiled, "You two have the nicest divorce."

Together, we chose a home for me in Park City. Dwight sent me alone to meet the realtor saying, "Go ahead, make a full price offer. I'll give you the money."

Together, we chose a condominium at the base of Emigration Canyon in Salt Lake City for Dwight. Alone, he remodeled it, putting in shutters and walnut floors.

Together, but separate, divorced, but in love, Dwight and I saw movies, went to dinner and celebrated holidays. After seeing *Something's Gotta' Give* starring Diane Keaton, Dwight asked me for my diamond ring. He reset it into my "divorce" ring, lowered the diamond and set it white and yellow gold so I could wear it everywhere.

Now I'm remarried and he's back in his home state of Michigan, with a woman whose heart he broke when she was twenty-three.

But Dwight is the love of my life. Dwight likes the idea that I will live a very long time and remember him, his stories, and our history for all of that time.

Still Flying Alongside Me
by Larissa Gula

I'M SITTING BY THE TROLLEY TRACKS at the Pennsylvania Trolley Museum, trying to talk to Evan over car #66's air compressor. I'm about to kick it—

It turned off. Wonderful. I can talk normally now. And I don't have to break my foot kicking the metal. Now I can hear him.

"You know what they called me in that class? 'Lord and master.'"

I laugh. Evan's just told me over the phone what his nickname in Imaginative Writing had been the year before.

It's already September. We broke up a year ago, now that I bother to think about it. After meeting when I was a freshman and he a sophomore, after growing closer and dating, and after breaking up…after I went through almost a year of depression…

I hadn't realized how much I had depended on him until he broke up with me. I hadn't realized he had reinstated my trust in men. My father and I had fought to the point that the confrontations had become more about personal insults than solving our problems. Eventually I had begun to feel his words wear me down.

And then, Evan came along—Evan, who wore glasses and kept his hair slightly roguish, who gave me my first kiss, who taught me about love. Not physical. That isn't love; it's lust. No. He taught me about true love, the art of giving and compromising, of keeping the relationship strong through every life obstacle.

I like to think we're closer than ever, a year after that breakup. He's nineteen and in college now. Jealous as I am, I'm happy for him. He deserved to leave our "bubble" community, as well as the family who treated him as badly as mine treated me. It'll be my turn next year to get out of my own nightmares and start anew.

Around my neck today is a necklace he gave me almost two years ago. I don't tell him over the phone. It's not as important to him as it is to me...probably. Besides, he's seen me wear it before. He knows I kept it.

What he doesn't know is that the necklace has been battered by vacuum cleaners, dropped down sink pipes, and fixed with super glue as much as my heart. It isn't in perfect shape anymore. But you have to look closely to tell the difference between its old and its new shape.

It's just like the bond we have now compared to a year ago. Evan the big brother is as good as Evan the boyfriend. Maybe better. Can I ask for more than to be loved for being me, even now?

I close my cell phone. I think back on a set of lyrics I wrote, titled "Second Heartbeat." I actually chuckle out loud there on the public bench, thinking about how depressed I had been back then. It was amazing that my parents never took me to therapy. I had been so convinced I would never recover from the break-up, so immature was I in my thought process.

But the breakup had never meant I would lose him. All it meant was change.

It also meant I could tell the difference between the lust and the love we shared. Still close, we are able to sleep side by side without having sex, to talk about sex and our bodies. We are comfortable with each other. We understand the other now, years later.

Maybe one day I'll truly be able to show Evan how grateful I am for that bond, for his lending me his wings when I needed a boost to fly up again, and for catching me after the long fall. Not to mention for still flying alongside me now.

But for now, I have to take care of myself as I promised. The best way to do that is to pick up the pen and start a new story, write a new song to go with it.

And that's just what I'll do.

HEARTSCAPES
CONTRIBUTORS & CONTACT INFORMATION

Danielle Abbatiello   danielle.abbatiello@yahoo.com
Diana M. Amadeo
Monica A. Andermann
John Anderson   poemhunter.com/john-emmett-anderson/
Lanita Andrews   lanitaandrews@hotmail.com
Anahi Arana

Kathryn Hackett Bales   kgb@frontiernet.net   Elko, NV
Dorothy Baughman   450 Fleahop Road, Eclectic, AL 36024
   dbaughman@elmore.rr.com
Madeleine Beckman   writedowntown.com
Carmen Beecher   hbeecher@earthlink.net
   carmenbeecher.blogspot.com
Luke Beling   lukebeling.blogspot.com
Connie Berridge   TulipProductions.biz@gmail.com
Indrani Bhattacharyya   ruu924@gmail.com
   4644 Avenue Dupuis, Apt. 10 Montreal H3W1N3 Canada
Ann Blanton   deb.blanton52@yahoo.com
   233 Shale Lane, Rineyville, KY 40162
Nanci Block   nanci.e.block@gmail.com
Patricia Boies   paboies@gmail.com
Diana Lesire Brandmeyer   dianabrandmeyer.com
   pencildancer.com (blog)
Bryan Braun   bryan.braun5@yahoo.com
Meagan Brooks

Joan L. Cannon   jlcannon28@att.net   hilltopnotes.blogspot.com
   207 B Ridgeside Terrace, Morganton, NC 28655
Beth Carlson   carlel01@gettysburg.edu
Albert W. Caron, Jr.   hatolincoln@yahoo.com
Dawn Carrington   dawnrachel.com
Laura Lee Carter   lauraleecarter.com
   MidlifeCrisisQueen@gmail.com
Gergana Vladimirova Chinovska   urban.fairytalez@gmail.com
   theblacksheep1.wordpress.com
Matukio OleAfrika Aranyande Chuma
   matukiochuma@yahoo.com
Mitchell Close   spit.fire@live.com
Autumn Conley   auntiej@gmail.com
Jill Cordover   jillcordover@gmail.com
Libby Cudmore   recordofthemonth.blogspot.com
Leslie Creek   lesliea1968@yahoo.com
   twitter.com/bookluvr68

John Day   luckytoons@aeroinc.net
Margaret DeAngelis   margaretdeangelis@gmail.com
   silkentent.com/Trees
Ellen Denton   finelifetoall@silverstar.com
Ann DesLauriers   WriteOnAZ@aol.com
Conda V. Douglas   condascreativecenter.blogsport.com

Katie Eichele   katieeichele@gmail.com
Terri Elders   telders@hotmail.com   Colville, WA
   atouchoftarragon.blogspot.com
Lyla Faircloth Ellzey   mslyla216@comcast.net

Deborah Finkelstein   DeborahFinkelstein.com
Drury Fisher
Alexandra Foxx   afoxx99@gmail.com
Suzanna Freerksen

David Galassie dgalassie@gmail.com
Jerry Gaube jerrygaube@gmail.com Madrid, Spain
Marcia S. Gaye St. Charles, MO
Jeanne Pafford Glasgow azglasgow@cox.net
    6949 E. Kingston Dr. Tucson, AZ 85710
Brian Greene brianjosephgreene@gmail.com
Larissa Gula
Roberta M. Guzman arguzman8@msn.com
    3930 N. Old Sabino Canyon Rd.,Tucson, AZ 85750-2119

Ariel Hafeman hafemana@hotmail.com
Heather Haldeman
Florence Haney 2501 Tudo Court Annapolis, MD 21401
Kelsey Hanson hanson.l.kelsey@gmail.com
Heather Haldeman
Janine Harrison southpawscribbler@hotmail.com
Judy Harwood jhar2@aol.com swimmingupriver.com
MJ Henry mjtexasrose61@live.com
    texasrose-strangeroses.blogspot.com
Taryn Henry-Latham taryn@yahoo.com
Sonja Herbert Germanwriter.com
Nhan Thi Ngoc Ho vivianho1992@gmail.com
Grace Hobbs gracemhobbs@gmail.com
Beatrice M. Hogg HoggPen57@yahoo.com
Julie Hooker julieannhooker@gmail.com Park City, UT
Juliana Hill Howard juliana2h@yahoo.com
    P.O. Box 370 Midpines, CA 95345
Thuy Hua thuybhua@gmail.com

Dickens Ihegboroh dickens@alfaregy.com (Nigeria)

Julia Jacques jrjacques007@yahoo.com
    P.O. Box 25 Deerton, MI 49822
Adna Jahic annamollydawn.tumblr.com
Katherine Johnson katherinekai@yahoo.com
    onespiritcoach.com
Emily Joyce ejoyce2@gmail.com emjmusings.blogspot.com

Beda Kantarjian bkantarjian@cfl.rr.com
    anhinga.wordpress.com
Diem Kaye drunkenmonkeyking22@gmail.com
Nadine C. Keels prismaticprospects@wordpress.com
Lisa Kempke
Leonard W. Kenyon acomedyofhorrors.tumblr.com
Michael Keyton baffledspirit.blogspot.com/
Jill Koenigsdorf New Mexico

James C. Landis landis@yosemite.net Mariposa, CA 95338
Marian Lane 2121 S Pantano Road, Unit 61, Tucson, AZ 85710

Michelle McAlister michellemcalister.com
Colin Matthew McClung colinwriter@gmail.com
B. Gael McCool gael@ifeelmorenow.com
Betsy McPhee betsymcphee@yahoo.com
Leslie Mastrianni lbroun@live.com
A. L. M. alm528@nyu.edu
Karen Monroe karem@comcast.net
    22756 Nona, Dearborn, MI 48124
Aaron Moseley moseleyofaaronj@hotmail.com
Liz Mugavero liz.mugavero@gmail.com
    Twitter: @lizmugavero.
Daniel Mullen danielmullen79@gmail.com
Maria B. Murad mbwriter@att.net mariamurad.com
Lee Ann Sontheimer Murphy labyline@att.net
    leeannwriter.weebly.com

Lori A. Nason
Ariella Nasuti theninthwavenovel.wordpress.com
Kaylie Newell kaylienewell@yahoo.com
    kaylienewell.com

Mary Oak   oak188@msn.com   maryoak.com
Juli E. Ocean   TheRadicalWrite.blogspot.com
Molly O' Day   cyourinnerlight@yahoo.com
Sylvia Outley   sylviaoutley@gmail.com

Karen Paul-Stern   karen@kpsdevelopment.com
     kpsdvelopment.com
Stephanie R. Pearmain   srpearmain@yahoo.com
James Penha   jamespenha.com
Kelley Walker Perry   kphoenix_3@sbcglobal.net
Rochelle Potkar   rochellepotkar@gmail.com
JoAnne Potter   joannepotter.weebly.com
     20110 Hidden Valley Rd. Richland Center, WI 53581
Samantha Priestley   www,samanthapriestly.co.uk
     twitter.com/#!/sampriestley
Fred M. Prince   24110 Rd. 379 Kiln, MS 39556

Sean Burnside Quigley

Kathryn Radeff   kradeff1@msn.com
Lynn Radford   radford.lynn@gmail.com
Judah Raine

Daphne Rice   riceburns@hotmail.com
     1214 SE Reynolds St. Portland, OR 97202
Frances M. Rooks   rooksfran@yahoo.com
     fmrooks.blogspot.com
Albert J. Rothman   albroth@comcast.net
     503 Yorkshire Drive, Livermore, CA 94551
VonQuisha Ann Russell   estopareann@gmail.com

Savita Sachdev   slak06@gmail.comJ.
Victoria Sanders   joshunda@gmail.com
     jvictoriawrites.tumblr.com
Mary Ann Savage   emmaysavage@gmail.com
D. S. Schildkraut

Xenia Schiller xeniaschiller@yahoo.com

Daniela Schirripa dani.dale@hotmail.com

Anna Seip annaseip@yahoo.com

Ariel Sky arielsky@live.com

Abigail Sprague asprague185@g.rwu.edu

Barbara Milstead Stanley babs@tds.net Blairsville, GA
  barbiescommonsense.blogspot.com

Lori Stott lori.stott@gmail.com

Sonia Suedfeld soniasuedfeld@yahoo.ca
  soniasuedfeld.com

Elaine Suelen

Amy L. Thomas amywriter46@gmail.com
  14 Pleasant Ave. Scarborough, ME 04074

Norm Titterington a-writer-in-progress.blogspot.com

Sam Turner samwriting76@gmail.com
  tobecontinuedbysam.com

Jeanne Waite-Follett jfollett@ptialaska.net
  gullible-gulliblestravels.blogspot.com

Barbara Walker eyepoetress.wordpress.com

Samantha Ducloux Waltz samanthawaltz@comcast.net
  pathsofthought.com

Laurie Weed laurieweed@gmail.com

Geraldyne R. Weiser gerryweiser@verizon.net
  9039 Sligo Creek Pkwy, Apt #912, Silver Spring MD 20901

Laura Grace Weldon lauragraceweldon.com
  bitofearthfarm.com

Sarah Bracey White onmymind.org

Susan White scwhite17@yahoo.com
  119 Summerglen Drive Ashville, NC 28806

Glanda Widger Vale, North Carolina

Gary Winters deerdance@sdmensa.com

Linda C. Wisniewski lindawis.com

Maryellen Wolfers   mewolfers@earthlink.net
    Mountain View, CA 94043
Sara Wolkow   2676 Crest Cove, Annapollis, MD 21401
Jim Womack (Harriet Powell Womack)
Shari' Wright   swright0326@gmail.com
    examiner.com/urban-arts-in-washington-dc/shari-wright

About the Editors

Kate Harper and Leon Marasco are the authors of *If Only I Could Tell You: Where Past Loves and Current Intimacy Meet*, an exploration of what people do with memories of (and feelings about) past loves in the context of a subsequent relationship. In *Heartscapes* they offer stories that further explore the intriguing world of "old flames."

A Note on the Type

This book was set in Palatino Linotype, a modern and easier-to-read version of the Renaissance faces upon which it was based. It is named after the sixteenth century Italian master calligrapher, Giambattista Palatino.

CPSIA information can be obtained at www.ICGtesting.com
Printed in the USA
BVOW040115311212

309284BV00001B/1/P